Teaching Approaches in Music Theory

An OVERVIEW of PEDAGOGICAL PHILOSOPHIES

Michael R. Rogers

SOUTHERN ILLINOIS UNIVERSITY PRESS

Carbondale AND *Edwardsville*

Library of Congress Cataloging in Publication Data

Rogers, Michael R.
    Teaching approaches in music theory.
    Bibliography: p.
    Includes index.
    1. Music—Theory. 2. Music—Instruction and
study.
I. Title.
MT6.R76T4   1984   781'.07'11   83-10169
ISBN 0-8093-1147-X

Contents

Contents

Preface

A REVOLUTION has occurred in the teaching of music theory during the past twenty years. Some teachers have become part of the sweeping changes, while others may be only vaguely aware of them. The information explosion, the dozens of new textbooks, new journals, the influences of newer or more widely disseminated theoretical viewpoints and analytical systems, the comprehensive-musicianship movement, reactions and backlashes against and even returns to older teaching goals and methods (fads and cycles), programmed instruction, innovations in technology, the rise of graduate theory programs, the ascent of cognitive psychology, and the formation of the national Society for Music Theory have all contributed to the growing activity and increasing respectability of music theory.

This is an especially exciting time to be involved in music theory and its teaching, since the discipline is just now beginning to come into its own and to determine its boundaries. In past decades, music theory was often thought of as a kind of offshoot or sub-category of music history or composition. It is now finally gaining esteem as an intellectual domain in its own right. In this respect music theory, in the 1980s, is at the same juncture in its academic and professional evolution as musicology was in the 1940s.

This book is an attempt to summarize and compare the more recent trends affecting college-level theory teaching. I do not espouse one particular point of view or theoretical bias but rather will (*a*) present an objective discussion of the similarities and differences among various types of undergraduate theory programs and curricular designs and teaching styles, philosophies, and approaches; (*b*) suggest a broad range of specific pedagogical techniques and strategies for specific topics in theory classes; (*c*) recognize and define the most significant issues and problems in college theory teaching today; and (*d*) identify and evaluate appropriate responses, solutions, and future directions for these matters. In other words, I will attempt to describe and explain the "state of the art" for college-level music theory in the 1980s.

One basic premise of this book is that a single best method for teaching music theory probably does not exist; most theory programs and individual teaching methods are a compromise among many possible approaches. In emphasizing one aspect of a course or a program over another, something else will necessarily be slighted or omitted. Good teaching, then, to a large extent, consists of recognizing the strengths and weaknesses—the values and limitations—of a wide variety of approaches and in being able to blend the greatest number of desirable features while compensating for inevitable deficiencies. An analysis of the pros and cons of various pedagogical orientations along with an understanding of the individual teaching situation (type of school, needs and background of the students, training and interests of the theory faculty, etc.) become vital elements in constructing and improving the level of college theory teaching.

I am not so interested in recommending particular philosophies as I am in providing a background for current or prospective teachers to be able to form their own beliefs, opinions, and attitudes. My advice should be taken as suggestions, not prescriptions. The mere raising of legitimate and relevant issues can serve as framework for discussion and thought. Just as thinking about music is the beginning step for understanding it, thinking about teaching is a prerequisite for improvement in that area.

Two topics for special emphasis will be (*a*) an examination and critique of the underlying and often tacit assumptions behind textbooks, materials, and technologies; and (*b*) a comparison and contrast of pairs of concepts and teaching approaches—some of them mutually exclusive and some of them overlapping. My comments are intended to be both general and specific, both philosophical and practical. I do not discuss

the vast subject of learning theory or the vast research in per- || *good*
ception (little of which actually relates to musical—as opposed || *point*
to acoustical—experience). The tone of much of the book,
then, is down-to-earth.

While I trust that my presentations are objective, I hope they
are not too objective. I assume and even wish that some of my
views will be stimulating enough to be debated and challenged.
My purpose in expressing thought-provoking opinions at times
is not so much to convert you to my view as to state the issues
with enough clarity that we can compare views; I am more
concerned that you understand my argument than that you
agree with it. An additional reason for presenting strong views
is to demonstrate, as a model, how to argue for particular
beliefs. While a certain amount of objectivity is necessary in a
book like this for all angles to be heard, eventually sides and
positions must be chosen for teaching to have force and con-
viction. Music theory teaching is not a subject that lends itself || ||
well to fence straddling. Teaching without commitment is like
a sentence without a verb.

If the book has a single underlying assumption of its own, it
is that the common distinction in theory teaching between
written skills (part-writing, composition, analysis, etc.) and aural skills (dictation, sightsinging, etc.) is an artificial one. This
thesis runs through almost every chapter like a red thread.
Finding ways to eliminate the distinction should be one of the
primary goals of theory teaching.

This book can serve two main functions. First, it should be
useful as a reference and research tool for theory specialists,
teachers, and graduate assistants—especially inexperienced
ones. Many college theory courses are taught by specialists in
areas other than theory, such as performance. These people
often have need, not just for factual information about theory
(which can be found in many basic texts or other theory
reference works), but for information about how to present
particular topics and the varying philosophies behind the
methodologies.

Second, the book can serve as a text for music theory pedagogy classes—the classes that teach college theory majors and
minors how to teach. Almost every major music school has
such a course—some even at the undergraduate level—but no
comprehensive textbook covering differing approaches pres-

ently exists. Information about the subject is scattered among hundreds of isolated (and sometimes obscure) sources, or in some cases has never even been identified, labeled, categorized, or organized in any coherent fashion.

Enough material has been omitted to fill two or three additional books; a whole volume could be written, for example, on just sightsinging or analysis. Within the necessary restrictions of a single work many topics, therefore, are presented in condensation or in passing. Through classroom discussion or lecture, pedagogy teachers will want to elaborate or fill in the gaps as they define them for the needs of particular classes. In this regard, I would like to draw attention to the extensive suggested reading lists for each chapter, which may be found in the back of the book. I hope this feature will enhance the value of the book beyond the actual content itself and will alert potential or present teachers to ideas or research sources with which they may not be familiar. Almost every topic in the book can be pursued in greater depth through these additional references. In our age of rapidly expanding frontiers of knowledge, merely knowing where to locate certain kinds of information is comforting.

The bibliographies consist of articles, treatises, dissertations, and textbooks. A small sample of unpublished papers is included as well; copies can often be obtained from the authors. I believe this represents the first attempt to pull together such background information about theory teaching all in one place. My intention in compiling the reading lists has been to make them broad but not exhaustive. The criteria for inclusion stresses the widest possible variety of viewpoints on the greatest number of differing topics, along with the normal standards of importance, relevance, and quality. Some especially notable entries are accompanied by brief annotations—often related to the terminology in the book. Textbook reviews are not included because much of pedagogy class time will probably be spent in that critiquing process. Detailed discussions of texts are best left to individual classes, but the conceptual categories of this book can help to provide a larger frame of reference for such discussions.

Notated musical examples are omitted from the book, although many specific compositions, composers, harmonic progressions, chords, rhythms, melodic patterns, and other concrete musical situations are mentioned—often in detail. The stress is therefore placed on the teaching principles themselves without locking a teacher or class into predetermined illustrations. Most pedagogy teachers will prefer the flexibility of using their own special or favorite examples to portray the main points. In addition, the articles and especially the textbooks in the bibliographies include an abundance of ready-made prototypes for illustration and elaboration purposes.

The book is organized very much like a sonata-form composition with part 1 ("Background") exposing the principal ideas or themes; part 2 ("Thinking and Listening") developing these ideas in the specific areas of mind training and analysis, culminating in the chapter on ear training; and part 3 ("Achieving Teaching Success") recapitulating some main points, but in new contexts and surroundings.

The actual content of the book is based on a combination of almost twenty years of personal teaching experience in a variety of college-level educational settings, and the collective wisdom of dozens of the most creative college theorists and theory teachers across the nation, gleaned through personal discussion, observation, and through their writings—both scholarly and pedagogical. My approach, accordingly, in both my own teaching and in this book, is frankly eclectic. The ideas expressed in these pages are therefore a survey of the best current thinking available on the most panoramic range of topics—blended, of course, through my own particular set of biases. This is not, then, just a "how-I-do-it" or a "how-it-should-be-done" book, but rather a compendium of possibilities—an overview of the whole field.

It would be impossible to sift and identify all the individual strands of influence and help that have gone into this book, including the hundreds of students who have helped me to learn what works and what doesn't. I can, however, single out a few for special mention. The historical theorists who have most influenced my thinking include Schenker (how can anyone not be affected by his ideas nowadays?) and especially Fétis, the first musician who seems to have understood the inner workings of functional tonality as a set of mutually supportive relationships. More recent theoretical influences include the writings of Edward Cone, Charles Rosen, Leonard Ratner, William Thomson, and especially Leonard Meyer.

Certain teaching colleagues have provided not only samples of organized and effective theory teaching but also many valuable insights into both the teaching process itself (Frederic Homan, Central Missouri State University) and the structure of music and analysis (Ralph Turek, University of Akron—himself the author of a remarkably comprehensive and innovative text: *Analytical Anthology of Music,* Knopf, 1983).

My thinking has been shaped most of all, perhaps, by my own graduate theory teachers at the University of Iowa: Marvin Thostenson, for his innumerable practical and helpful teaching tips and hints; D. Martin Jenni, for his deep understanding of musical analysis (and many of whose terms and ideas I have borrowed directly for this book); and W. T. Atcherson, for his sure grasp of what music theory is and why and how we do it. Peter DeLone of Indiana University should also be thanked for his thoughtful readings of preliminary drafts and his constructive suggestions and encouragement.

In one sense, this whole book is an attempt to define, not more precisely, but more broadly, the field of music theory. I will consider it a success if readers of the book finish with an enlarged feel for the vigor, beauty, subtlety, and range of its thought. There is no way to pass on these values to students without first being captivated as a teacher by their appeal and enchantment.

PART ONE

Background

ONE

The Purpose and Goals of Music Theory

Defining music theory is almost impossible. Every college theory teacher in the country has an opinion—or should have—about why it is taught or even what it is. These opinions often vary tremendously from school to school and sometimes from individual to individual within the same department. This is not necessarily cause for alarm but is rather a measure of the diversity and richness of the discipline. Despite the difficulty of defining such a broad domain and before discussing teaching approaches to specific topics, it is essential to consider the nature of this diversity. The most important place to begin a book about teaching music theory, then, is with a discussion of its purposes and goals.

Many theory teachers proceed from tacit or hidden assumptions formed and colored by their own undergraduate theory classes rather than from concepts based on reflective and mature personal conviction. These early opinions are usually instilled long before the student imagines that he may be teaching theory himself some day. As we shall see later on, many textbooks and courses are also based on tacit assumptions—ones about which the author or teacher may not even be aware.

Whenever "theory" is mentioned, almost all students and even some teachers think of scales, do-re-mi, roman numerals, and key signatures. While these items would be part of almost any beginning level of college study, they really represent a pre-theory stage. They are no more a part of the genuine study of music than knowledge of the alphabet, verbs, or commas is a part of the study of literature.

Rudiments and fundamentals, while absolutely indispensable, are most important for establishing an essential background that leads to the eventual study of other things. Those "other things" constitute the essence of music theory. It would be a mistake, I think, to define theory too narrowly in terms of preliminary basics—no matter how crucially important—rather than by the fuller scope of meaningful inquiry that is possible. Development of a feel for this fuller scope along with information about presenting the basics are both prerequisites for successful theory teaching. Development of perspective concerning the necessary relationship between first and succeeding steps is an important goal of this book.

One irony of many undergraduate curriculums is that the two- or three-year required sequence of courses allots all its time to acquiring the background (terminology, labels, etc.) for doing music theory but runs out of time just as the topic becomes interesting—resulting in an extended introduction that leads nowhere. Under such conditions of all motion and no arrival, students are never exposed to what real theory is all about and carry with them a biased and limited notion of the subject. It is difficult for them to see why the courses are even taught if the background materials become an end in themselves.

On the other hand, it is equally pointless and frustrating for students to be pushed too quickly into advanced and overly sophisticated projects without preparatory intellectual supports in place. A distinction between two levels of pursuit—forging conceptual tools for thinking (knowledge) and then actually using those tools (the thinking itself)—is necessary even as we realize that the two are inseparable components of a meaningful overall program.

Theory is also often defined by course descriptions like harmony, counterpoint, form, analysis, orchestration, sightsinging, and dictation. Too much emphasis on narrow course content and acquisition of knowledge once again obscures the more far-reaching goals of theory instruction—goals that should spill outside the strict boundaries of the courses themselves and affect serious musicians throughout their lifetimes. This kind of shortsightedness leads, in my judgment, to a pernicious, yet prevalent, misconception: that theory consists primarily of a body of factual information to be learned or memorized. Of course, one purpose of theory courses is to teach data and terminology—the proper names for processes and events—so that communication and discussion about pieces can take place. But a more substantial and inclusive view of theory should also admit the possibility of learning how to ask questions as well as how to answer them. In fact, one of the most important goals of any theory class ought to be discovering which questions about music are most worth asking in the first place.

The natural inclination to weight those aspects of musical experience that are the most "teachable" and "testable" should be carefully examined. Theory teachers, too often, tend to overstress topics or questions that permit only clear-cut right or wrong answers while avoiding those gray areas of ambiguity that can be so treacherous. Channeling of the thought process into black-and-white categories is important at a beginning stage so that basic concepts can be established, but eventually a theory program must move ahead to create tolerance and enthusiasm for the discovery, exploration, and comparison of a wide range of *differing* musical ideas and must promote the ability to back up decisions and judgments with logic, consistency, and imagination. In the long run, most questions that do have unequivocal answers turn out to be insignificant, whereas those that allow a variety of interpretation have the power to kindle real musical insight.

This notion is forcefully and succinctly expressed in Bierstedt's Paradox: studies that are reliable (statistically rigorous) are usually trivial; the most valuable studies are scientifically unreliable.[1] Blatant examples include the doctoral dissertation that proved that high school students who read newspapers regularly are better informed about current events than those who do not, and the infamous $100,000 government study that brilliantly associated convicts' attempts to escape from prison with their desire for freedom.

Teachers are often hesitant to use assignments or instigate discussions that involve creative thinking or that touch on sensitive aesthetic issues since it usually means more work (or embarrassment) for themselves. Many students also prefer the psychological security of situations that are obvious and explicit, although those with mental fertility usually relish the opportunity for probing deeper or more controversial matters.

5

The value of results that can be conclusively proven, however, is often overestimated at the expense of the values of speculation, reflection, and contemplative imagination which are, perhaps, more helpful in unveiling novel patterns of thought. These uncharted byways, then, in turn, often lead to still more discovery. Their certainty or even truth is less important than their potential for enlarging the scope of our conceptions. Finding loose ends can be as important as tying them up. "It may be that for certain intellectual purposes cogency is more important than truth. . . . Unconfirmed conclusions, when they are cogent, can be more significant than verified truths, when they are trivial. . . . [The more that researchers refine methodological precision], the more inconsequential are the items of knowledge that result. It is as if they had put together the best butterfly net in the world and were able to catch with it not butterflies and not even an occasional moth, but only a miserable species of gnat."[2]

To continue Bierstedt's line of reasoning by paraphrasing what he says about contemporary sociology: it is possible, of course, that in the study of music theory we shall never achieve that measure of truth that characterizes a verified proposition in the sciences. This, however, may have to be recorded as one of the accidents of the universe. It just seems to happen, so far as present capacities can disclose, that the physical world can be captured cognitively by mathematical models, tools and methods, whereas the world of music, in many important respects, evades a similar capture. It may be that this is a situation to which music theorists will have to respond with a Stoic acceptance. It may be one, on the contrary, that they will want continually to challenge and to try to overcome.

That the most important issues in theory can never be pinned down neatly at all four corners is simultaneously the cause of both theory's frustration and charm. The frustration can be used creatively as a goad to spur us on to continual inquiry as we leapfrog from insight to insight. In a subject like theory that deals with provisional, debatable, and even fallible responses, it seems likely that not all proposed questions will receive a conclusive or absolute answer; in fact, as some answers are suggested, additional questions will bob up. According to Meyer, however, this situation should not be cause for despair:

Disheartened and perhaps dismayed by the speculative uncertainties of theory . . . too many humanists, particularly those in music, have tended to follow the well-worn path of safe scholarship. But to choose prospective certainty over present insight is both mistaken and misguided. It is mistaken because the search for final, definitive answers is an unattainable goal for those disciplines concerned with understanding and explanation. For since the future is open and influential, it can change our understanding both of past compositions and of past historical events. It is misguided—paradoxically so—because the enduring monuments of scholarship, which have shaped men's minds and beliefs, far from being cautious and circumspect, have been those which illuminated a relationship, a work of art, or a past epoch through a bold encompasing hypothesis. Though in all probability they will subsequently be revised, or even rejected, such works and theories endure because they are exciting and seminal: they lead to new discoveries and further formulations, and thereby continue to affect language, thought and behavior.[3]

That answers for this subject are necessarily elusive is no excuse for failing to grapple with the questions. Viewed in this context, the ultimate value of the endeavor will lie as much in the quality of new questions raised as in the answers given.

In any event, we may say that music theory appears to be more like philosophy than mathematics. Theory, then, is not just something to learn but is also something *to do*. It represents not just a cluster of answers but a range of options for thinking about and listening to music. Music theory, in my opinion, is not a *subject* like pharmacy with labels to learn and prescriptions to fill, but is an *activity*—more like composition or performance. The activity is *theorizing*: i.e., thinking about what we hear and hearing what we think about—and I would include even thinking about what we think.

A music theory program must distinguish between means (short-term goals) and ends (long-term goals). The acquisition of musical knowledge (facts), skills (performance techniques), and literacy (music reading) is *what you do* to make the final goals possible but does not represent the goals themselves. The purpose of all music training is to teach for musical understanding (to perceive, organize, and then conceptualize what you hear) and consequently to learn how to create musical expression and how to develop an aesthetic response to that expression.

7

Success in a music theory course cannot be measured by a grade at the semester's end but only by the strength of the reverberations from the course for decades afterward. A college theory program is only the beginning of a lifetime process in establishing, then revising and refining, a set of attitudes and modes of conceptual/perceptual operation for responding to music. After formal course work has been completed, this process is not usually called music theory, except by theorists, but it remains nevertheless at the core of any serious teacher's, performer's, composer's, or listener's growth as a musician.

Just as a balance must be achieved between learning the content of pre-existing theory (what others have thought about music) and, at a more advanced stage, creating original theory (how to think for oneself about music), a balance—or more precisely an integration—must be fashioned between the conceptual and perceptual components of students' training. It is handy to construct the following simple diagram as a way of picturing and discussing how these elements relate:

thinking / listening

This image illustrates the inseparable bond between these two principal aspects of all theory programs. These are not simply two sides of the same coin but the fusion of a single entity. This wholeness is separated into two parts only so that the internal interrelationships can be identified and more fully explained.

This association will be examined throughout the book and especially in the three central chapters, "Mind Training" (thinking), "Musical Analysis" (the link) and "Ear Training" (listening). Regardless of their correlation in the curriculum (from course to course, within the weekly teaching schedule, or even within the daily class routine), the dominant thesis of this book is the interdependence of thinking and listening. "No instruction in music can be valid unless it constantly relates intellectual understanding to aural experience."[4]

As represented in the diagram, each part of this "thinking/ listening" duality feeds into the other: the more thinking that takes place, the more there is to hear; the more listening that takes place, the more there is to ponder. Which aspect comes first is a "chicken-and-egg" problem that is beyond the discussion for now; either activity can, at times, lead to the other. Musical analysis is usually the operation that sets this cyclical and spiral process into motion. The goal of analysis is to understand from the inside out *how* and *why* a piece of music works and therefore, by extension, how it might have been composed, how it might be performed, heard, or taught.

"Thinking/listening" musicians, then, are prepared for more meaningful experiences in composing, performing, listening, and teaching. The above duality and the ultimate and most profound goals of music theory and analysis are stated most eloquently by Leonard Meyer: "to refine the aural imagination" and "to sensitize the cognitive ear" so that both our minds and feelings are expanded and enriched and experienced in ways *that otherwise might have been missed.*[5] To come in contact with music (and all the arts) is to apprehend more fully what it means to be human.

The teaching of the conceptual half of the twin pairing perhaps can best be thought of as intuition enhancement. In introductory remarks to beginning students Bruce Benward writes that

> *Intuition* is knowledge that comes to a person without conscious remembering or reasoning. Your music intuition includes a vast storehouse of familiar sounds, established patterns of melody, harmony, and rhythm, and an instinctive consciousness that you draw upon thousands of times in the performance of a single composition. Bits of information you have accumulated since your first musical experience are stored in your memory and are shaped into thoughts or judgments that you apply daily. You make split-second decisions about the phrasing of a melody, the application of dynamics (louds and softs), and the tempo of the music you play. And yet, you are seldom able to say precisely where this knowledge came from. Your musical intuition has become a part of you through your experience and, indeed, is one of the most valuable gifts in your possession.
>
> As your musical intuition has already told you, music is a complex and highly organized combination and arrangement of tones. Besides providing a rational knowledge of music, a study of music theory interacts with intuition—honing, sharpening, and enhancing it with further insights and perception not available from any other source. Much of what you learn . . . will at first be simply surface information that you apply in a cursory manner, but as the concepts and ideas mature in your mind they

9

will become a part of your musical makeup and will eventually amplify and broaden your musical intuition.[6]

Benward concludes that music theory might be defined as the study of artful designs and inventive patterns in music that are transformed by the mind into aesthetic experience. This transformation is achieved, of course, through performing and listening.

I have purposely chosen the term "listening" rather than "hearing" to underline the active nature of musical perception. William Thomson, in writing about the goals of music study, stresses this point and also the idea that reading and talking (i.e., thinking) about music without listening will prove to be empty:

> Even though the listening is more important than the talking, nevertheless, having one without the other robs us of much of the enjoyment, and prolongs the journey as well.
>
> Knowing a piece of music is much like knowing a person. It is one thing to observe and respond to skin-deep qualities. It is quite something else to make contact with the inner life—those deeper traits that make one person (or one composition) unique and prized. We seek this latter kind of knowing.
>
> An in-depth knowledge of a musical composition is not easy. Even Leonard Bernstein, one of the most gifted musicians of all times, acknowledges that "Music is hard." He means that getting "inside" a piece of music requires more than a passive hearing of its sounds, more than tapping one's foot to its pulse. He elaborates by saying that music ". . . may be easy to take, or pleasant to hear for many people; it may evoke fanciful images in the mind, or bathe in a sensuous glow, or stimulate, or soothe, or whatever. But none of that is listening." [*The Infinite Variety of Music*, pp. 19–20]
>
> [Music study should] help you become a listener of the kind Bernstein had in mind. Don't settle for less.[7]

In another introductory essay, Frederic Homan extends discussion of some of these points by speaking simply but persuasively about the purpose of theoretical study:

> Because music is so abstract—you can not touch or smell it, only hear it—we tend to listen as though we were having some sort of tonal bath. We hear the sounds in our head. Unlike words, there is no dictionary to define or explain what the

sounds "mean." We simply react to the sounds. The music washes over us and soon fades away leaving us pleased or irritated, interested or bored, elated or indifferent.

Similarly, when we learn to perform a piece of music we tend to move from note to note—in effect reading letters, not words—until the music is learned technically and somehow it begins to "make sense."

The problem to be addressed in [music theory] is, very simply, how sounds are put together to create music. The process is two-fold: what we hear when we listen to music and what we see on the printed page when we are performing. We seek to develop more awareness for ourselves of these two aspects of music.

Assuming that our ears function normally, our problem, then, is awareness and identification. Unfortunately most music study does not train us to listen (really), identify or even remember the music sounds we hear or use. This is left to accident. The student must put it all together alone and often by accident. And we say some are born with good ears and some are not. This is only partly true.

Some of us hear more precisely than others just as some see well without glasses while others require them to improve the clarity of their vision. But there is no use in improving our vision if we do not know what we are seeing.

There is a distinction between color blindness (the inability to recognize the difference between red and green, for example) and color ignorance (not recognizing carmine or magenta). There is a similar difference in sound perception. Few can not distinguish different pitches; many are sound ignorant, even people with considerable experience with music.

It is easier to overcome color ignorance or word ignorance than sound ignorance, especially if in our music background we have been allowed to ignore the specific characteristics of a sound or a piece of music. We develop the habit of not listening or confidently hearing the sounds.

Be fully aware of what you hear. Listen as you practice for lessons, in ensembles, attend concerts and recitals, watch television or listen to the radio. Look with your ears for the different characteristics of sound. Joyce Carey [*sic*], the novelist, suggested that when looking at a painting, feel it with your eyes. Can we "feel" the music with our ears?[8]

William Schuman has suggested the unforgettable term "virtuoso listener" for this goal.[9]

Once again, the connection between thinking and listening is explored by Peter Westergaard in his essay on the role of the theorist and his relationship to the chain of communication from composer to performer to listener.[10] Westergaard concludes that theory involves explaining the sense-making process used in imagining and hearing sounds—a process that flows through the entire chain. Music theory teaching, by implication, should then relate this process to a student's own experience of music so that this experience can be sharpened, heightened, and broadened.

The listener may be the key element in this communication chain since he is not simply the final link, but his function is also embedded in the role of the composer and performer. The theorist observes the whole chain internally by playing each role himself—i.e., he listens first as a composer, then as a performer, and finally he listens as a listener. To communicate and share with another person mutual pleasures in these experiences and to fill in one another's gaps in understanding is what is meant by "doing" music theory; it represents those "other things" about which I spoke earlier.

Sometimes theory goals are described in terms of musicianship. This important, but vague, concept is as elusive as music theory itself and—like a slippery bar of soap—is difficult to grip. Its meaning is so broad as to be almost useless. Most usage seems to center on skills and abilities that practicing musicians must have: connecting notation with sound (or sound with notation), reading music, conducting, performing at the keyboard and/or with one's major instrument/voice, developing historical perspective and analytical techniques, using appropriate terminology, learning music literature, etc.

Acquiring musicianship, however it is defined, is intimately bound up with theory training, of course—and most of a student's other music training as well. It all finally comes down to the competence to use our thinking ability to improve listening and our listening ability to improve thinking. As long as this cycle can be kept in motion, real education takes place; we learn so that we can learn even more. Each new accomplishment leads to yet more sophisticated and more challenging levels of investigation and perception that were never even imagined before. The helix is never completed which is why music theory, in this sense, is endlessly intriguing.

The concept of musicianship implies the practical application of skills rather than the ivory-tower philosophizing that is sometimes implied by "theory." Some teachers, in fact, would prefer to drop the word "theory" altogether and substitute "musicianship." This seems to put too great a burden on a theory program, however, since musicianship training includes other courses.

Some prefer "music practice" or simply "music" as the object of study. Even here, though, the aesthetic problems are plentiful. Do we define music as printed notation, the sound projected by the score in performance through physical wave vibrations, the psychological temporal experience of *one* particular performance as it is happening in the listener's mind, or the meaning of a piece as symbolized by the composer's pre-score mental sound image? This last possibility introduces yet a new problem (what is meaning?) and the can of worms is opened once again. All of these views can be true in different ways.

Regardless of what music theory is called, I believe that most teachers would agree that undergraduate classes can include both thinking about ideas (or even theorizing about theory—metatheory as it is called) and direct study of the music itself. These are not mutually exclusive any more than are the concept-forming and listening components. Common-sense balance among a wide range of mind-training and ear-training assignments and classroom activities with real music at the core is a desirable goal.

Theory does have some value, I think, as an end in itself. Since curiosity is a part of human experience, to investigate compositions just to see and hear how they are put together and why they sound like they do—why they qualify, in fact, as music and not something else—is a valid activity and should require no apology or elaborate defense. This might be called the "man-climbs-the-mountain-because-it's-there" view. Sometimes these conjectural or visionary undertakings do lead eventually in roundabout ways to more pragmatic and utilitarian ends (spin-offs); sometimes they are satisfying simply as stimulating and creative outlets in their own right.

Most students, however, will look for practical relevance. Recognition of music theory as a creative activity—like composition and performance—can be used to tremendous advantage in relating theory to these and other branches of music study. Like a drop of ink in a glass of water, music theory should infuse and permeate all aspects of a college music curriculum.

The urge—powerful because it makes our work easier—to teach theory in a box-like compartment should be vigorously resisted. Of prime importance in the overall university setting is the responsibility of the theory teacher (*and* the whole music faculty) to make connections between the content of a theory program and the entire range of a student's other musical experiences, such as performance, aesthetic response, and teaching preparation, so that all of these activities, including classroom instruction, applied lessons, rehearsals, concert attendance, etc. are mutually reinforcing. It is in this context that music theory can be one of the most meaningful and exciting aspects of a total musical education and it is in pursuit of this goal that teaching music theory becomes a fascinating, challenging, and rewarding profession.

TWO

Philosophical Orientations

T HE PROBLEM of defining music theory continues in this chapter, but from the viewpoint of conceptual pairings that represent the shaping characteristics of textbooks, curriculums, and teaching styles. These characteristics mold and control the content and even the choice and naming of course offerings and can bias and color—often in veiled and insidious ways—a teacher's presentation of materials.

I am not arguing here in favor of one particular slant but that such preconceptions be the result of planning, not accident. The elimination of prejudice is not necessarily a goal so long as that prejudice is acknowledged and can be defended against a background of alternative possibilities. Unyielding and narrow-minded dogmatism is rarely attractive, but strong, well-formed beliefs, partialities, and preferences are almost always a part of enthusiastic theory teaching. It is the extraordinary teacher who can go even one step further by combining conviction with tolerance for other views.

One central idea of this book is that all aspects of theory teaching—from the presentation of lecture material and drill practice to the construction of curricular models and statements of objectives—should be patterned by design and not by chance. It is not possible to avoid the question of philosophical orientation by eliminating the preliminary (actually constant) soul-searching that is a normal part of setting up or teaching a course; to *not* decide on a particular approach is itself a decision—a decision for confusion and for a course with no bearings.

Like the myth of objectivity in journalism, even the most

neutral courses will have hidden biases. The simple choice of a textbook (or none), type of assignments and exams (or none), and course content and order will involve partisanship of some kind. What is important is an awareness of the biases and their opposite counterparts or complements so that they are thought of as part of some larger context and range of options. While a philosophy may remain unspoken, it should never remain unknown. The very best courses incorporate their philosophical underpinnings into the content of the courses themselves by bringing them into the open for comparison with competing possibilities. This chapter, then, will attempt to provide a framework for discussing these underpinnings and how they may differ.

Integration versus Separation

Probably the most crucial issue facing a theory faculty is the proper relationship of thinking and listening activities in the design of an undergraduate theory program. The traditional view of coordinating written and aural skills has been to consider either an integrated or separated approach. According to this viewpoint, the integrated approach mixes ear training, analysis, and composition within a single unified course each semester. The musical advantage of this blending of topics is intended to guard against the potential danger of producing "paper-and-pencil" musicians, who purportedly are the result, for example, of a course devoted only to part-writing or analysis. Such individuals frequently are extremely proficient at manipulating the pitches of a figured-bass exercise or in placing roman numerals under chords but have little or no understanding of what the given progression sounds like or its musical sense. The study of music should include more than black dots and lines on white paper. If any meaningful grasp of written work is to be accomplished, then this work must be immediately reinforced by, and correlated with, its actual sound by related ear-training activities involving dictation, sightsinging, etc.

On the other hand, proponents of a separated approach argue that intellectual comprehension and hearing abilities develop at completely different rates—the ear, generally, lagging behind the eye and mind. The weekly or even daily lock-step correlation of intellectual and aural work can sometimes, in the integrated approach, impose a rigid and unnaturally slow pacing on written topics. For practical teaching reasons, then, and because of the inherently different nature of these skills, they must each be placed, according to this argument, on individualized time tracks in separate courses for maximum pedagogical effectiveness.

An additional thorny problem (frustrating to all who have ever tried fairly to make final student evaluations) involves the mechanics of grading, weighting, and averaging separate skills. The separated approach allows for the separate assignment of grades in separate courses for these distinct abilities. It also permits a more clear and strict monitoring of standards. Students in a separate sightsinging class, for example, could be held back if minimal proficiency levels were not achieved, while at the same time passing on to more advanced analysis courses if their written work were adequate. In the integrated approach, however, where not only topics but grades must be combined, the awarding of a single final grade for a variety of different activities frequently allows deficiencies to masquerade as real accomplishment, as inferior work slips through the grading net semester after semester.

To acquire a broader perspective it will be necessary to explore the narrowness of this traditional "either/or" approach and to suggest alternative possibilities by redefining "integrated theory" as a teaching method or technique rather than as a way of organizing or scheduling classes. Real integrated theory involves using written projects and analysis to develop a set of principles that can explain (as Noam Chomsky has done in linguistics) how a competent listener makes sense out of a piece of music. This set of principles is then used as the basis of an ear-training program that emphasizes not merely accuracy of performance or response but also the understanding of what is heard along with the attempt to hear even more. Through the kind of cyclical process discussed in chapter one, the hope is that both the thinking and listening aspects of ear training (and analysis) can nourish one another: the more that music is studied, the more there is to hear; the more that is heard, the more there is to learn.

Using both this newer and the more traditional definition of integration, then, curriculum design can take one of four rather than just two different forms: (1) integrated teaching within integrated classes; (2) integrated teaching within separated classes; (3) separated teaching within integrated classes; and (4) separated teaching within separated classes. Integration, then, has to do with making connections and establishing relationships between thinking about and listening to music and does not necessarily or automatically require a coordination of timetables for the two topics in the semester outline or a blending of results in assignment of final grades. Integration and correlation, in other words, are two different things.

It is quite possible, as the above fourfold outline suggests, for ear training and analysis to coexist within the same fifty-minute class and still be treated as isolated topics. It is likewise possible for a separate ear-training program to be devised, with an independent syllabus and grading procedures and separate course description, and still make use of integration in the teaching sense.

It is possible, in other words, to have the best of both worlds: the musical validity of relating sound to symbol and the practical advantage of individualizing the ordering and pacing of materials for both topics. The danger in separating theory into two different courses is that true integration will never happen, but that danger is always present anyway. The simple placement of two topics side by side within the same class does not guarantee their merger. Integration doesn't magically happen; it's created. What I am proposing, of course, is simply that solid cross-referenced teaching be emphasized regardless of course labeling or surface division of content. Types one and two of the above four choices, then, are the preferred models.

Analysis both leads the ear and is led by it. This dual process is endlessly spiral, although the analytical segment usually occupies a higher level of sophistication. Analysis must always be done in relation to sound, and listening (for improvement in the classroom) must always be done in relation to analysis. This can happen or fail to happen regardless of curricular structure. In spite of the important and often crucial role that drill and repetition play in building aural skills, ear training is primarily *mind* training—it's what goes on between the ears that counts. Knowing *how* to listen and *what* to listen for are the key ingredients. A basic repertoire of memorized patterns is often useful as a starting point for listening, but the application of melodic, harmonic, rhythmic, and formal procedures provides the student with the desirable and attractive option of "intelligent guessing"—i.e., bridging the gap from what can be heard to what can almost be heard by making predictions based on the most fundamental structural processes and operations of pitch and time.

Real integration is not a matter of course scheduling (this is correlation) but is a manner of presentation that uses conceptual frameworks to entice the lagging ear forward like the proverbial carrot in front of the horse. Full application of such frameworks for listening need not happen at their initial introduction in analytical work. It is their eventual use that is essential. Their effectiveness in ear training is dependent not on a correlation of weekly calendars but on that necessary connection between cognition and percpetion.

Although dozens of analysis and ear-training textbooks are available, few of them include the kind of integration discussed above. Chapter 5 ("Ear Training") will discuss in more detail these materials and approaches.

At one time (1950–60), the fashion in curriculum design leaned toward integration as a corrective to the splitting apart of theory programs into numerous fragments (part-writing, dictation, sightsinging, and keyboard, for example, each taught as a separate class, often even by separate instructors with little use of common or shared analytical principles). This type of organization was characteristic of theory teaching in most schools up through mid-century and often beyond. More recently, as the pendulum swings again, the trend at many schools seems to be back to separate aural-skills classes in an attempt to pin down student achievement. This probably reflects the influence of the competancy-based learning philosophy of the 1970s and which itself is part of the "back-to-basics" movement that pervades much of current educational practice.

Comprehensive Musicianship versus Isolation

Trends in teaching styles have also accounted for the rise and more recent decline in popularity of the comprehensive musicianship (CM) approach.[1] Like theory itself, CM means quite different things to different teachers and can be defined in many ways. CM grew out of the Literature and Materials theory program begun at Julliard in the late 1940s and early 1950s and received its greatest boost through the sponsored Contemporary Music Projects of the 1960s and early 1970s.

In general, CM (in undergraduate theory programs) refers to a curricular arrangement that attempts to include and interrelate at least four subjects that otherwise might be taught more conventionally as isolated courses. These subjects are music literature, harmony, counterpoint (and melody), and formal analysis. They could be set up as separate courses with a close coordination of outlines and concepts or, more ideally, combined in a single course taught by one individual or team.

A more complete and ambitious CM program might also combine music history, conducting, orchestration, keyboard skills, and even applied music (i.e., performance studies) and ensemble rehearsals with theory topics. A full-blown interdisciplinary flavor is achieved with the inclusion of formal, textural, and stylistic analogues from painting, sculpture, architecture, and poetry. As we have already seen, the integration of ear training with written work is a separate issue and is not necessarily part of the CM idea. CM programs both with and without integration of aural skills are possible. The underlying philosophy behind all CM plans is to bring together discrete elements and ideas from the various branches of music study so that students are taught to understand music as a unified whole rather than as detached fragments.

Most CM programs include the following specific traits:

1. All style periods are treated as being equally important. This progressive development has resulted in the rightful inclusion of both twentieth-century and pre-tonal music in the theory curriculum along with jazz, ethnic, and non-Western music in some programs. The undue emphasis on the common-practice period in traditional theory curriculums has been a shortcoming long in need of adjustment.

2. Real compositions in a variety of textures and mediums, as opposed to artificial exercises in four-part chorale style, form the core of study. Thus, the learning of music literature (although not necessarily in a chronological sequence) assumes

a central role as a goal of its own along with synthesizing basic theoretical principles.

3. Parametric analysis—both written and aural—is prominently featured. The traditional weighting of pitch relationships (especially harmony) in analysis is thereby balanced and augmented by attention to rhythm, timbre, texture, and other properties.

4. Composition and/or improvisation projects, not just mechanical note-pushing drills, are stressed. Exercises can often be important, especially for acquiring basic technique and facility (e.g., voice leading, control of dissonance/consonance, scoring, etc.) but real compositional work—both style imitation and purely original creation are useful for different reasons—can, once again, make a closer connection to real music and also add interest.

5. Rehearsing and performing of student or other compositions in class is a part of many CM programs. Just as swimming cannot be learned from a book, real music learning rarely takes place without this live contact; composing, analyzing, and then hearing and playing actual pieces is the musician's equivalent of jumping in the water and actually getting wet. "To play" music literally means to have fun by moving around sounds.

6. The most important aspect in the CM philosophy is that all of these activities and components be related to one another and lead to a unified and complete understanding. To rectify the compartmentalization of music study and to substitute holistic learning is the ultimate goal. All facts are originally learned one at a time, but genuine musical insight is usually only achieved when facts and ideas are *brought together* and seen in *true relationship* by totaling more than the sum of their parts.

At schools where CM theory programs have been tested, problems have sometimes arisen. While the following points cannot necessarily be considered weaknesses, they are nevertheless serious considerations that must be taken into account whenever modified or total CM curriculums are set up:

1. CM demands extensive preparation from the teaching faculty. Like integrated ear-training texts, published teaching materials for such an approach have been slow in coming. (See chapter 3 for a discussion of available texts.) Teachers are

often forced to construct homemade materials. And to arrange and correlate the vast network of interrelationships that is part of the philosophy can become an overwhelming burden. Frequently, the mechanics and organization of a CM course can become cumbersome, and grading factors are often difficult to calibrate.

2. CM requires unusually fine teaching. Superstar teachers whose background is broad enough to see the relationship between details and the larger picture are extremely rare. Most do not have the required expertise in enough different areas of music (theory, history, literature, performance) and more importantly lack the overview frame of reference to make all the interconnections; few have even the expertise just within theory itself to relate all of its branches and sub-branches (analytical systems, aesthetics, acoustics, psychoacoustics, pedagogy, history of theory, etc.). Under such conditions, team teaching may be required, but even here extremely close cooperation and unanimity of purpose are essential.

3. CM requires unusually committed, serious, and sophisticated students. Learning both patterns and associations, in addition to bits and pieces of information, implies that every course has built within it layers of meaning. When each item ties in with every other, it becomes difficult to trace all the intertwined strands of knowledge. A small student/teacher ratio can help but is unlikely in these economic times.

4. With so many topics to cover, a lack of time for in-depth study can become troublesome. The potential loss of detail and thoroughness raises the issue of breadth vs. depth. How to balance these two concerns in any kind of theory course cannot be answered by a pat formula. What is important is that this issue be acknowledged, brought to the surface, and worked out in some way that is consistent with the needs of students and philosophy of the faculty.

The risk of too much breadth is that vagueness and superficiallity can keep students afloat in a sea of overgeneralization without enough supporting anchors of data. The danger of too much depth is that they will drown in a flood of detail having too few basic principles with which to connect. A value, then, of isolated courses is that information can be packaged in convenient bite-size chunks for ease of sorting and intellectual digestion.

5. Another result of many topics in one course is that some tend to get lost in the shuffle. This is particularly true of ear training and sightsinging. Guarding against the slighting of real achievement with these important topics should be a high priority.

6. Finally, a more subtle problem is that eventually dogma can set in and work against the spirit of innovation and experimentation that is at the heart of the CM philosophy. A resolute effort should be made to sustain the fresh approaches and imagination that the CM movement has brought to college music theory programs.

In fairness to proponents of CM, it should be observed that many of the above problems are applicable not just to CM but involve difficulties of music teaching in general. As was suggested with integrated teaching earlier, perhaps it would be best if CM were defined as a teaching method rather than as a way of naming courses or organizing curriculums. Many of the goals and ideals of CM can be achieved, in other words, in courses that appear (on paper in a college catalog) to be narrow in scope.

Master teachers—those who are able to relate their specified subject to a wide range of others—have existed much longer than the term "comprehensive musicianship." It should be possible, for example, for an instructor in a traditional "isolated" harmony class to bring up aspects of counterpoint (linear approaches), simple orchestration (scoring of exercises), and even aspects of form (extension of principles operating at the phrase level to a whole piece)—all animated by reference to excerpts and complete compositions from the literature and within the context of psychological and compositional procedures broad enough to permit comparisons, as necessary, with pieces from a variety of style periods. Aspects of texture (register placement, density, timbral balance, etc.), pacing of climax points (control of tension/stability, contour, long-range shaping, etc.), the changing historical evolution of a pitch or rhythmic language, performance suggestions, and many other relatable topics can all be skillfully interwoven at appropriate moments; the subject of any harmony class can be just chords, or it can be music. (See the end of chapter 4 for a sample analysis that illustrates—among other things—how some of these topics could be worked into the study of a specific composition.)

23

The only boundary on a course should be one limited by the teacher's imagination and not one imposed by the course title, the department of origin, or the specialty of the instructor. Effective teaching, even in "isolated" courses, is not only cross-referenced to other courses but actually overlaps them in content occasionally. It is my strong feeling that enlightening education often exists most dynamically in these little pockets of overlap between courses—in those too-rare moments of proverbial mental "bell-ringing" when two teachers in different classes, perhaps, have explained the same idea in different ways and a student suddenly realizes the link between theory and history, theory and aesthetic pleasure, or theory and interpretation.

In a choir rehearsal, for a simple example, the tenors might be asked to crescendo slightly while holding a suspension across the barline so that the effect of the dissonance is not lost. The mere fact of actually using the terms "suspension" and "dissonance" and referring to metric placement will, for the student who has heard these terms before in a theory class, help to make that kind of a link (i.e., will ring a bell). Thousands of other similar examples could be cited for both inside and outside the theory class; good teaching within every area of a music department consists of finding and using such examples.

The performance studio and rehearsal hall rather than the theory classroom are probably the best places for pulling everything together. Golden opportunities abound here for coordinating the skills of aural perception and the knowledge of style and analysis with creative musical expression. It's disappointing that applied teachers and conductors are as timid in doing this coordinating as theory teachers.

Too often, the private-studio teacher manages little more than a lesson in forming embouchures, pushing valves, holding bows, correcting wrong notes, superimposing a canned interpretation learned from the teacher's teacher, and then assigning the next etude in the book, just as the theory lesson often never goes beyond naming the key, singing the interval, writing roman numerals, or labeling the formal mold. The private lesson is more than learning to play the violin or piano; it is learning to play music. The theory class likewise is more than about music theory: it is about music; it is about comprehensive musicianship.

The danger of isolated courses, then, is obvious: that this admirable intermingling will never happen. Putting the label of CM on a class or program will not automatically make it happen, though. And teaching one course on a single well-defined topic does not rule out the possibility of touching on a multitude of other related issues that will also be covered by another teacher at a different time in a different class, perhaps even from a different or even opposing point of view.

The real danger is not isolated courses but isolated learning. Synthesizing knowledge, thinking, experience, and feelings (i.e., comprehensive learning) is, of course, a lifetime process that goes on far past our schooling. Like integration of aural and written skills, CM is a teaching style that transcends curriculum design.

Historical versus Astylistic Approaches

Two different questions are connected with this pairing of terms. First, should a theory curriculum that compares historical style periods make use of a chronological or non-chronological ordering? And second, should the differences among style periods even be stressed at all or should more universal principles applicable to all music be taught?

The value of beginning with plainchant, for example, and continuing through the medieval and Renaissance periods leading eventually to the twentieth century would be greatest for those curriculums that either are correlated with a separate music history course or incorporate one directly. Even without the support of a detailed historical component, though, the chronological sequencing encourages study of the developmental aspects of theoretical principles. To trace the evolution and interrelationships of polyphony, pitch focus, intervallic usage, meter, timbre, dissonance, temporal proportion, or any important concept across the centuries not only increases understanding of the concepts themselves by establishing perspective and continuity (how each topic fits into the larger view of historical flow) but introduces additional topics such as the nature of musical style itself and style change—important elements in their own right.

To study a topic in relation to what it emerged from and

where it leads to involves the same kind of integrated and comprehensive learning that has already been mentioned—in this case linear (i.e., historical) connections from period to period while in the earlier cases (of ear training) vertical connections between simultaneous courses within a curriculum. For example, the early twentieth-century atonal language of Schoenberg, Berg, and Webern can only be properly understood as an outgrowth of the late nineteenth-century dissolution of tonality which, in turn, can only be properly understood as an outgrowth of the modal system (sixteenth and seventeenth centuries) and its succeeding gradual expansion, then undermining, through chromaticism, of functional pitch relationships (eighteenth and early nineteenth centuries). Do we finally need to go back to Gregorian chant to understand tone rows? Is the stream of music history as goal-oriented as musical compositions?

On the other hand, some may argue that the study of music should begin with examples that are most well known or most relevant for undergraduate students. The argument based on accessibility rather than chronology suggests beginning with the common-practice period (Bach, Beethoven, and Brahms) and depends on the psychology of moving from the simple (most familiar) to the complex (least familiar). Some theory teachers advocate beginning with twentieth-century music, since this is the music of our own times and therefore has the most meaning for us.

Yet another view recommends a teaching approach based on more fundamental concepts that cut through superficial stylistic distinctions and center on factors common to the music of all times and places. Style traits, in this view, are simply peripheral matters that mask the true universals of all epochs and cultures. For example, pieces by Machaut and Webern might be studied side by side to look for common features, such as handling of registral space, use of silence, motivic germs, rhythmic relationships, individual line independence, intervallic restrictions, density, time spans, cadences, etc. It would be normal in such a course of study to begin with an idea (defining a term, establishing an analytical category, pursuing a formal process, or discussing a compositional procedure) as the point of departure rather than a historical era or single piece, and then jump—often rapidly—from period to period, or composer to composer to illustrate the wide applicability and significance of the concept—not just for a style or particular composer but for music in general. The issue here seems to be whether differences or similarities are more important when comparing pieces.

There is no reason, of course, why a choice must be made. Both historical and astylistic aspects are necessary; these categories are not mutually exclusive. It is possible to teach historical context and awareness without necessarily a chronological ordering. The more important issue is not choosing which philosophy to adopt but in learning what *combination* of both can be effected and balanced in a particular teaching situation. In a chronological course it is important to remind students that certain basic features will always be present simply because of how music is defined and how listeners' minds are organized; in a concept-oriented class, it is necessary to notice how the stylistic assumptions and background of a composer can subtly (or even grossly) alter the working out of some underlying technique or expressive gesture. The hazard of universals is that they might become too universal by forcing principles of one style period inappropriately on another. The same goal—learning how pieces both correspond and contrast—can be achieved in more than one way. To borrow linguistic terms, the deeper inner structure *and* the transformations that lead to gradual changes in surface details are both essentials regardless of course orientation.

Concepts versus Skills

A final brief comparison in teaching philosophies attempts to distinguish between curriculums that stress speculative thinking and those that highlight practical application of knowledge. The concepts approach features reading, discussing, analyzing, and thinking about music. We can practice thinking in the same way we practice an instrument. The intellectual gear that is accumulated gradually becomes a part of our habitual thought process—a kind of mental posture that is taken toward issues. I am not talking about having a ready-made stereotyped response for every subject or simply teaching an immense vocabulary so that students become walking lexicons. But I am referring to developing the ability to think for oneself, to have informed opinions and strong convictions, yet to appreciate other viewpoints.

Musical understanding of real depth encourages growth[2] since it provides a backdrop against which new ideas, pieces, or listening experiences can be placed and eventually assimilated. The kind of inflexibility that characterizes some analytical systems or theory programs recalls the well-known Emerson quote: "Foolish consistency is the hobgoblin of small minds." Too often teaching styles foster rigid conceptual molds that restrict the consideration of alternate questions and answers. It is easy to fall into the old trap of accepting the facts that support one's preconceived molds and rejecting those that do not. A wide variety of thinking approaches to meet a wide variety of musical situations is the goal. The psychologist Andrew Maslow says that if our only tool is a hammer, we view every problem as a nail.

The skills approach views the learning of music theory as "doing" things such as singing intervals, aurally recognizing a chord, transposing a scale, harmonizing a melody, performing a keyboard progression, composing a fugue, conducting an ensemble, arranging an exercise for string quartet, etc. These activities are sometimes referred to as practical musicianship.

It should be obvious by now that it is not necessary to choose an "either/or" approach. Concepts and skills can be mutually compatible and reinforcing. An amalgamation of the two is the only sensible solution. The reason for even mentioning this pairing of approaches is to avoid the imbalance that can result when both components and their relationships are not recognized. Perhaps it would be good to remember the earlier distinction made between means and ends. While understanding by itself can rarely lead to improvement in skills, the practicing of skills can often aid in the development of understanding. This is not to argue for the priority of either item but rather for their shared dependence.

"If one were to ask any number of people to state the purpose of an education, the answers, though varied, would express the concept that an education prepares the individual for something he will do after his education is completed. I make a subtle switch by saying: I do not educate the individual in

order that he might do a particular thing, I have him do a
particular thing in order that he might become educated."[3]

Summary

All theory programs, then, are colored—consciously or un-
consciously—by a teacher's or faculty's stance on these four
issues: (1) integration vs. separation; (2) CM vs. isolation; (3)
historical vs. astylistic approaches; and (4) concepts vs. skills.
These pairings, in a way, have presented false issues by suggesting that choices rather than blendings are required in theory teaching. The pairings were purposely set up in this way,
however, since this is how they are often viewed by teachers. It
seems to me, though, that many of the values of these approaches are not contradictory at all (as implied by the use of
"vs.") but rather complementary.

To mix and unite these values in the correct proportion for a
particular school requires the same degree of craft in theory
teaching that is required for doing theory itself. Nearly every
solution will involve compromises of some kind merely because our time is so limited; to emphasize one topic or method
necessarily slights something else. To take advantage of the
strengths and to protect against the weaknesses of one approach, we must also be aware of the strengths and weaknesses of its counterpart, just as in playing the beginning
moves for the white pieces in a particular chess opening, we
must also know the corresponding moves for black. To com-
pensate for defects or gaps in the structure of a class or the
presentation of a teacher involves, first of all, a knowledge of
what those shortcomings are, why they are there, and what
different pattern of shortcomings might spring into existence
with corrections of one kind or another. A delicate web of
counterbalances is continually being spun in creative theory
teaching. It is not possible in a book of this type to specify
exactly the structure of this web. It must vary from situation to
situation since theory teachers themselves vary in temperament
and background, theory students vary in ability and needs, and
music schools vary in goals and mission.

The central concept in successful theory teaching is *synthe-*

sis. CM, integration of ear training and analysis, and all the others are more like teaching attitudes than underlying course layouts. This is why effective theory learning can be accomplished (or fail) in such a wide variety of curricular settings. First-rate teachers are always able to outfox the inherent flaws of imperfect course blueprints by working around the problems even as they are mindful of new difficulties that might arise from the adjustments they make. Poor teachers are rarely successful in the most perfect program design since they are unlikely to know how to squeeze all the benefits from its soundness—in some cases the concepts of strength/weakness and similarity/difference are absent from their world view.

To have a method for comparing and contrasting teaching approaches, to have a frame of reference for measuring one's own favored system against the others, to develop a steady personal credo, yet remain flexible and receptive to new or auxiliary ideas, is to take the beginning steps in teaching music theory with impact and finesse.

PART TWO

Thinking and Listening

THREE

Mind Training

Mind training is teaching the musical concepts, ideas, and terminology that are used in talking about and thinking about music. Composition and analysis are two of the skills and activities that depend on conceptual knowledge. And most important of all, music reading and meaningful listening are totally dependent on the ability to conceptualize what is heard. Likewise, ideas about music have little chance of being fully understood without aural illustration and reinforcement. It is probably easier to achieve intellectual comprehension (it can begin, for example, at the simple level of definition) than aural comprehension, so our discussion will start with mind training rather than ear training. However, the interdependence of the two cannot be overstressed.

Fundamentals

The fundamentals of pitch include scales, intervals, key signatures, and triads. These four topics are so elementary that they are often hastily skimmed over as necessary evils before the real work of the semester begins. In fact, many college teachers (and books) assume that entering music majors will be sufficiently acquainted with these topics and therefore begin immediately with harmony study, melodic analysis, etc. with perhaps a token nod in the direction of fundamentals in the form of a quick one- or two-week review. The frequent casual suggestion found in theory texts that a supplementary book should be assigned, if necessary, gives the impression that these preliminary matters are incidental—almost optional.

It is true that most students with performance experience and the ability to read notes (know letter names) in treble and/or bass clef have picked up some knowledge of these fundamentals from their pre-college background (e.g., in a high school ensemble or even theory class; private applied lessons—especially if piano—or summer music camp). But it has been my experience that this knowledge is almost always a mile wide and an inch deep. They often know a little bit about many different things but nothing about connections, reasons why things work in a particular way, precise and discriminating terminology, or the long-range significance of the information for future study.

For example, students will often be aware of differences between major and minor scales and may even be familiar with the spelling and terminology for the three forms of minor. They usually will not know, however, *why* alterations of scale degrees 6 and 7 exist or, more importantly, that in real music distinctions among minor scale forms—sometimes even between major and minor—are usually artificial. They may know terms like parallel and relative but not the different comparisons that are implied by the concepts.

Thorough knowledge of fundamentals can almost never be assumed; it must be taught as any other subject. A superficial grounding in the basic elements of pitch will cause more problems later on than almost any other form of negligence.

An opposite miscalculation is to indulge a class by stretching out the study of fundamentals for months and months. Students will gladly take all semester to learn just scales if given the opportunity. There is no need in theory teaching to prove the wisdom of Parkinson's Law, "work expands to fill the time available." The optimum time for covering fundamentals seems to be about four to six weeks (with obvious modifications for unusually weak or strong classes, curriculum structure, type of music department, and other background factors).

I stress the word "master" rather than learn since an important distinction—especially for this topic—should be made between mastery and knowledge. It is not enough for a student to be able to figure out the answer for spelling a triad or recognizing a key signature. Understanding the principles behind such questions is, of course, essential since the same principles will often be involved in more complex questions in later study. But eventually the information must be so totally engraved into the natural thinking grooves that responses are swift, sure, and automatic. Like a basic two hundred word vocabulary in a language, or the multiplication table in mathematics, certain facts in music (e.g., all major and minor scales, whole steps, all P5s, all major and minor triads, and all key signatures), once they are understood, must then actually be memorized.

Some students never catch on that information computed from scratch each time is useless. Unless spelling or recognition of these constantly recurring pitch relationships can be instantaneous, simple analysis and composition assignments will take so many hours that no connection will ever be noticed between musical events occurring just seconds apart aurally or an inch away visually. We have all had the awkward experience in beginning foreign language study of translating a sentence into English by looking up almost every word in a dictionary; by the time we get to the end, we have forgotten the beginning.

Fundamentals study occurs in three stages: (1) understanding the concept behind a topic (e.g., the whole-step/half-step pattern of a major scale—the two identical tetrachords); (2) developing accuracy through practice; and (3) developing speed. The culminating goal at this third level is *fluency*—a smooth and instant melding of comprehension, precision, and quickness so that the desired information is always confidently at one's fingertips.

This insistence on mastery should remind students (and teachers) that if preliminary or background rudiments are whisked aside too nonchalantly in the early phases of training, the resulting gaps or weaknesses will invariably come back— maybe in a week, a month, or a semester—to haunt the offender. Sometimes a slower and more thorough pace at the beginning permits more rapid development later on. Much of theory teaching unnecessarily involves moving three steps forward and two steps back. If special attention is given to making the initial steps steady ones, the need for time-wasting zigzags is greatly reduced and a sense of straight-line progress can be achieved. Too many theory programs sadly begin on the wrong foot altogether by ignoring these simple truths.

Fundamentals, then, are the foundation for all further tonal study. Even more advanced beginners can profit from this preparatory stage since a particular slant in presentation can often shed new light on familiar material, suggest a coupling with some more subtle idea, provide exactly the correct term for communication, or even clarify misunderstandings. My own theory experience corresponds with that of W. Francis McBeth: "Every student that I have had who had trouble with theory was weak in fundamentals, fundamentals being thinking in keys, building intervals and chords, etc. I have never had a student who was strong in fundamentals and weak in theory. Speed in fundamentals is imperative. Theory study is like building blocks—no one block can be omitted or skipped."[1]

Teacher impatience and the desire to move to more interesting or more "important" topics, and teacher reluctance to leave the safety of fundamentals—thus postponing the pitfalls and confrontations of substantial analysis—often account for either the skimming or the sluggish saturation that characterizes the pacing of fundamentals in some curriculums. It is true that rudiments represent only the outer layer of a vast and unfathomable discipline, but there is no way to reach the inner depths of any subject without first passing through the surface.

A dilemma often facing teachers of fundamentals is whether to study scales or intervals first. Standard textbooks can be found supporting either choice. Using the idea of presenting new topics as outgrowths of previously studied material and simultaneously as preparation for future topics seems to tip the balance in favor of doing scales first.

The distinction between whole and half steps and between different kinds of half steps (m2 vs. A1) would be an essential preliminary condition for constructing scales. Before continuing to larger intervals, however, by measuring them as sums of whole and half steps, it seems to me to be more logical to use these tiny building blocks immediately for the creation of a larger structural unit that can itself be exploited for yet additional purposes. A foundation of major and minor scales sets up perfectly the continuation into more comprehensive interval study since all the larger sizes can be generated easily, quickly, and accurately from some scale by using the proper tonic reference pitch (sometimes requiring half-step adjustments for quality or change of direction from the reference note). To study intervals before the framework of scales has been erected forces the student into the complicated ritual of counting large numbers of semitones—a chore that is time-consuming, tiresome, highly inaccurate, and that offers little opportunity for double-checking against another pitch scaffold. To think of a P5 as seven half-steps rather than as the tonic/dominant backbone of all major and minor scales—at least for simple spelling purposes—is inefficient at best. P5s, of course, occur in other locations within tonal scales and in nontonal contexts as well, and for analysis purposes it is often necessary to picture or hear the more abstract non-functional size. Knowing both the scale reference and the half-step distance does provide that double check, if necessary, at the simple level of beginning spelling. Once familiarity (and *mastery*) with the standard intervals is achieved, reference systems of any kind are rapidly discarded anyway. Intervals are then no longer counted or figured—they are known directly with certainty as you would know your own name.

I prefer introducing minor scales by comparison with the parallel major since the adjustments and changes in scale degrees 3, 6, and 7 can be made more vivid. More important, the functional similarity in various scale degrees can be made clear even while these coloristic modal interchanges are substituted. Parallel relationships underscore the unity of tonality by showing two "different" scales existing within a *single* functional system.

In tonal music there is only one scale, the major/minor scale, with many cross-borrowings. Leland Smith goes so far as to say, "in tonal music the minor mode has no separate existence, but represents merely a fairly consistently applied group of alterations—flattings—of certain parts of the major mode."[2] His contention (although not all will agree) is that, while minor did not originate historically in this way, its functional use is best understood from this point of view. This combination of teaching surface differences (three minors and one major) *and* underlying similarities (functional meaning) is useful as a technique for many topics both simple and advanced.

Relative scales are important for studying key signatures and as a prelude to modulation. The concept of pitch reinterpretation is involved here as (almost) the same pitches assume different relationships—different pulls and attractions—toward one another. For example, the pitch B (as leading tone) in the scale of C has an upward tendency (or stylistic probability) while in the changed context of A minor is more likely to move down toward tonic.

Key signatures are probably the easiest basic to memorize. First, they are limited in number, and second, they exist within such an evident larger pattern (circle of fifths, and interlocking tetrachords). The whole topic is loaded with ready-made teaching tricks: flats and sharps in reverse order; the second half of one scale becomes the first half of the next (or vice versa); the same letter names add up to seven accidentals; the relative tonics are a m3 apart; parallel minors always have three more flats (or three fewer sharps); etc. All of these facts must be understood as part of the network of relationships—a network that has additional properties and meanings beyond key signatures. For facts this simple, though, the whole network should not have to be assembled anew each time. Key signatures must be recalled instantly and especially for minor should be known directly, not as a spin-off of the relative major.

Once scales, and then intervals, are learned, triad study follows naturally. In fact, there is hardly anything new to learn except defining the four basic qualities. True facility with scales and intervals pays enormous dividends in accuracy and speed with triads. Students can quickly develop the ability to think of a triad as a single unit rather than computing each note individually. At an early stage the distance of root to third, third to fifth, and root to fifth must be detailed. Then, however, the constituent parts should be brought together as *one* thing just as first graders are initially taught the letters, C . . . A . . . T and then the word "cat."

Triads should be memorized in groups of letter names sharing common configurations of accidentals. For example, in major triads, the family that requires no accidentals (or all sharps or all flats) is CEG, FAC, and GBD; and the family with sharps on the middle note: DF#A, EG#B, and AC#E, and their photographic negatives with flats on the outer notes. Similar topographies of white-and-black keys on the piano can be made for minor triads. Particular care must always be taken with triads (and with P4s and P5s) including the letter names B and F since these represent a special family of their own.

By memorizing all the common major and minor triads (about thirty-five chords) once and for all, a tremendous gain in speed and ease of thinking can be attained. If the major and minor ones are known, then all diminished and augmented triads can be readily calculated as a variation of a more familiar type. Soon the common ones (e.g., BDF) of these categories will be thoroughly learned as well.

The final follow-up step of fusing notes into chords (or melodies) that occurs at the memory stage is frequently never achieved in the opening weeks of a course resulting, months later, in students whose minds and eyes (and ears) shift from pitch to pitch in little jerks instead of long smooth sweeps. These pathetic (and I'm sure frustrated) students can be recognized easily at exam time as their pencil tips touch each note one at a time laboriously building up vertical and horizontal fragments that never quite make sense. What takes tedious minutes of piecing together for some, others can see at a glance.

The goal of fluency in fundamentals is not speed as an end in itself but as an aid to continuity. Having continuity in reading and hearing music means being able to collect and connect the separate bits of conceptual and perceptual information into groupings that coalesce. Below a certain threshold of quick response, pattern recognition is simply unlikely since the separate parts will never be held together long enough to form into something bigger. Knowing about notes, we can build scales. Knowing about scales, we can learn intervals and can imagine them against this backdrop. Knowing about both scales and intervals, we can learn chords, melodies, and the larger groupings like progressions, phrases, sections, and all the rest—but only if the patterns of these early links are literally memorized. Otherwise the whole chain must be reconstructed each time in the student's mind and even then is usually so heavy that its weight becomes overwhelming as it is dragged to each new piece.

I am dwelling on fundamentals because I am convinced that the secret of learning succeeding topics (e.g., roman numerals, non-harmonic tones, 7th chords, secondary dominants, modulations, advancd chromatic harmony, even formal analysis) lies in having each preceding stage totally anchored.

A vigorous internal continuity in a curriculum can be realized by slanting a presentation to foreshadow approaching subjects which share common features. In this regard, good theory teachers often resemble chess grandmasters by thinking ahead many moves—or lessons. For example, at that relatively early point when triad spelling and roman numerals are first encountered, students can be asked to identify the quality of a given triad and to place it by roman numeral in as many keys as possible. In addition to the obvious values of label matching, this exercise also prepares for the flexibility in mental imagery required for proper understanding of pivot chords in modulation—a topic that is not likely to appear until much later but for which the student has been primed in advance. At the earlier stage, the student will not even know what a pivot chord is; yet, at the proper time the skillful teacher can ease in this concept most naturally. It will be, by then, in the student's repertoire of thinking habits about music.

Music theory taught in this manner is almost painless, since the additional doses of truly new material are always relatively tiny. In this sense, real growth in understanding is cummulative and graduated. Almost never is it necessary to start a "new" topic from square one. Music theory is simply one long continuum and actually becomes more comprehensible the further one travels. As with a jigsaw puzzle, the borders are sketched first and as more pieces are added, the bigger picture becomes easier to see. Those last pieces really fall into place quickly. This rush of excitement in finally finishing a puzzle is analogous to experiencing the "aha" response in theory when separate facts or thoughts are brought suddenly together and seen for the first time in kinship. Unlike working puzzles, theory never finally ties together all the loose ends, since the picture itself is constantly expanding. Each new achieved goal becomes a springboard for additional study.

Frequently trouble occurs in an assigned task (such as spelling a secondary dominant 7th) not because that current topic itself is misunderstood, but because some previously assumed knowledge is incomplete, missing, or just insecure (such as simpler primary dominant 7ths, just a plain dominant triad, or given scale knowledge, etc.). To remove the stumbling block, all of the steps leading to that task must be retraced—steps that supposedly were established earlier in the course. By eliminating difficulties one at a time, like peeling layers of skin from an onion, attention can be focused on the precise location and nature of the hindrance. These earlier flaws must then be mended or the required information (re)established before additional information augments the load; the foundation must be able to bear the weight of the structure being erected above.

To achieve fluency in fundamentals, a variety of assignments and drills can be employed. To promote mental agility and complete proficiency, it is desirable for questions to be asked in as many ways as possible, not just the obvious ones. For example, problems should be concocted so that predictable patterns and familiar habits of thinking are skewed by situations that are inside out, upside down, and backwards (question and answer reversed)—to be specific:

1. Instead of spelling scales just from tonic, also provide a note in the middle of the scale; identify it by number, syllable, or function and have the student complete the given spelling from the internal evidence. For example, spell the harmonic minor scale that uses G♭ as the 6th degree.

2. Provide a given tonic and mode and have the student locate a specific note within its scale. For example, what is the mediant (or 3, or mi) of E major?

3. Provide a four-note step-wise scale fragment with accidentals; have the student list all possible scales where this fragment might occur (as a beginning, middle, ending, or overlap into the next octave).

4. Provide a set of random pitches (two, three, or four notes) perhaps in different registers; have the student list all possible scales that include these pitches. These last two items provide good class discussion—especially when students are required to outline the steps that led to their answer.

5. Have students name the five chromatic pitches that do *not* occur in a given scale.

6. *Recite* aloud and quickly the letter names and accidentals of given scales, intervals, or triads.

7. Identify intervals by changing clef signs, keeping pitches and accidentals on the same lines and spaces.

8. Spell intervals both up and down from a given pitch.

9. Spell a whole series of different intervals all from the same given pitch.

10. Spell a whole series of identical intervals from different pitches.

11. Combine operations by identifying intervals between given scale degrees.

12. Construct a spelling chain: what is the third of the next-to-last chord in a plagal cadence in the relative minor of the major key with five sharps key signature? Hundreds of similar examples either less or even more complicated are possible. Since a single error in such a chain can result in a wrong final answer, these questions can be unfair. There is no way to distinguish a near miss (one weak link) from total failure (a whole series of inaccuracies). They do, however, mimic superbly real-life musical situations where reliable judgements demand that every step be correct. Musical analysis is not like ping-pong where one can start over on each point but more like chess where nineteen brilliant moves can be undone by a blunder on the twentieth.

13. Flash cards, although reminiscent of elementary school, provide excellent practice for drilling key signatures, triads, scales, and maybe even some intervals. Just writing them out on the cards is practice in itself. They can be rehearsed both front and back (question and answer).

14. Keyboard reinforcement is one of the best ways to instill knowledge of fundamentals (see later section in this chapter).

15. Familiar tunes (besides, of course, substantial musical examples) can be used to quickly illustrate simple concepts. For example, "Greensleeves" (in its various versions) is ideal for demonstrating the possibilities of raised and lowered sixth and seventh scale degrees.

16. Timed classroom quizzes, if not overdone, can encourage—almost force—the mind toward nimbleness. For example, spelling forty triads (M, m, d, A; two clefs; root position only given the root and quality; no roman numerals) in five minutes is not unreasonable after sufficient preliminary explanations, practice with flash-card drill, and worksheet assignments have been completed. To write eight triads per minute requires that the hand make circles about as fast as possible. At this level of proficiency, thinking of separate intervals and notes is eliminated. The mind works on automatic pilot with as little thinking as possible—which is the point. Compe-

tence of a lower order is practically useless for later harmonic analysis and composition.

The pressure of constant nerve-racking speed tests can be detrimental to the progress of some students. When used judiciously, though, most students can eventually be convinced of the long-range benefits. Diligent drill work early can substantially reduce homework time later and, more importantly, amplify understanding.

Achieving mental fluency in pitch relationships is only one of the reasons for perfecting fundamentals. The rudiments also embrace concepts—often in an embryonic state—that emerge with crucial importance during ensuing study. A conceptual grasp of the material, in addition to development of the automatic response, will set the stage logically, then, for the follow-up phases. One of the best ways of tuning up the understanding is to scrutinize fine distinctions among and between groups and pairs of commonly confused terms. Developing an appreciation for discriminating and articulate comparisons is a habit worth cultivating for all aspects of theoretical study and can be launched from the earliest stages. The following list provides some starting points:

1. Relative vs. parallel scales
2. Natural vs. harmonic vs. melodic minor (ascending vs. descending)
3. Major/minor scales vs. church modes vs. whole-tone (or pentatonic, octatonic, synthetic, etc.)
4. Compound vs. simple intervals
5. Consonant vs. dissonant intervals (a good place to introduce the concept of contextual sensitivity in discussion of the P4 and historical evolution/changing function of P4s, 3rds, and 6ths)
6. Key signature vs. key
7. Key (or scale) vs. tonality
8. Meter signature vs. meter
9. Meter vs. rhythm
10. Chord vs. triad
11. Chord inversion vs. interval inversion
12. Root vs. bass (extremely important and almost always misunderstood at first)

13. The seven scale-degree functional names
14. Leading-tone vs. subtonic
15. Seven functional names vs. three harmonic functions
16. Melodic tendency tones (active vs. passive); crucial for tonal hearing
17. Enharmonic equivalence in spelling

One final purely practical goal can be accomplished during fundamentals work: as precision of thinking is gradually entrenched, precision and neatness of notation can follow. Two facets are involved: (1) correctness of manuscript writing (i.e., following the proper conventions regarding signatures, stems, beaming, ledger lines, rests, expression marks, etc.); and (2) calligraphy (i.e., the *art* of making legible and even pleasing written notation in the size and shape of note heads and clefs, proper alignment among parts, thickness and straightness of lines, etc.). Sloppiness is a bad habit that probably doesn't encourage clear, organized thinking. There is no reason why careful, accurate notation cannot become a habit also. But it won't happen without asking.

Tonal Harmony

Many courses contain common-practice harmony as their main topic. Certain critical issues about teaching approaches must be faced in such programs:

1. ROMAN NUMERALS VERSUS FUNCTION

Placing conventional roman numerals under chords has frequently been criticized as mere labeling. These labels in themselves simply identify the pitches belonging to a chord and that chord's location within the scale of a defined key. Since the roman numerals represent only rather trivial descriptive tags, some teachers have chosen to underplay their role in harmonic analysis by substituting or supplementing with other symbolic systems. Some of the prejudice against roman numerals is a reaction against the chord-grammar approach of most textbooks from the early to mid-twentieth century. These books usually had chapter after chapter of figured-bass exercises in unvarying four-part texture with little or no reference to real musical examples, resulting in a sterile and distorted view of both music and music theory.

In moving toward a more meaningful approach to harmony instruction, however, roman numerals should not too readily be ridiculed or discarded. In working with beginning harmony students, the limitations of such symbols—of any representational signs—should be fully recognized just as the values should be fully exploited. Roman numerals do provide an excellent and comprehensive means of codifying the raw materials of tonal music. Although this descriptive level represents only the first stage in explaining pitch operations, it certainly represents an essential stage. Just as some courses skim over fundamentals too quickly, some harmony classes move to sophisticated concepts before students can reliably and accurately identify the simple pitch facts of those more advanced relationships. If roman numerals are to be used at all, then, or used in combination with other methods, it is vital that students be adroit at their manipulation.

The issue of whether or not to use both upper- and lower-case symbols is more slight but still germane. Two sizes permit finer distinctions in assigning quality and therefore require more discrimination in analysis. Reliance on just upper-case symbols is simpler but one size is less specific and less finely tuned. Some teachers will especially want to stress figured-bass symbology for part-writing—i.e., the use of arabic rather than (or in combination with) roman numerals.

It is important, as students become skilled in using and recognizing chords (through spelling drills, part-writing and composition activities, and old-fashioned harmonic analysis), that they move to the next stage and put this information to some worthwhile purpose. If we pretend for the sake of argument that roman numerals really exist in music (as we make similar assumptions about numbers having true existence in the real world as opposed to being just convenient constructs of our minds), then we can probably say that their most important duty is to bear harmonic function. These functions are conventionally described as predominant (or dominant-preparation), dominant, and tonic. It is through these functions that functional tonality (late 1600s to late 1800s) can be distinguished from broader tonal applications of tonality that are often defined as a group of pitches revolving around a focal note (and

45

that include the modal language of medieval and Renaissance periods, some twentieth-century styles, and those of most non-Western cultures as well).

These three functions are just categories into which chords can be lumped, like sorting out vegetables into bins, and unless thoughtful definitions can be established for these classifications, we are back to labels again. But what do the labels mean? For the labels to be useful, they must explain how one event (chord, interval, pitch) leads to another and how each succeeding event grows from what came before. The study of harmonic progressions in tonal music is the study of logical continuity and psychological flow. Understanding the inner fluctuation of tension and stability is the core of harmonic analysis and is the reason for converting the descriptive but inert symbols of roman numeral analysis into functional carriers of dynamic musical motion.

The concept of function is the essence of the common-practice tonal system. It is an outgrowth of cadential action in that the three primary functions are those that operate in a key-defining cadence: *link/preparation* (predominant); *cadence signal* (dominant); and *arrival/repose* (tonic). It is possible to categorize this harmonic action in terms of three psychological and/or kinesthetic states: (1) the sensation of rest and finality of the keynote itself (tonic); (2) the state of dissonance that evokes or attracts this sensation (dominant); and (3) the set-up environment in which such attraction is likely to take place (predominant).

Tonal music's forward thrust derives from projections-in-time of the harmonic energy generated by primary functional relationships. These *relationships,* not the chords themselves, are responsible for our sensations of tonal centers and the establishing of keys. They infuse tonal music with the potentialities of movement towards and from specific goals and of arrival. These sensations are perceived, thanks to cultural conditioning, even without our discovering their special mechanisms. But unless we are consciously aware of them, they are only vaguely felt, and their nuances and structural importance escape us. It is essential that these sensations be heard through the reinforcement of visual and intellectual experience—through mind training.

Tonic function is possessed only by stable chords (major and minor triads). In triadic music, the tonic function is produced by the tonic triad most definitively in root position and with the tonic note doubled at the octave in the uppermost voice. Inverting this structure successively reduces its conclusiveness.

This function is most frequently the first event you hear in a tonal piece. After that, when it is prepared and signalled, you can always hear it coming. That's what makes surprises, cliff-hangers, and elisions possible. A strongly prepared tonic may often be detained by a momentary substitute, which makes its eventual arrival all the stronger. It may also be waylaid, dislodged, or reinterpreted.

Pitch reinterpretation illustrates the beautiful simplicity and remarkable flexibility of functional tonality. Tonal inflection (e.g., secondary dominants) and modulation depend on the chain-like linking and pivotal action of functions in which a single sonority does double duty as the tonic member, for example, of one function-group and the predominant or dominant member of another.

A functional dominant must contain at least the leading tone of the tonic it resolves to. Consequently the dominant chord must contain a major third. (A minor dominant triad may act as a point of arrival for the key scheme of a piece but will *not* be the functioning dominant chord of the piece.) This function is also shared by extensions of the dominant chord (vii°; vii$^{\varnothing 7}$;vii^{o7}). It should be emphasized that the tonic $\frac{6}{4}$ chord, in spite of its common roman-numeral designation, is a dominant-functioning chord. The $\frac{6}{4}$ act as dissonances to the $\frac{5}{3}$ of the dominant chord. Therefore, a roman numeral by itself is not a reliable indicator of function.

The dominant function is most strongly represented by the dominant-seventh chord since the intervallic attraction of the tonal tritone (scale degrees 4 and 7) summons its resolution to the simpler sonority of the tonic chord. The function is somewhat weaker in the simple V chord unless the leading tone is exposed (by position or timbre); then, the leading tone's directional tendency of rising to the tonic note epitomizes the sense of resolution.

Predominant function creates the backdrop for the telling movement of dominant tension to tonic stability. Consequently it is a function shared by many sonorities including the subdominant, supertonic, augmented 6th chords, Neapolitan 6th, and V/V; these chords are all related structurally (i.e., they

47

all include scale degrees 4 and 6 implying linear convergence inward toward the dominant, and all are slight variations of one another in terms of spelling). Notice that the function of this family of chords can only be perceived in context. In isolation, and especially by ear alone, they are either functionally neutral (e.g., a simple triad) or deliciously ambiguous (IV_5^6 or V_5^6/V or Ge^6 might all sound alike but work in quite different ways). It is not unusual to find several of these predominants in tandem—the effect being a stretching of the set-up: an augmentation or braking of the harmonic rhythm.

In fact, all the functions are capable of being spaced out over the course of a phrase; they are rarely as dense as in a harmony exercise. The spacing out of functions—called prolongation—is one of the most important concepts of harmonic analysis and is also an important element of form. Tonal music can be considered (and heard) as a mapping out in time of functional relationships. This happens on many structural levels. The time involved in projecting a simple cadence is related to the importance of such an event in the overall plan of a piece. On a larger level, key areas themselves may be understood and related to the central tonic in terms of large-duration prolongations of cadential function.

Just as roman numerals are the link from fundamentals to harmony, functional analysis, in turn, is the link from harmony to musical form. Roman-numeral analysis is only valuable when used for something besides chord identification. These other things include key areas and their large-scale relationships, transitions vs. arrival points, strength and weakness of events, connections between events, use of purposeful ambiguity, and especially the initiation and eventual achievement— through all kinds of obstructions and embellishments— of musical goals.

Of all these uses for functional analysis perhaps the most practical is the simple task of key identification in those passages where the prevailing key does not match the key signature. In my experience, the greatest analytical weakness of incoming graduate students is their frequent inability to recognize key areas (either cadentially realized or ones just passed through) in conventional tonal pieces even though their application of correct labels is just as frequently quite accurate *once the key has been determined*. But determining that key in the first place is their problem. For example, they invariably will be totally lost if set down in the middle of a typical classical development section—especially if given the score only with no aural clues except their own powers of imagery (which points out a deficiency of ear training as well for most of them). This problem suggests that meaningful harmony classes should devote as much attention to recognizing keys (in places other than the beginnings and endings of pieces) as to placing labels under chords.

Quick recognition of keys and key changes is an absolute prerequisite and foundation for all analysis of tonal form. And the most helpful clues are the appearance and disappearance of accidentals, the usage and resolution of tritones (the most candid method of establishing pitch focus), the directional steering and patterning of bass lines (by itself an almost foolproof indicator of key), and the ultimate regulator of tonic definition: the "P-D-T" train of thought that is controlled by functional relationships.

2. HIERARCHY VERSUS EQUALITY

Another potential danger in teaching harmonic analysis is to treat every chord (or key area) as equally important. This is especially likely when roman numerals are asked to carry too much of the explanatory burden. The remedies for this problem are reliance on function (as described above), movement between chords rather than the chords themselves, context, and grouping of chords into larger patterns. All of these approaches can be subsumed by an important concept already mentioned—prolongation. This idea, first thoroughly developed by Schenker, has begun gradually, since the 1960s, to seep into, if not dominate, harmony textbooks.

In fact, one of the striking trends of recent music theory pedagogy (along with the influences of CM) has been the penetration of undergraduate courses and materials by topics once reserved for graduate seminars (e.g., the ideas and terminology of Schenker, Babbitt, Meyer). To what extent these more advanced concepts are appropriate at the lower levels of study (can they be adapted without being diluted?) is still an issue of discussion among theorists. The idea of prolongation—that a pair or even whole cluster of chords can serve a single function—is closely related to the concept of hierarchy in pitch structure. According to this view, levels of importance can be identified and sorted. Some chords act as pillars for a progression, section, or whole movement, while others decorate or extend (i.e., prolong) these props. Some chords, or notes, are close to the foreground while others are background directors of large-scale motion or definers of key focus. Still others represent an in-between middleground level by connecting the surface details to the underlying support points.

Simply placing roman numerals under chords gives the false impression that all the symbols carry equivalent import. Some system for making distinctions among levels and for distinguishing between the embellishments and what is being embellished must be established eventually so that pitches click into place in our understanding and hearing like tumblers in a lock. In general, points of departure, goal points (secondary vs. primary; strong vs. weak; etc.), chords leading to or leading away from or joining goals are the kinds of events to identify and distinguish.

The visual or analytical apparatus for making such distinctions is less important than recognizing their existence. A full-blown Schenkerian structural-reduction technique is not necessarily suitable for all classes, students, or teachers. Sometimes just verbal discussion of a given passage can bring out relationships not fully revealed by the roman numerals alone. Sometimes three or four roman-numeral analyses underneath one another can provide, more or less, symbols at various levels closer or farther from the music itself. Sometimes simply placing some of the chord labels in parentheses or within brackets will indicate the secondary position of subsidiary chords.

In making elaborate charts or tonal-map diagrams of whole movements, false impressions are also often conveyed by listing all key areas in a piece as if they were equivalent. Failure to distinguish between passing through a key vs. arriving, and, subsequently, failure to distinguish between degrees of strength or weakness in an arrival is the cause of such superficiality. Charles Rosen, with characteristic wit, describes this approach as the "Railroad Timetable School of Harmonic Analysis":

> We used to find a lot of this in program-notes, and unhappily it still hangs on in some music departments and conservatories. It

goes something like this: "At measure 200, Verdi starts in F minor, moves to A flat by 225, arrives at F flat at 240, and ends in D flat in measure 270." The trouble with this school is that they are unable to distinguish between express and local trains: it does you no good to know that all the trains from New York to Philadelphia go through Princeton Junction, if you have no idea which ones stop there. That, essentially, was my criticism of Porter's approach [in his *New Grove* article on Verdi]: he cannot tell when Verdi stops at F flat, and when he just slows down there going past the station. The metaphor breaks down, of course, because the nature and character of the final tonality changes according to whether one has stopped somewhere else on the way.[3]

3. HORIZONTAL VERSUS VERTICAL

Some approaches to teaching harmony vary in the relative attention given to horizontal and vertical relationships. A traditional view (one perhaps growing out of Rameau's lingering influence) considers the triad—stacked in thirds from a generative root and sometimes inverted—as the main structural component of tonal music. An opposing attitude, articulated by Leo Kraft, considers this harmonic (i.e., vertical) approach to be virtually useless:

Supposedly, harmony deals with the study of chords, counterpoint with lines. But such a statement overlooks the basic fact that lines flow together to make chords, and the only reason that chords follow in a certain order is that the lines lead them there. If harmony books make any sense it is because they deal with musical motion—that is, counterpoint. The linear approach . . . does away with the artificial distinction between harmony and counterpoint. Of course, you must learn all about chords. And there is much more to learning about chords than writing Roman numerals under them. But the way to learn about chords is through learning about the lines that generate the chords.[4]

One outcome of the difference between horizontal and vertical emphases is the amount of pitch information that is encoded into the roman numerals. Some teachers (and their students) will attempt to account for almost every note as part of some vertical unit producing an analysis that is thick with symbols. Others will use fewer roman numerals by interpreting many pitches as part of the horizontal context having no real independent vertical status and therefore the result of purely linear operations. Many notes, then, can be explained as non-harmonic (an unfortunate term) tones, connectors or links, coloristic (non-functional) tones, or as chromatic slippage (half-step, suspended, delayed, or out-of-alignment alerations). When several of these effects occur simultaneously the temptation is especially strong for many to add them together and find some explanatory label or root. Many teachers are uncomfortable with gaps in the string of roman numerals.

One extreme in either direction (horizontal or vertical), however, is unlikely to reveal as much as both together. Like a crossword puzzle, pitch relationships must make sense both down (up in music?) and across. This is another clear case, then, where choosing one approach over another is not necessary. Both vertical and linear associations are important and, in fact, complementary.

Even in analysis that stresses chord quality and intervallic content, it is prudent to remember that chords always move forward in time. The freeze-frame method of isolating individual chords out of the context of an ongoing progression, although still popular in some circles, should be carefully monitored. A motionless chord—like a snapshot of the middle of a dive—has little meaning by itself. Halting the movement may be necessary to glimpse a detail that might otherwise pass unnoticed in the rush, but placing it back into the living flow of action is necessary to hear and understand its role as part of a continuous chain of events. By joining two approaches, theory teachers can emulate psychologists who waste little time arguing the influence of "nature vs. nurture" but rather concentrate on the *interaction* between both innate and learned capabilities.

For some styles (especially Renaissance and some of the baroque), harmony clearly seems to be a byproduct of horizontal activity. For other styles (especially some nineteenth- and twentieth-century pieces), composers are just as clearly reveling in the coloristic possibilities of simultaneous sounds although here too the "chords" can be heard as offshoots of linear factors. In some late eighteenth- century samples, certain melodic styles (chordal outlines and skipping) seem to be a result of triadic influence. Examples can be found to support any viewpoint. It is more important, though, to find viewpoints that will support the examples.

4. HARMONY VERSUS TONALITY

Bach's music is often cited as representing an ideal balance between the vertical and horizontal, and it is interesting to note a gradual revival of interest in Bach's four-voice chorales in some recent texts. At one time these pieces were avoided (perhaps as an overreaction against the excesses of SATB textures in earlier texts), but these compositions are now becoming recognized as minor masterpieces of artistic construction and expression.

The textbooks of McHose,[5] by their very titles and with their detailed studies of Bach chorales (prevalence of certain chords, progression types, inversions, root movements, etc.), imply that the chorales are valuable only for increasing our knowledge of eighteenth-century style traits—or perhaps some nineteenth-century composers. The remarkable thing is that these chorales (or any body of tonal pieces such as Beethoven piano sonatas, the Chopin preludes, Brahms symphonies, Mozart operas, etc.) could be used, if taught in the proper way, for revealing a broad set of principles applicable to the whole tonal realm—and for many aspects beyond.

The issue, for courses that feature pitch analysis of the common-practice period, is whether harmonic style or the more global subject of functional tonality will be highlighted. It is surprising that even though dozens of harmony books are available, no current textbook includes the words "functional tonality" or even just "tonality" in its title.[6] The word "harmony" connotes the study of chords. Tonality covers this topic but also includes a whole spectrum of related concepts that encompass the movement, control, expressive values, and meaning of chords in addition to mere content. Harmony resembles simple grammar (structure of words and phrases) whereas tonality parallels a whole language system or even the field of linguistics (phonology, morphology, syntax, and semantics). Harmony, then, is just one facet of the more inclusive province of tonality.

The other facets involve counterpoint and melody (to be discussed shortly), rhythm and meter, and musical form. Some of the specific concepts that enhance harmony instruction (in the narrow sense of chord usage) and that should be part of a complete course of study include the following:

1. Centricity—a pitch structure in which one tone is made to serve (and be perceived) as referential to all the others.

2. Tonality—the sum of relationships and attractions that projects the centricity of a keynote. Functional tonality includes among its many relationships the three harmonic functions discussed earlier.

3. Polarity—tones other than tonic serving as secondary focuses or goals, thus providing the basis for tonal movement: departure and return.

4. Tonicization—a momentary strengthening of secondary elements (treating them as if they were temporary tonics) but within a stable key.

5. Modulation—a more sustained breakdown in tonic control resulting in a new tonal center set up as a distinct arrival with cadential realization.

6. Dissonance—the basis of tonal musical motion (almost more so than rhythm itself) and arguably the single most important expressive device in the development of tonality throughout history; implies a vertical unit that *requires movement* to a sound-complex of lesser tension. The environmental influences of context and historical style should always be acknowledged. Dissonance can work through single pitches (e.g., non-harmonic tones), intervals (e.g., tonal tritone), chords (e.g., fully diminished 7ths) and also on a larger level as the tonal dissonance brought about, for example, by the conflict between opposing key areas in the exposition of sonata form. Rhythmic dissonance is a possibility, too, as in the extended metric disturbances often found in Beethoven and Brahms (large-scale syncopations and hemiolas).

7. Consonance—the equilibrium (steadiness, stability, and sense of rest) of certain vertical pitch situations (and by extension melodic factors).

8. Resolution—the movement from dissonance to consonance or the result of such movement.

9. Chromaticism—includes modal borrowings (from parallel scales), functional alterations, and various embellishments (non-functional and coloristic effects). Chromatic alterations are frequently learned in harmony class by studying each indi-

vidual type of chord—chapter by chapter—that includes such alterations. An alternate approach is to study the broader causes of chromaticism as a topic of its own and afterwards fit the chords into the appropriate categories.

10. Ambiguity/neutrality—the purposeful disguising of function, sometimes through tantalizing vagueness, sometimes through presentation of two or more simultaneous meanings.

11. Cadence—a shaping or articulation of a sound event that is either partially or fully reposeful and involving the full range of sound parameters (rhythm, dynamics, color, etc.), not just harmony or melody.

12. Point of arrival—a structural goal cadence that closes off a large section of a piece.

13. Macrorhythm—the temporal proportions of structural events (phrases, periods, sections, transitions, the stretching of major arrival points, the plotting of densities and climaxes); how the piece is shaped in time.

14. Harmonic function and prolongation—see earlier discussion concerning linear operations, structural pitches, embellishments, etc.

When a harmony class is filtered through the above concepts, it is transformed into the more extensive study of tonality—the functional kind of the eighteenth and nineteenth centuries or the more universal type of many eras and cultures. Just as Fux, in his counterpoint approach (*Gradus ad Parnassum,* 1725), discovered many of the fundamental workings (rhythmic control, dissonance/consonance interplay, musical motion, etc.) of all tonal music—even though he thought he was describing just Palestrina's style—the study of Bach chorales or other materials can transcend their narrow slot in history and illuminate a broader range of musical issues. For some classroom situations, it may be profitable to center on specific late baroque style traits (e.g., root-movement types, harmonic rhythm, appropriate use of non-harmonic tones and chromaticism, voice leading and range restrictions, etc. of the chorales). For other classes, the application of general principles will be more appropriate. Just knowing such choices or combinations are available is a substantial beginning step in teaching harmony.

A more stylistic or chronological approach to teaching functional tonality might examine the stages through which common-practice harmony has evolved. One interpretation of these stages follows:[7]

1. Unitonic (late 1600s)—the end of the modal system as signalled in the music of Corelli. Functional (as opposed to just triadic) progressions, major/minor scales, circle of fifths, and consistent leading tones are used, but no clear means of large-scale modulation is yet apparent (occasional meanderings to relative or other closely related keys).

2. Transitonic (early 1700s)—the discovery of functional dominant-7th harmony (through the natural dissonance of the tonal tritone) as exemplified in the music of Bach. Modulation now controls and shapes overall musical form.

3. Pluritonic (early 1800s)—the concept of a distantly related key emerges in Beethoven through chromatic enharmonicism (respelling; fully diminished 7th chords, etc.).

4. Omnitonic (middle to late 1800s)—any vertical situation becomes instantly relatable to any other through the devices of chromatic alteration, linearity, coloristic chords, lack of direct resolutions, as found in Chopin, Wagner, Liszt, etc.

At least three other important pitch languages of Western culture besides functional tonality could be the foundation for various parts of an undergraduate curriculum and each one itself includes numerous sub-categories:

1. Modality—medieval, Renaissance, and early baroque periods using the church modes. Contains centricity and triads but not harmonic functions. Includes historical phases involving the evolution of polyphony from single-line chant through the works of Josquin, Palestrina, Byrd, Monteverdi, and Schütz.

2. Extended tonality—late nineteenth- and early twentieth-century outgrowth of conventional tonality. Also contains centricity but not harmonic functions. Involves extension of major/minor scales (chromatic, octatonic, whole tone, pentatonic, synthetic, and return to modes), non-triadic harmony (quartal, added tones, clusters, and microtones), polytonality, systems for control of dissonance/consonance, etc. This covers composers such as Debussy, Stravinsky, Bartok, Hindemith, Copland, Ives, etc.

3. Atonality (or pantonality)—conscious lack of pitch focus (control and unity through intervallic means often achieved). Serial and non-serial forms in the music of Schoenberg, Web-

ern, and Berg, and more complex applications by Boulez, Babbitt, etc., cover most of the twentieth century.

Presenting New Material

Good theory teaching—not just in harmony, but all phases—constantly pursues opportunities for presenting one topic as an offshoot, variant, or relative of another. Modulation, for example, can be presented as an extension of secondary dominants, but involving greater emphasis (i.e., a more complete functional cadence, stronger arrival, longer time spans, etc.). These two topics, surprisingly, are often treated in textbooks—even in adjacent chapters or paragraphs—as isolated matters. They are, in fact, varying degrees of the same phenomenon of pitch-focus shift although with quite different long-range meanings in the overall structure: one acting at a local level and the other more fundamental.

In introducing the N^6 "chord," for another example, the resemblance—almost exact correspondence—in spelling, usage, and predominant function to the simple iv (or IV) should not only be mentioned but spotlighted. Properly presented, the N^6 does not represent a new chord but is more accurately a kind of variation or continuation of procedures and contexts already studied.

An automatic review mechanism can be designed into a course or a whole theory curriculum by drawing on concepts already mentioned earlier in the semester or program so that the same few ideas can be constructively recycled again and again at increasingly sophisticated levels. Some textbooks have this spiral-learning technique built into their structure. This is highly desirable since it forces selection of central concepts—such as the tonality list just presented—on which a course can be erected.

Another way of promoting learning is to emphasize similarities as much as or even more than differences; link appropriate topics together by common traits. For example, augmented-6th chords are frequently presented by stressing and fussing over the minute internal differences of their spelling/notation and resolution (Italian vs. French vs. German vs. doubly-augmented; major mode use vs. minor; voice leading and use of tonic 6/4 chords; roman numeral labels vs. simple naming; inversion vs. root position; etc.). All of these "extra" issues should either be aired or eliminated through discussion in due time.

The important point to emphasize at once, however, is that all of these "chords" (some would call them linear byproducts) work in the same way. They are all very slight variations of a single process; they do not represent separate or different situations. The common properties include: (*a*) a technical one—the dynamic horizontal expansion of the augmented 6th to the dominant octave (half-step resolution in contrary motion); and (*b*) a musical one—the intensified forward thrust of its set-up function to the dominant goal (increased momentum). Both the similarities and differences are important. In this case, though, and in many others, the similarities overshadow the differences because they express what is essential about the operation.

Non-harmonic tones also represent many opportunities for getting bogged down in differences. In this case, though, differences in definition and function are not just important but crucial. But even here opportunities for making comparisons and establishing connections can be lost if advance planning in explaining the connections is lacking. For example, the basic difference between a suspension and anticipation is that the suspension delays the arrival of the eventual goal tone so that it appears "too late" while the anticipation arrives at the upcoming goal tone "too early." The similarity is that a temporal adjustment has occurred in both cases. In fact, their difference here has been highlighted by a single important concept that unites two quite different-looking and different-sounding types of dissonance; a difference has been explained by reference to a similarity.

Another obvious similarity in this same example is the appearance of repeated notes. The balancing difference is that for the suspension the repeat leads into the dissonance, while for the anticipation the repeat leads into the resolution; here a similarity (repeated notes) has been explained by reference to a difference (order and location). Simple charts can be constructed to list and summarize the differences among NHTs by identifying intervallic surroundings, metric placement, etc. The perceptive teacher will go one step beyond these pigeonholes by drawing attention to the interrelationships between and among items and by cross-referencing the individual definitions with the applicable partner situation(s).

Oversimplification, of course, should be avoided as much as overcomplication. In general, though, a desirable goal is to attempt to cover the greatest number of circumstances that are different on the surface with the smallest number of underlying explanations. This has been the goal of all great theoretical systems—music, philosophy, science—for centuries. It can also be a goal in teaching about these systems.

Another recommendation is to identify and spotlight the essence of a topic; separate and distinguish the core ingredients from all of its other more marginal aspects. Some incidental issues can often be woven into a course at later points after the initial exposure and the heart of a subject have been revealed. The focal points for a given subject will not always be agreed upon by all theorists and teachers. Nevertheless, for a particular teacher in a specific situation, students must be made aware of the teacher's assumptions about levels of importance; the hierarchy of primary and secondary information must be clear.

To clarify the relationships between the individual strands of knowledge that meld into a complex topic does not necessitate dilution of the material. Most topics can be simplified without distortion if care is taken. The trick is to balance between making the presentation as simple as possible (by eliminating non-essentials or placing them in perspective) and making it as thorough as necessary (by inclusion of all relevant fundamentals). The key point here is to differentiate between non-essentials and fundamentals even when both are presented.

Knowing what to omit in an initial lecture can be pivotal in students' understanding of what is presented. Too much elaboration or too many different kinds of examples too quickly can detract from the main points that must be set in the student's mind at once. For example, in the presentation of non-harmonic tones, the passing tone would normally be thought of as a simple (even elementary) type. By discussing immediately, however, all possible sub-categories of the PT (some books list 10–12 different situations), this simple topic quickly becomes impossibly and unnecessarily complex.

The subtleties of PTs such as diatonic vs. chromatic, unaccented vs. accented, accented vs. appoggiatura, filling in a third vs. a fourth, dissonant vs. consonant, use in one-voice, two-voice, and four-voice contexts, combinations with other NHTs in the same voice, combinations with other NHTs in another voice, choice of chord tone or PT in melody harmonization, etc., are all worth pursuing—eventually—perhaps in a follow-up lecture. But plunging at once into all of the special cases, exceptions, interesting sidelights and byways usually overwhelms a beginning student to the point where he can barely articulate a simple, yet complete definition of a PT.

In this example the essential factors to emphasize would be: (*a*) the basic dissonance or existence outside of some more stable background chord structure (true of all NHTs); (*b*) the step-wise environment (both approach and resolution); (*c*) continuation in the same direction (to distinguish from a neighboring tone); and (*d*) the mildness of the dissonance caused by the usual non-stressed metric placement.

Frequently the necessary approach involves breaking down unwieldy complex topics into a series of separate graduated steps, each one of which can be tackled as a simple individual problem. Whole textbooks and most computer-assisted approaches, of course, have been based on this method of programmed instruction. It is not necessary, though, to adopt all of programmed instruction's tenets or materials to take advantage of its rewards. Sometimes the situations that could most benefit from this procedure are not even thought of as being unwieldy or complex at all by theory teachers. This occurs because teachers usually blend together automatically and extremely rapidly the discrete parts of their thinking process in solving theory problems. These items, though, can be singled out, identified, put into order, and numbered for the student with a little self-analysis on the teacher's part.

Even elementary topics can be split into a logical sequence. For example, the spelling of a given secondary dominant in a given key seems to be a reasonable request. We all know, however, the confusion and bafflement that can result from a student's involvement with this "simple" exercise. Since theory teachers themselves often entirely omit the beginning steps in this type of question, it seems an effort to even list the separate stages. But one plan of attack might look like this:

Question:

Spell a V_5^6/ii in the key of D major.

Answer steps:

1. Notate the key signature of the given key (2 #s).

2. Look at the roman numeral *underneath* the slash (ii).

3. Notate this as a pitch on the staff (off to the side or on scratch paper); this represents in a tangible way the temporary or secondary "key" (pitch E).

4. Construct the dominant-seventh pitches of this temporary key starting a P5 above E, like for any V^7; be sure the accidentals chosen belong to this key (e), not the original key (D); add or subtract from the original key signature as needed (chord = B, D#, F#, A).

5. Convert to first inversion (D# in the bass). All of these steps assume that the basic concept of secondary dominants has already been explained. If students already know how to spell ordinary dominant sevenths—this may not always be a safe assumption and frequently is the main stumbling block—then, this question, D: V$^6_5$/ii, in terms of pure spelling, translates into e: V$^6_5$ (although the meaning in the larger context is, of course, not equivalent).

Students frequently make the mistake of jumping to the final steps too soon—worrying about the inversion before the pitches have even been calculated, or generally getting lost in the intricacies of proper accidentals (or forgetting that such intricacies even exist). They fail to clearly picture the secondary key to which the accidentals relate or confuse the secondary key with the primary key or try to think of both keys simultaneously. Numbering the steps puts order into all of these mental gymnastics and is especially useful for pinpointing exactly where a confused student may have strayed off the track. The ultimate goal is to put these broken-apart stages back together again so that the reasoning chain will be whole, smooth, and swift. To scrutinize each link under a microscope is tedious but also immensely helpful for both learning the skill in the first place and for diagnostic purposes when things go wrong.

Another example—this one truly unwieldy—concerns how to harmonize a melody. In a situation as potentially convoluted as this, specific steps are absolutely vital. One sequence, among many, could run as follows:

1. Sing, hear, or play the melody.

2. Identify the key.

3. Determine tempo and style and decide appropriate harmonic rhythm.

4. Analyze cadences, phrases, secondary-dominant implications, modulations, etc.

5. Translate the implications of melodic structure into corresponding harmonic cadences, key changes (brief or long term), etc.

6. Examine melodic content for possible NHT interpretation.

7. List all of the available chord choices for each melody note or group of notes (this step can be eliminated as more experience is acquired).

8. Establish tonality clearly at the beginning and choose progressions that (*a*) move normally through the predominant/dominant/tonic cycle of functional families; (*b*) mix secondary and primary triads by substitution; and (*c*) maintain an appropriate balance of root-movement types.

9. Write a musical bass line against the given soprano that (*a*) balances step-wise and skipping motion (including inversions for smoothness and variation in degree of weight); (*b*) avoids static effects (by covering a reasonably wide range and maintaining clear goals—i.e., has shape and direction); and (*c*) reacts with the soprano in four basic motion types (especially contrary motion).

10. Fill in the inner voices and add NHTs as desirable or necessary (not just as decorative overlay but as an intrinsic part of the overall conception).

11. Revise, revise, and revise.

Some of the above steps could be re-ordered, combined, eliminated, or expanded; many other equally valid schemes could easily be designed. Each one of the steps consists of many more sub-steps that would have been pursued at earlier times. The topic of melody harmonization by its nature is one that pulls together and coordinates matters that originally were studied one at a time. The main point here is not to argue for this particular set of steps but to accentuate the importance of approaching any large undertaking with some organized, coherent blueprint.

Not all compositional or analytical problems lend themselves so neatly to such a rigidly quantified approach. To some, making such lists may seem to squeeze all imagination from a project or rule out the possibility of divergent solutions or the possibility of changing plans in midstream. This is probably true for completely creative work (including many kinds of analysis). From another point of view, though, having a basic framework—a point of departure, checkpoints along the way, and some final goal—may, for some, enrich intuition and spur originality by providing ammunition for the subconscious. At any rate, my suggestions are aimed mainly at those situations that have reasonably clear-cut, predictable outcomes toward which students can be gently nudged through a series of carefully chosen, measured levels of accomplishment.

While I hope that these suggestions can prevent problems from happening in the first place, when misunderstandings and failures do occur, one final recommendation can be made. To diagnose and resolve difficulties, backtrack through the original series of steps until some successful response can be accomplished. If a student flounders at an assigned task, make it one step simpler, then another step simpler until finally a stage of comprehension is reached. The steps should then be retraced one at a time leading forward again toward the desired objective.

To use the above example of spelling a given secondary dominant, the process might break down like this:

1. Try spelling just a primary dominant seventh (in given inversion).
2. Spell the same chord in root position.
3. Spell a Mm seventh chord from a given pitch independently of any key context.
4. Spell simple M triads and m7s separately.
5. Spell just M and m scales.
6. Spell just half steps and whole steps.
7. Names notes on the staff.

At some point of simplification, the student will be successful; at that point the process is turned back around as the student is led forward again.

Occasionally pauses need to be inserted into a course in the form of gathering up facts that may have been in the air for some time. Topics are often scattered over so many chapters or months that overview summaries are required to pull together loose ends. The information in these kinds of collections are rarely found in textbooks all in one place but can be constructed by a thoughtful teacher. Frequently older items can be combined with newer so that fresh relationships are established.

One example, among many, involves the very broad topic of chromaticism. One way to supplement and enrich the conventional chord-by-chord approach is to list (after study of all relevant sub-issues is complete) the reasons for accidentals appearing in a composition:

1. Altered 6th and 7th scale degrees in minor
2. Modal borrowing (minor to major—always *parallel* keys—or vice versa as in the Picardy third)
3. Chromatic non-harmonic tones (embellishment)
4. Non-functional chord-member alteration (e.g., lowered 7th, raised 5th, etc.) changing quality or urgency of voice-leading tendencies
5. Secondary dominants (functional change)
6. Modulation
7. Traditional altered chords (N^6, augmented 6ths, etc.)
8. Chromatic mediants (3rd relationships)
9. Unusual scales

Such a list not only summarizes important causes of chromaticism but provides a handy analysis checklist. One of the best analytical exercises is to sift out specific chromatic pitches in a given composition and match them with the appropriate explanation. Some obviously will have multiple causes.

All of these teaching principles are applicable, of course, to many other aspects of theory teaching besides harmony. By reminding ourselves about the plain virtues of planning ahead, clarity, organization, and continuity, we can analyze our lectures, discussions, assignments, and course outlines for teaching improvement in the same logical way that we analyze music itself.

Counterpoint

As with harmony, counterpoint can be taught stylistically or with relevance for all historical periods. Stylistic approaches usually center on the sixteenth century (Palestrina), eighteenth century (Bach), or twentieth century (Hindemith). Such courses can include both style-imitation projects and general principles, such as climactic contour in a single line, independence of voices, activation and fulfillment of melodic/harmonic goals, and intervallic control.

Counterpoint can also be viewed as something more than the study of polyphonic textures in a particular century. All tonal music is contrapuntal in that it is generated by a constant lining-up between the top and bottom voices (soprano/bass polarity) whose sense of action and pause depends on the adjustments of consonance and dissonance. Imitative counterpoint, in which interdependent voices are organized melodically by the stating and answering of motives, figures, and subjects is a more restrictive use of the term and is associated with certain compositional procedures like canon, fugue, invention, ricercare, or motet.

Two tonal pieces, then, of widely different textures or styles can be reduced to controling outer voices and understood through identical techniques of voice leading and procedures of rhythmic alignment. This linear approach—often used in conjunction with harmony training—can also be the basis for a separate one- or two-semester counterpoint class. This concept of counterpoint is so broad as to encompass an overview of all tonal theory. Its strength lies in its wide applicability to the entire span of Western music history—especially in Salzer's extensions of Schenker's ideas—including many twentieth-century composers (but excluding the twelve-tone school). The obvious weakness of the non-stylistic brand of counterpoint training is the minimizing of differences among composers. Some object that these differences are not just skin deep but penetrate to the essence of informed comprehension and therefore cannot simply be dismissed. There should be room in the teaching of counterpoint (as in the other areas we have discussed) for a blending of approaches, even though one may predominate, so that both resemblance and individuality among composers can be observed.

One final issue that affects the teaching of counterpoint concerns the use of the species approach. With this method, students are in effect fleshing out pieces of music from given structural reductions—the opposite of the analytical stripping away of details. The metering out of dissonance control in small but increasing rations of rhythmic freedom is viewed by many as not only a means of keeping students out of trouble at each stage of their compositional development but also as a means of making clear the precise relationships among pitches at various levels of structure. An inside (i.e., a composer's) view is thereby brought to life by showing how a piece is built up with support points and elaborative particulars all contributing to the whole.

Although it seems difficult to question an approach that provided the musical foundation for most of the important eighteenth-and nineteenth-century composers, some maintain that species counterpoint is inherently unmusical, constricting creativity by rigid adherence to solving a time-consuming series of tedious exercises. Especially in a sixteenth-century style, where durational flow and flexibility are critical, the predictable metric regularity of the early species might stifle the elastic feel for nuances and gentle differences between rhythmic lifts and landings.

While jumping directly into suspensions, intricate syncopations, and other florid effects would be foolhardy, exciting the interest of a class at the beginning of a course is an important consideration. Spending inordinate amounts of time on mechanical note manipulations could easily dull the latent enthusiasm of those wishing to contact living pieces of music regardless of the theoretical validity of the teaching approach.

Believing as I do that good theory teachers must also use subtle but compelling salesmanship in promoting their teaching views, it may turn out that the power of belief will establish in the student's mind the justification for a specific system. If convincing reasons and goals for particular assignments are thoroughly explained, most students are willing to try them out. As is true for most other subjects, the theory teacher himself is often more important than the method. And the most successful ones are often those who most effectively solve that tricky problem of remaining at the same time fervent about their present teaching and yet open-minded about the future.

Melody

Overlapping both harmony and counterpoint is the study of melody. In proportion to the amount of time spent in most courses (and books) on harmonic analysis, it is amazing how little time is devoted to melodic study (perhaps because of our impoverished nomenclature in the melodic realm). This is especially regrettable considering that most student are performers in a single-line medium that provides easy entry into a variety of analytical areas.

One type of melodic analysis is simple key identification. Many students are taught to look at the key signature and perhaps the final pitch. Key signatures, of course, do not confer tonality; they only summarize accidentals that belong to a key already established by other means. A more musical approach encourages students to look for patterns (outlining of triads; background step progressions, up-beat to down-beat; dominant to tonic; leading tones; etc.) and stressed notes (first, last; highest, lowest; longest; loudest; metrically strongest; etc.) so that keys are seen as an outgrowth of a melody's internal construction rather than something imposed from outside by accidentals on a staff.

Nothing is more important in tonal theory than learning how keys are set up (directly, gradually, strongly, weakly, deviously, ambiguously, etc.), sustained, revitalized, broken down, contrasted, passed through, returned to, reconfirmed, etc. All of these effects can be studied with single-line melodic examples—in many cases before harmonic progressions are even introduced. The best method is to give students dozens of melodies with no key signatures (necessary accidentals written in the music) or false key signatures (with appropriate cancellations or additions in the music, of course). Most important is to provide examples that usually start and end on pitches other than tonic (implied half cadence; 3rd of tonic chord; etc.) or are interrupted—in musical chairs fashion—before the end. Students are then forced to search through the *entire* example for clues that define the pitch centers. Actually making lists of supporting evidence to shore up their own answer and to rebut alternate possibilities—like a lawyer in court—is the very best training for understanding what tonality is all about; and melodic study is ideal for instilling such habits of critical thinking and analysis from the beginning.

Conventional melodic analysis also includes study of contour types, interval content (sizes; disjunct vs. conjunct), motives and sub-motives, cadences, phrases (antecedent vs. consequent; parallel vs. contrasting), periods, sections, overall form, harmonic implications, and polyphonic implications (of two or more embedded lines). These are all worthwhile pursuits and especially good for demonstrating both expressive components and how longer units are built up from shorter ones. But it is in the area of reductive technique that melodic and tonal analysis become most valuable. This is because the concepts of prolongation, and embellishment vs. structural function (that have already been discussed in relation to harmony and counterpoint) can be presented most simply and persuasively. Single-line melodies do not include all the distractions, competing voices, complications, and confusions found in longer pieces or thicker textures.

I am almost prepared to say that the single most important point to learn about the pitch organization of tonal music—and other systems as well—is that all notes do not carry equal weight. This is not to say that some are important and others are not, but rather that some notes give meaning while others take it. Distinguishing between at least these two levels is at the heart of all tonal analysis.

Some pitches seem to exist independently of the others by forming guideposts (frequently through the unfolding of key-defining triadic tonality frames and/or step-wise scalar connections) around which the rest cluster in various patterns. These secondary pitches are dependent on the primary guideposts for their meaning and cannot exist alone. Various shadings of in-between types, including pitches with dual or ambiguous or even conflicting roles, are also possible. The final result will show that every note has a place (or places) in the hierarchy and relates in some special way to all the others just as every line in a drawing is part of a larger sketch. This is that network of relationships and attractions projecting the centricity of a focal note that we have already defined as tonality. These very basic principles can be beautifully and plainly demonstrated in simple and short examples and then applied to longer, more complex melodies, harmonic progressions, and eventually whole pieces.

Everyone will recognize that I am recommending an approach to melodic analysis that derives from Schenker. I am not necessarily recommending, however, adoption of the elaborate and highly technical graphing and notation system that accompanies much of his own work, full acceptance of all his views, or exclusive use of the reductive technique. Simple reductions can be used in combination with other methods or as complements or alternatives. Many of the tacit and underlying assumptions behind Schenkerian analysis remain controversial. Almost every major theory textbook since the middle 1960s, however, has been influenced in some way—many extremely so—by his concepts, so it no longer seems truthful to refer to his methods as a fad. Schenkerian principles must be fully recognized as a dominant force in the contemporary teaching of music theory. Some will wish to contrast his ideas in a pro-and-con way with more traditional approaches or with other contemporary views; some will prefer to find areas of common ground between differing approaches by mingling methodologies as I have recommended for so many other situations; but none can afford to ignore his contribution through ignorance or prejudice. I hope that all students will be exposed in some way to Schenker's profound insights into structural levels.

Keyboard

Keyboard skills have traditionally been included in most theory curriculums (often in the ratio of forty percent for analysis/composition; forty percent ear training; and twenty percent keyboard). Some schools have keyboard labs with electronic pianos and even incorporate the keyboard portion of theory into a sequence of separate courses (usually required of all music majors). This can be tremendously beneficial since it gives back about one extra day per week to a theory program that is constantly fighting for time. The potential disadvantage is that if the theory curriculum and piano-class curriculum do not share at least some goals, terminology, and pacing through communication and partial correlation, opportunities for mutual support and efficiency will be missed. The correct balance between a desirable overlap and unnecessary duplication of content is very delicate.

Piano classes usually incorporate many goals, including.not only theory-related skills but functional and practical skills, such as acquiring moderate technical proficiency, correct fingerings, sight-reading, performing simple accompaniments, etc. From the standpoint of a theory program, however, the central justification for a keyboard component is not learning how to play the piano—essential as this is for any musician— but as *reinforcement* of conceptual skills.

Reinforcement occurs in other ways, too, such as in regular written assignments, worksheets, ear-training drills, performance studies (other than keyboard), rehearsals, and even during out-of-class discussions with teachers and classmates (often the most instructive but overlooked aspect of education). There is something extraordinary, though, about the melding of tactile, visual, and aural sense modes with ideas that elevates the importance of keyboard work to a special status. The tangible act of pushing down keys, seeing distances, and hearing resultant sounds can cement a concept to the mind and ears in a way that no amount of paper work or talking can ever accomplish. The talking and writing are important counterparts, but the keyboard activities actually involve (although at an elementary level) making music: playing with sounds in both the amusement and performance sense.

Scales, intervals, triads, 7th chords, progressions, melody harmonization, and figured bass all provide opportunities for the mastery of the fundamentals mentioned earlier. Playing intervals and triads up or down from a given note is just a more concrete form of the timed spelling quiz; completing a scale from a given internal note is just another type of "inside-out" question. Solving these problems at the keyboard (i.e., with the implied pressure of a quick answer demanded by any performance situation) encourages the "thinking-on-one's-feet" attitude that is required of all committed musicianship. For more advanced students or classes, score reading with its on-the-spot reduction and simplification combines analysis and hearing skills simultaneously. Keyboard work can, like ear training, be generally correlated with written work without a lockstep week-by-week matching schedule (i.e., the same general order but not necessarily the same pacing).

Perhaps the primary benefit of keyboard work, in fact, is for ear training. Too often, students sit at the piano plodding through the required harmonic progression, assiduously keeping track of chord spelling (am I pushing the correct buttons?), voice leading (is the correct finger moving to the correct

70

note?), inversions (is the bass line correct?), but forgetting to notice the sound and musical meaning of the assigned exercise. Some present-day computer programs and tape labs would be less necessary if students could be taught that keyboard lab is one of the best places to learn to hear. Other aural drill opportunities are necessary for interval and chord identification, but the keyboard class is helpful (especially for all those single-line melody people) for hearing and producing two or more voices together and for exploring various textures (SATB; melody and accompaniment; Alberti bass; two-part imitative; etc.).

Even sightsinging and dictation activities can be combined with keyboard work with immediate feedback and solutions available. Improvisation drills, playing by ear, and transposition exercises are especially good for coordinating thinking and listening. The ultimate purpose of the keyboard component, then, from a music-theory point of view, is to train the brain, not the fingers; the goal is to become a musician, not a pianist.

Twentieth-Century Music

Twentieth-century music at the undergraduate level can be taught as a separate class (usually at the junior level) or as part of a two-year program. Since students now in college will be spending the majority of their musical careers in the twenty-first century, it seems reasonable to expect twentieth-century music to receive prominent attention in the curriculum. It is regrettable that some schools still relegate this topic to the final few weeks of the sophomore year—almost as if to alleviate the guilt feelings that would result from ignoring it altogether. Occasionaly twentieth-century music is made available, but only as an elective. Some schools spend so much time with tonal music that post-tonal music is never reached, while other schools begin with the twentieth century so that it won't be overlooked or for other more philosophical reasons. Twentieth-century techniques and literature cannot be treated as an afterthought. Its inclusion must be planned in advance and made conspicuous—not stuck in if time is available. The reasons for knowing the music of our own century and times are too obvious to need reiteration here.

The matter of teaching approach is especially problematic since the outstanding feature of twentieth-century music is its diversity. One obvious possibility is chronological. This is likely to make good sense if the earlier semesters have followed a historical progression. Beginning twentieth-century developments can easily be presented as outcroppings of late romantic trends. At least two branches of evolution are discernable (splitting off as early as Wagner): the extended-tonality camp and the atonal/twelve-tone group. The branching after 1945 becomes extremely dense and ultimately unmanageable, although influences of technique and style can be traced for almost any topic or composer. The chronological approach for music of more recent decades becomes, then, a series of individual mini-histories for each separate subject.

Another approach might take composers, one at a time, from their early to late works. Stravinsky's output, for example, spans many of the important trends in this century. With each composer the tracing would begin anew, resulting in a course that repeatedly overlaps itself. Grouping by styles would provide an alternative: impressionism, expressionism, neo-classicism, for example. Geographical areas are another possibility: Americans (Ives, Ruggles, Cowell, Varese, Cage, Copland, Babbitt, Partch, Carter, Crumb, Rochberg, etc.), Germans, the French, etc.

Yet additional approaches choose to downplay historical context by stressing analytical or structural elements—often jumping back and forth from early to recent composers for intriguing comparisons, much like some CM approaches do for the entire stretch of music history. Some course outlines group around parameters (harmony, melody, rhythm, form, timbre, and texture), while others investigate, in turn, various compositional techniques or philosophies (serialism, indeterminacy, minimalism, etc.), mediums/forms (opera, string quartets, electronic music, etc.), or even particular compositions important for special innovations, for being influential landmarks, compendiums of compositional procedures, or simply masterpieces of communication (e.g., *Afternoon of a Faun, Rite of Spring, Mikrokosmos,* or *Wozzeck*).

Most teachers end up combining approaches, perhaps by taking each parameter in a roughly chronological order or by taking one piece at a time and viewing it through a variety of analytical lenses. The greatest danger of twentieth-century classes is that they can easily become schizophrenic and lose continuity or direction. Regardless of approach, threads of connection between topics, composers, or analyses must be constantly searched for, and decisions must be made concerning what to omit. There is always too much to include in one semester and many questions need answers: should more recent music be omitted? (many courses barely make it past Bartok); should less innovative composers be skimmed (e.g., Vaughn-Williams, Shostakovich, Britten)? what balance between breadth and depth should be achieved?

The main point is that some approach be chosen—that a rationale exists—so that a course does not ramble from topic to topic and issue to issue but is bound together by a predetermined view or governing philosophy that provides some bearings—and that students perceive what that philosophy is.

Strongly analytic approaches are most effective when they stress that much of this century's literature can be understood through concepts, techniques, and procedures that work for other periods as well. The thinking proccesses, expressive goals and gestures, and structural operations and concerns of many twentieth-century composers are not nearly as different from earlier composers as the surface of the music often suggests. On the other hand, it would be a mistake to underestimate the importance of change and true innovation when it occurs—especially in experimental and avant-garde circles. And it would be just as misleading and dishonest to fail to acknowledge the corresponding new methods of analysis that are needed to explain such innovations. Frequently, not only are new analytical methods and categories necessary, but analysis itself needs redefining to be able to meet the challenges of the music (in some cases of the background philosophy) that is being probed.

It is not often recognized that analysis (what it is and how to do it) has changed over the centuries and is still changing—or should be—to fit our transforming concepts of music itself. Analysis is probably the most all-embracing concept in music theory, since it is from our notion of it that most of our other concepts about music are formed and through it we are able to both think and listen. It is toward the task of developing a clear, flexible, and workable idea of musical analysis that we now turn.

FOUR

Musical Analysis

Philosophy

ANALYSIS is the activity that links mind training to ear training and therefore occupies the central position in theory teaching. The most basic problem in defining analysis is to distinguish it from description. Confusing the two has probably resulted in more feeble student work and more misguided analytical teaching than almost any other issue.

Description is an indispensable first stage of musical analysis but is incomplete by itself; it is a necessary but not sufficient beginning phase through which an analysis must pass but not stop. Description is a preliminary fact-gathering enterprise that answers "*what* happens?" and "*where* does it happen?" Listing features, identifying raw data on a time line, naming events with labels, etc. are all descriptive activities. Description can be recognized by statements like, "The introduction ends on a V^7 in measure 14;" or "This piece is an ABA;" or "The second theme enters in the oboe at 39;" or "The texture becomes polyphonic in the middle of the development just after the diminuendo in the strings;" or "The prevailing timbre of this electronic piece is dark and tubby." The goal of description, then, is to collect information.

It is astonishing (and disappointing), though, how often such descriptive commentary is displayed in texts and professional literature under the guise of analysis—the poverty of insight often camouflaged by needless technical jargon. A description of events cannot substitute for musical analysis any more than a plot summary can substitute for an analysis of character development, interaction, and motivation in a Shakespeare play. An analysis—in music or literature—goes beyond the facts, takes a particular slant, or demonstrates a point by using details to illustrate their larger significance or uniqueness. Points need explanations in light of a particular theoretical stance.

True musical analysis includes some or all of the following specific characteristics:

1. Explanations—analysis seeks to answer "how?" and "why?" questions. In his autobiographical novel, *Si le grain ne meurt . . .*, André Gide relates a childhood experience with a kaleidoscope, an instrument whose infinite variety of complex, symmetrical color patterns fascinated him for hours on end and led him first to experiment with the speed and direction of rotation, and ultimately to take apart the rosette, examine each semiprecious stone individually, put the kaleidoscope back together, take it apart again, substitute tiny objects for the original stones, and above all—as he puts it—to discover "le pourquoi du plaisir" (the "why" of his pleasure).[1] This is the point, and the method, and the ultimate satisfaction of analysis: to come to understand, from the inside out, *why* and *how* a piece of music works, to recreate the process by which it grew to life in the composer's mind, and to learn a little more about ourselves.

2. Connections—except for the obvious exception of indeterminate forms, events in music both grow out of what came before and lead toward what comes next. Analysis seeks to understand the causal logic behind such alliances and is therefore concerned with process, change, and motion.

3. Relationships—how events in one part of a piece are affected by or affect events in another part often involves long-range perception. Matters of balance, temporal proportion, and retrospective hearing (reinterpreting past events on the basis of new information) fall into this category.

4. Patterns—individual events tend to group together to form larger events. Analysis discovers the relation of part to whole, thereby aiding recognition of predictability, novelty, etc.

5. Hierarchies—out of pattern perception grows an aware-

ness of *levels* of connection or relationship. Events can have quite different meanings on different levels, or, conversely, might coincide on several levels at once. A weakness of immature analysis is to try to connect on incompatible or disparate levels (the "apples-and-oranges" confusion).

6. Comparisons—the disclosure of similarities and differences between sections, between details, or between one whole piece and another can often be revealing. This is especially so when looking for differences among pieces that have obvious similarities (e.g., two Mozart B♭ piano sonatas) and similarities among pieces with obvious differences (e.g., a dance movement from a Bach French suite vs. a Strauss tone poem).

Descriptive work is necessarily favored in the early stages of theory training since it makes no sense to *explain* facts if the facts themselves are not correct. Gradually, during the freshman year and increasingly from the sophomore year on, the accumulating experience of new terminology, information, concepts, and listening capabilities should be extended as much as possible into the analytical realm. Students should be taught to recognize the differences between description and analysis so they do not misinterpret the role and relationship of each or mistake one for the other. A further distinction is made by Meyer between critical analysis and style analysis:

> For these disciplines, though complementary, involve different viewpoints, methods, and goals.
>
> Critical analysis seeks to understand and explain what is idiosyncratic about a particular composition: how is this piece different from all other pieces—even those in the same style and of the same genre? It is concerned with the implications of this specific motive or process, the function and structure of this specific harmonic progression, the relationship between this particular slow introduction and the Allegro which follows it, the reason why there is a *sforzando* on this note or why this theme is interrupted at this particular point. In short, criticism tries to discover the secret of the singular—to explain in what ways the patterns and processes peculiar to a particular work are related to one another and to the hierarchic structure of which they form a part.
>
> Style analysis, on the other hand, is normative. It is concerned with discovering and describing those attributes of a composition which are common to a group of works—usually ones

76

which are similar in style, form, or genre. It asks, for instance, about the characteristic features of late Baroque music—its typical textures, harmonic procedures, and formal organization; or it inquires into the features common to diverse movements in sonata form or different types of operas. Style analysis, in its pure form, ignores the idiosyncratic in favor of generalization and typology. Consequently statistical methods are as a rule more appropriate in style analysis than in criticism. For style analysis, a particular composition is an instance of a technique, a form, or a genre.[2]

Style analysis is similar to music theory itself since it helps to discover the general principles that govern typical stylistic procedures and schemes. Critical analysis, on the other hand, uses these general principles to explain how and why particular events in a specific composition are actualized—or even evaded. Two different views are represented by John White, who claims the essential purpose of both theory and analysis is the understanding of musical style,[3] and William Thomson who, at the other extreme, has written about the trivialization of analysis when it is reduced to finding and discussing style traits rather than more organic and enduring features and constructive and aesthetic operations.[4] In actual practice the two approaches often overlap or even interpenetrate, but the distinction is still useful since it pinpoints that analysis can offer differing goals and methods.

The context and reasons for analyzing music will, of course, affect both method and result. Any of the following purposes can find their way into the music classroom:

1. Re-creation of an epoch—used by music historians.

2. Attribution—both for an unknown composer or to place the work of a known composer chronologically.

3. Explanation/understanding—one valid purpose is to satisfy curiosity, certainly a welcome trait for any thinking musician.

4. Performance—an adequate theory of performance relating the specifics of interpretive decision-making to analysis has not yet been written but most would agree that such a connection does exist.

5. Composition—there is more to writing music than studying how others did it, but creativity is surely not harmed by

the intuition-enriching experience of analysis. It would be difficult to cite a single top-rank composer who was not immersed in the music of his predecessors and/or contemporaries.

6. Evaluation—perhaps no musical activity is more enigmatic or risky than making value judgements about compositional worth, yet it would be impossible to even begin without some analytical framework.

7. Aesthetic response—conditioning the hearer for perceptive listening is the one goal that runs through all the others.

A distinction between map-like vs. time-like views of analysis can emphasize either the synchronic or phenomenological side of music. Analysis can either work from the inside out (surface to background) in a way that explains its unity and wholeness after the fact—the static overview; or it can work from the beginning to end by explaining the dynamic experience of the listener as it happens.

The format for presenting the results of analytical inquiry will also affect our approach and mental set while working. The possibilites are numerous: features can be listed, summarized, and grouped; scores can be annotated, reduced, or exploded (isolated fragments pasted together showing related elements); continuity lines and sounding scores (an aural version of the exploded score presenting items for side-by-side comparison) can represent the listening experience; graphs (of contour, dynamics, densities, etc.), statistical tables, letter and number symbols, diagrams, and charts can often visually depict relationships that would be cumbersome in written form; and conventional verbal discussion is normally reserved for expanding on subtleties that can't be handled in more compressed layouts and for interpretation of emotional and expressive values—values that are often overlooked or ignored in much contemporary analysis (perhaps because they cannot be scientifically quantified).

The limitations of analysis are often never mentioned at all in theory classes, but to understand these shortcomings helps us to appreciate its strengths. Merely choosing which analytical categories to use will skew the results in some way. Changing our analysis (or categories—should I use pitch, time, color, or some combination?) will simply skew the results in a different direction. Since music is so much more complex and multifaceted than our analytical means of capturing it and pinning it to a board like a butterfly, we will always be perverting our experience of it in the very act of selecting an approach and conceptual classifications.

Another danger is fragmentation. Too much breaking apart tends to separate detail from detail, section from section, listening from thinking, and finally even feeling from thinking. In addition to courses in musical analysis, we also need courses in musical synthesis where the music is recreated again after being dissected. Doing analysis is like solving Rubik's Cube: sometimes the patterns in one part need to be destroyed before all six sides can be put back in order. Perhaps listening is the re-creative act that can synthesize for us what talking and thinking have separated.

It is true that because of its selective nature, analysis of any type is a distortion of real experience. But communication and therefore education would be impossible without it. All learning would have to be acquired privately through pure mystical insight. Explanations and knowledge, however, can be documented, debated, corrected, and passed on. Distortion is a risk that must be taken for understanding to be shared.

One of the most important, yet most overlooked, goals of analytical training is the practice it gives in making interpretational decisions—not about performance necessarily but about judging conflicting evidence, measuring significance, discovering appropriate supporting clues, sifting out clutter (knowing what to omit is as important as knowing what to include), and arguing convincingly for a particular point of view. Beyond the descriptive level, almost all good analysis involves interpretation and much of skillful teaching involves searching for classroom opportunities and outside assignments that raise questions permitting two or more analytical solutions. Forcing students to argue both for and against a particular answer is one of the best methods of developing a discriminating and analytical mind. Using factual information (i.e., description) to sustain an opinion with the healthy give-and-take of follow-up classroom comparisons of views should be a goal of all theory teaching.

Some teachers will feel reluctant to pursue more uncharted leads, preferring the safety of questions with explicit answers. These questions are important too for emphasizing the merits of accuracy and rigor. But students who are never exposed to the dangers (and delights) of speculation may be *learning* theory but they will never be *doing* music theory. They will simply be repeating the thinking of others who have gone before rather than developing their own ideas. The stimulation that flourishes from genuine theorizing is the kind of thinking that is vital for meeting new music situations long after the formal class has been finished.

Under conditions of debate and deliberate controversy, the teacher will often play devil's advocate or will simply referee the exchange of ideas among students by directing the drift of argument and granting equal time to all sides. The evaluation of responses to such uncertain situations should be based not on agreement with the teacher or a pre-selected "correct" answer key, but on the quality and pertinence of corroborating data (being speculative does not give one the right to be far-fetched), compelling logic, consistency, persuasion, imagination, creativity, and musical insight. These same qualities are desirable also in composition, performance, listening—and teaching.

This type of interpretive analysis suggests the idea that *doing* analysis is more important than the *result*. What is written down on paper and turned in to be graded is often viewed in the student's mind as the final goal of analysis. It is important in teaching, however, to stress the values of the preliminary phases that lead to the final answers being possible. The intangible process of trial and error; testing, revising, and discarding hypotheses; weighing and weighting facts; endlessly debating with oneself; exercising the mind and ears—these are the values of analysis that accumulate, through experience, the habits of thinking and listening that we label musicianship.

The final step of actually writing up an analysis is important too, since the act of verbalizing and organizing our thoughts often aids the clarity of our thinking. Once an idea hits the cold light of day (i.e., appears on paper), it can either evaporate in the glare or grow into something worthwhile as expansions and elaborations come forth. Students are often surprised at the depth of their own thoughts. Writing of personal and shared feelings and perceptions about music—doing analysis—is both exciting and revealing since we usually end up discovering as much about ourselves as about the music.

80

Method

The stages of musical analysis can be outlined. The following sample plan represents just one of many such outlines but can be used as a demonstration of how analysis can be learned (and taught) by taking one step at a time. Beginners will necessarily be involved more with the early stages, while those with more experience (some will be ready by the sophomore year) should be encouraged to ponder the deeper levels of later stages as they come up. This plan is a general and flexible one and could be combined with any of the more specific systems such as reduction technique, style analysis, implication/realization models, thematic unity, musical form, or set theory.

STAGE I—GETTING PREPARED: SOME BASIC PRINCIPLES

All analytical work is based on presuppositions that are not often verbalized or even acknowledged. These background assumptions—like all teaching issues and attitudes—should be fully recognized and brought to the surface before analysis is begun. The idea is not to eliminate all biases or try to adopt some magic set of beliefs that will insure perfect results and correct answers, but to be made aware of their consequences. The following list of ideas is presented as an illustration of how background assumptions—my own, in this case, as samples—can be stated in the form of principles and thereby be more fully exposed. Improved awareness of such underlying issues can help to orient both teacher and student to implied prejudices (and possible corrective measures) in a particular analytical system.

1. Structure in music, as external form, is the organization of the events of a composition. From the composer's point of view, it is the process he discovers in his material, by which the piece evolves into a whole. It is the *unifying idea* that all his other ideas for the piece have led him to.

2. How the events of a composition react to each other, how they generate similarities, or strike up contrasts, and how strong or weak those similarities or contrasts may be, has to do with musical *rhetoric*. This art of logical argumentation, emphasis, clarity, and persuasion, generally associated with speech, is also applicable to music. Composers assume they are dealing with

81

knowledgeably curious auditors—and every composer's "primary listener" is himself—and rest their reputations on concepts of craft, deftness of expression, and musical structure. That is why art music bears careful study, and why its richly complex nature is less exhaustible than music made primarily for casual passive enjoyment or short-term popularity. Serious music is, of course, made to be enjoyed, but the best of it demands the listener's total involvement.

3. Patterns in tonal and modal music grow out of the fundamental premises of the functions of the major/minor key system and/or centricity. Since the concept of a focal point (as both a site of departure and ultimate goal) is the nucleus of these systems, recurrence patterns are most typical of such music. When the patterns of tonal music are applied to newer, non-key music, it is usually the rhetorical (see above) aspects of the older music that make the patterns work with new sounds. Sometimes this gets hokey because we sense that the structure is not growing out of the music but is being slapped on. This has led twentieth-century composers to discard stock patterns and recipes in favor of more organic kinds of structures, or process. Since our culture likes to hang on to its old masterpieces, this has had an interesting effect on how we understand the past. By listening with twentieth-century ears, earlier pieces are often redefined and rediscovered for us through these newer processes.

4. Musical events take on significance in a piece in several ways:

    a. By their acoustical nature (surface, density, transparency, brilliance, placideness, spacing, register, movement, duration, etc.)

    b. By their relationship to the immediate context (which they may seem to emerge from, or contrast with)

    c. By their early or late position in the overall time-span

    d. By their recurrence or singularity (an important decision for the composer to make is whether to emphasize by reiteration or uniqueness)

5. Some basic structural processes:

    a. Continuum (continuation of an idea—a relatively stable process)

b. Accumulation (to a point of greatest density or complexity; then: cessation, or a winding down of tension)

c. Cycles (recurring patterns offset by increasing contrast
or distance)

d. Transformation (the music flowers into something new
and unforseen)

6. Additional processes especially applicable to more recent
music:[5]

PROCEDURES OF CONTRAST

a. Stratification (layering of texture, or the independent
operation of more than one parameter simultaneously)

b. Juxtaposition (abrupt change of elements)

c. Interpolation (abrupt change of elements with [almost
immediate] continuation of the first idea)

PROCEDURES OF CONNECTION

a. Gradation (gradual change within one parameter, or
an overlapping of two blocks of sound)

b. Amalgamation (the synthesis of sound events into an
inter-parametric unit where parameters act together)

c. Dissolution (the separation of an inter-parametric unit
into its component parts, where each part is developed
independently)

7. Because time is irreversible, music is balanced on a knife
blade of tension between persistence and fade-out. Memory
allows us to grasp the totality of the experience-in-time of a
piece, to hold it together while it happens even while everything we remember is being constantly reinterpreted by what
comes next. The further we get into the time-span of a piece,
the more forshortened its initial events seem (as we remember
them). Recurrence of early events is a kind of measure of the
distance traveled in time.

STAGE 2—GETTING STARTED: SOME FIRST STEPS

Students often have trouble knowing where to begin in doing
analysis. Of course, when a list of questions is provided by the
instructor, these will be the point of departure. Directed assignments of this type should always be a preliminary step before

throwing students on their own. After studying classroom and/ or textbook models, though, it is essential for students eventually to be handed a piece and told, "Now analyze it."

When specific questions are offered, the student will be locked, more or less, into the teacher's train of thought. A series of assignments can be devised (e.g., in a junior level form-and-analysis course) that will gradually wean the student from such strictly supervised work. The long-range goal is to create students who are independent of the teacher's guidance. Many students (and performers) do well so long as their teacher stands nearby cuing their analysis or listening (or interpretation). Some teachers—classroom and studio—cultivate this dependence because of the resultant ego boost.

The ultimate goal is for students to learn more than how to answer analysis questions devised by someone else. They must be taught a set of flexible and comprehensive analytical approaches so that their information about and understanding of music comes directly from the music itself and not from teachers or even from theory books such as this. It is in this spirit that the following list of starting points is offered—both for the teacher who might need suggestions for concocting questions or for the student who has been given none:

1. Prepare the score by numbering the measures (if necessary) continuously from the first full measure to the end of the movement. These numbers are needed for reference points throughout the movement.

2. Become familiar with the scoring (instruments, clefs, transpositions, if any); consider the various timbres, articulations, and dynamic weights of the sound sources. Note the details of tempo and meter (which determine the number of strong pulses per bar and their sub-divisions) and how these relate to harmonic speed. Determine the pitch language or key.

3. Hear the music: translate notes into sound; imagine the work from the score; listen to a recording if possible both with and without the score; play and sing at least the principal lines (including the bass). Let the ear provide a guide to the central or characteristic elements of the composition.

Some theorists object to beginning with the sound of the music rather than the score since the sound (i.e., a performance, either one's own or another's) itself is already a kind of analysis—the score has been tainted by passing through the interpretational filter of an intermediary. The unadulterated notation, on the other hand, is a pure objective source of information about the music that has encoded into it all potential and possible analyses (or performances)—even bad ones—not just the single analysis implied by one particular interpretive version.

The counter-argument then continues discussion by pointing out that many clues and hidden relationships are apparent only through an aural presentation—the visual appearance of the actual notes being just a pale shadow of the real music (real music being defined as the listener's experience and not circles and lines). This is obviously another "chicken-and-egg" issue and is reminiscent of the ancient riddle: if a tree falls in an empty forest, is there a sound? (It depends on how sound is defined: vibrations in the air or impingement on consciousness through eardrum contact.)

The score and sound should support and complement one another; each offers insights that the other can't provide alone. Visual and aural glimmers often appear simultaneously while listening with score in hand. It is my view that since listening is often the most neglected component of analysis (this can easily be confirmed by just cursory examination of professional journal articles and current textbooks), it should be given priority just to give it a fair chance of maintaining parity.

4. Let the nature of the piece (sound sources, genre, style, formal plan, expressive character) generate expectations and questions. Discover and follow musical expectations throughout the work; how are they set up, delayed, avoided, extended, interrupted, fulfilled? Look for goals (melodic, harmonic, rhythmic, etc.). How are they prepared and achieved? What factors of resistance impede or postpone their realization? Are non-goal-oriented aspects of musical construction present?

5. Look for the big picture first; don't start by moving from beat to beat and measure to measure. Get an overall idea of the work; recognize large structural divisions, contrasts of texture, sonority, tonal areas, movement towards and arrival at goals, cadence points, etc.

6. When the interrelationships among large events are heard and seen, examine subdivisions and then, finally, details. If the harmonic language suddenly seems elaborate or complex, figure out what is happening at that moment and why.

85

7. While pitch operations are a fundamental concern of both tonal and nontonal music, remember that all aspects (texture, dynamics, silence, macrorhythm, timbre, etc.) of the music contribute to articulating its structure and expressiveness. A common weakness of much student work is lack of attention to non-pitch factors.

8. Take notes, make diagrams, and mark the score whereever something interesting or problematic is found. Continuously look for places about which to ask questions.

9. Be sure to understand the terminology, procedures, and devices of musical analysis, form, and style. Make sure that the basic factual information about the piece is correct. Although a description cannot replace an analysis, an analysis cannot be constructed without the foundation of meticulous preparatory work.

STAGE 3—GETTING DEEPER INTO THE MUSIC: SOME QUESTIONS

All musical analysis boils down at some point to knowing what questions to ask. Often the answers are easy once a line of investigation can be initiated. The following list is intended to stimulate awareness of issues that are often crucial to the success of an analysis:

1. What kind of piece is it? Aggressive? Lyrical? Witty? Dramatic? Ponderous? Profound? Trivial? Boisterous? Subtle?

2. What are the piece's generating ideas? Do they have to do with specific sonorities, with notions of development, contrast, recurrence, gradual unfolding, sudden transformation, with the manipulation of time?

3. Why is the piece as long or short as it is?

4. What are the proportions in terms of relative duration? What is the difference between *getting to* and *being at* events? How do these events shape the composition?

5. If the structure is thematically articulated—if the various sections or events are marked off by different themes or by varying aspects of a central subject or motive—how is this related to the overall pitch plan or key areas?

6. What are the proportions of thematic assertiveness vs. areas of transition (developmental or linking events)? Distinguish between transitions (musical events that lead from—and often break down—one area of stability, to another) and main sections which are articulated initially by thematic contrast,

changes in texture, dynamics, mood, or modulation and are often closed off by goal cadences.

7. Where are the primary arrival points (structural downbeats) and how are these set up, reached, balanced, expanded, departed from, etc.? Which ones are strongest and weakest and why?

8. How is the flow of tension regulated? Which areas are most stable or most unstable?

9. How do densities and dynamic highs and lows relate to the tonal and thematic structure? Do events in different parameters (harmony, melody, rhythm, etc.) reinforce or detract from one another?

10. If the composition is for more than one sound source, how does the treatment of the sound sources relate to the structure as a whole?

11. If there is only one sound source, what are the elements of contrast? If the music is organized linearly in two or more voices, how does the ordering and combining of these voices form patterns in the work?

12. If the work has a (sung) text, to what extent does the composer's interest in projecting (or responding to) the sense of the principal images of the text, and/or its poetic structure, influence his decisions about pitch, duration, dynamics, articulation, texture, density, etc.?

13. If the piece is part of something larger (a movement from a suite, sonata, quartet, concerto, or symphony; an aria from a cantata or opera; a Lied from a song cycle, etc.) find out how it figures in the overall scheme.

14. Distinguish between the content of the composition and the compositional system (theoretical background) upon which it is based.

15. Put yourself in the composer's position: consider the challenges and potentialities of the medium, materials, and formal design. What might he—or *you*—have done differently?

STAGE 4—GETTING STILL DEEPER: SOME AESTHETIC ISSUES

Analysis discussions and projects can become either bogged down or enlivened—depending on both the skill, attitude, and temperament of the teacher—by consideration of the following spin-off questions. These questions, because of their tendency to lead to yet additional and even more murky questions are of the "can-of-worms" type and therefore more appropriate for advanced students or classes (perhaps graduate level at many schools), but they raise issues that ultimately cannot be ignored. Whether they are faced directly or by evasion, they will influence and tint the results of an analysis—even from behind the scenes.

There are, obviously, no right or wrong answers to the following questions. Student responses will reflect the degree of thoughtful consideration (and probably the amount of time) they have devoted to the issues that are raised. In the course of an analysis project, some of them may be answered in a fairly spontaneous way, but those answers wouldn't necessarily appear as part of the analysis. An analysis can be composed of even preliminary responses to these problems and to the music itself. In three months, or in ten years, responses to these questions, to music in general, and to specific pieces will have changed—perhaps significantly. Ideas, like music, continue to develop as long as they are pursued. But it is important for students to commit themselves as early as possible to a stand in analytical work, so that they can more easily see where they are and from where they've come.

1. How is "what do I hear?" different from "what am I listening to?"

2. How does it make sense? What is musical sense? What is the sense-making process that we use to make sense out of music?

3. How is the sense of a piece affected by its style, duration, medium, purpose, etc.?

4. How much does what you're supposed to hear in a piece—or what you expect to hear—*interfere* with a full experiencing of that music?

5. How much more could you get from a piece (on hearing it) than you usually do? What prevents you? Isn't it all there? If not, where is "it"?

6. How is our perception of music colored by (auto)biographical associations, cultural prejudices, our analytical conceptual categories, or immediate environment? Are we passive victims of such things?

7. Which is easier: overcoming our reactions to unfamiliarity, or hearing something familiar in a new and fresh way?

8. What makes a piece of music boring, or vivid? Do composers think of parts of their own music as being more insipid (or absorbing) than others?

9. How is the design (idea, conception, intention, shape) of a composition made clear?

10. What elements of musical design change from one era (or style, or culture) to another? Which change somewhat, altogether, considerably? Which remain constant?

11. What can we learn from the music of other cultures, about them, about our own music, about ourselves?

12. Can we empathize (imagine, re-create) the composer's experience, retrace his steps, understand the composition as a microcosm of the related choices he has made, share his excitement at having discovered the right sound at the right moment, find *the* moment (sound complex, idea, turn of phrase, timbre, etc.) that particularly turned him on?

13. How is music short, or long?: as we hear it, or as we remember it?

14. How does music articulate time?

15. To what extent is the success of a joke, the effectiveness of a drama, and the ultimately convincing quality of a musical composition a matter of timing?

16. How does the composer regulate the flow of time? What kinds of devices make time seem to stand still, or rush by?

17. How is our time-experience affected when we sense the approach of something important—what makes a musical event important?—or when the direction of the music seems temporarily lost or ambiguous? What is musical direction?

18. What similarities can we find between music and the cinema as temporal experiences?

19. In any specific piece of music (or film), how does real time differ from experienced time, or from remembered time? Why?

20. How does (musical) structure determine our perception of time? Does it make any difference if we are conscious of that structure?

21. How does being able to anticipate something in a piece differ from its being predictable?

22. How does a composer engineer our anticipations and expectations as we participate, through listening, in his music?

23. How, for the listener, is the evolving of a musical work a function of memory? How does the evolving of that work in the composer's imagination differ from the listener's experiencing of it?

24. How can a composer participate in an established style of cultural convention and yet maintain individuality?

25. How is it possible for one hundred paintings of a sunset, or one hundred sonnets on eternal love, or one hundred sonatas in G major, to be each a unique aesthetic experience?

26. A major triad in the midst of a composition by Penderecki would elicit a different response from that caused by the same triad in a Mozart symphony. Why? What does this suggest about triads, about musical (stylistic, historical, systematic) context, about the function of informed expectations?

27. If music is a symbolic language, what do its symbols symbolize?

28. Language is a socially conventionalized system of symbols and structural relationships. When we think in a language (which is probably most of the time, and which differs from non-linguistic feeling or reacting), are we really translating something (what?) into language, or are we performing a habitual act in its own right? To what extent are our thoughts channeled by the relational modes available to us in any particular language? Of what significance is it that there are some things that are possible to formulate in one language that simply cannot be thought (i.e., conceived of) in another?—like, for example, aspects of time, space, and condition that characterize certain American Indian languages, for which there are no direct or exact concepts in English.

29. When a composer thinks in sound, is he translating?

30. Consider the following zooming in on a thematically structured work for large orchestra, of considerable duration (say, forty-five minutes):

   a. The work as a whole
   b. The last movement, *Finale*
   c. A climactic résumé of the work's principal theme, scored "tutti"
   d. The melodic line of that theme (without its environment of harmony, counterpoint, context, etc.)

   e. A fragment of that melody: a fairly rapid passage in
     16ths (given a quarter-note pulse of 60 per minute),
     presented in the violins and doubled an octave higher
     by two flutes in unison
   f. One note from that passage, with all acoustical charac-
     teristics intact
   g. That note only as it occurs in one of the flutes
   h. An identical note in a piece for solo flute
   i. That same note represented graphically in notation
   j. The same, represented as 1760 c.p.s., 250 milliseconds,
     at 92 decibels

How does each stage of the breakdown alter the relevance of
the item under consideration?

31. Is the aesthetic whole equal to the sum of its parts?

32. How would you describe the surface of a composition?
How does it relate to the structure of the music?

33. What procedural differences would you expect between
a multiple-sound-source work (say, a piece for orchestra) and
a relatively monochromatic medium (e.g., a work for unac-
companied cello)?

34. To what extent, and on what level, do we understand
the gestural aspects of a piece in terms of interpersonal relationships—like a kind of musical psychology?

35. Compare a Beethoven piano sonata with one for piano
and violin; compare a two-voice invention by Bach with a
three-voice one. How does the presence of another sound-
source, in the former, and an additional voice, in the latter,
alter basic compositional and structural concerns?

36. How do we recognize the structural phases of a work—
for example: transition, goal preparation, arrival, derailment,
denouement, etc.? To what extent is such recognition the result of previous musical experience? To what extent is it the
result of the specific operations of the piece itself?

37. Which tends more to shrink the experiential time span:
continuity or (isolated) dissimilarity? Why?

38. Compare several performances of the same work (including, perhaps, your own). Assuming all the notes are correct in each, what constitutes the best performance? In what
sense is an intelligent performance an analysis of a work?

39. What kind of gear shifting is necessary in order to perceive subtle nuances of expression peculiar to particular historical and/or generic styles?

40. To what extent is a composition, or any work of art, a matter of posing and solving problems? What is the nature of such problems, and of what interest is that to the listener?

STAGE 5—GOING ABOUT IT: WRITING AN ANALYSIS

Writing up an analysis project should be the result of having listened to and thought about and lived with the music for some time. The prose portions must reflect careful organization, lucid thinking, and a concise, forceful writing style. The pretentious, pompous verbosity that is current in much academic writing about analysis and theory is deplorable. One brief sample will suffice: "With the understanding that this book is about *music,* none of whose structural elements often assumes independent manifestation, it will be acknowledged that there is a methodological advantage and common didactic purpose in individuating at provisional stages identifiable and classifiable element-actions for singular emphasis and for explication of conceptual and practical ideas relating to each such element-structure in turn."[6] This leaden, opaque, and tortuous monstrosity translates, I believe, into: "It is helpful in musical analysis to examine elements one at a time."

G. M. Trevelyn has stated clearly the notion that it is easy to make something difficult to understand but difficult to make it easy to understand: "The idea that histories which are delightful to read must be the work of superficial temperaments and that a crabbed style betokens a deep thinker or conscientious worker is the reverse of the truth. What is easy to read has been difficult to write. The labour of writing and rewriting, correcting and recorrecting, is the due exacted by every good book from its author, even if he knows from the beginning exactly what he wants to say. A limpid style is invariably the result of hard labour, and the easily flowing connection of sentence with sentence and paragraph with paragraph has always been won by the sweat of the brow."[7]

Just as performance without practice or musical composition without revision makes no sense, writing about music without rewriting is unworthy of all the time spent in discovering what to write about in the first place.

Most of all, students must be encouraged to be musical detectives, psychologists, and theorists; they must find clues, interpret reasons, and make discoveries. They must be spurred (some will need to be toned down) into speculating on the *purpose* and *function* of unusual, perplexing, or intriguing events—but always with the backing of those attributes already mentioned: supporting evidence, logic, persuasion, consistency, imagination, and pertinence. Analytical boldness, even when pushed too far, is more in keeping with the spirit of music theory than the kind of caution that is technically correct but excessively constrained by timid and shallow boundaries of safety and propriety.

STAGE 6—THE FINAL GOAL: ANALYSIS AND MUSICAL
EXPERIENCE

The contemporary American painter Ben Shahn defines form as the shape of content. In the same way that the structure of a language makes meaningful symbols of phonemic sounds, structure in music—which ranges from the acoustical envelope of a single sound to the shape-in-time of an entire composition—transforms relatively pleasant noises into significant designs and ideas that have the power to move and delight listeners to the degree that they are totally involved in the experience of *listening* and *reflecting*. In the "Overture" to his book on the science of mythology, *The Raw and the Cooked*, the anthropologist Claude Lévi-Strauss writes with remarkable insight about experiencing music:

> The musical emotion . . . springs from the fact that at each moment the composer withholds or adds more or less than the listener anticipates on the basis of a pattern that he thinks he can guess, but that he is incapable of wholly divining. . . . If the composer withholds more than we anticipate, we experience a delicious falling sensation; we feel we have been torn from a stable point on the musical ladder and thrust into the void, but only because the support that is waiting for us was not in the expected place. When the composer withholds less, the opposite occurs: he forces us to make the movement ourselves, but it always exceeds what we would have thought ourselves capable of achieving alone. Aesthetic enjoyment is made up of this multiplicity of excitements and moments of respite—a multiplicity

resulting from the challenges made by the work and from the contradictory feeling it arouses that the tests it is subjecting us to are impossible, at the same time as it prepares to provide us with the marvelously unpredictable means of coping with them. The intention of the composer, ambiguous while still in the score . . . becomes actual . . . through and by the listener. The relation between transmitter and receiver becomes reversed, since in the last resort the latter discovers its own meaning through the message from the former: *Music has its being in me, and I listen to myself through it.*[8]

One of the most important and difficult (but alluring) goals of analysis, then, is to try to explain and understand these mysterious processes of assertion and response, departure and arrival, expansion and contraction, continuity and evanescence, and motion and stasis that are present in the music of all cultures and periods. In focusing on specific pieces, we can discover how these elements operate within a specific system of pitch and temporal order whose typical patterns are often familiar to us, and to many of whose operations we already have conditioned expectations.

It seems desirable for a book about teaching theory to include at least one sample analysis. As a summary for this chapter I have chosen Chopin's Prelude in E minor, Op. 28, no. 4 because it is brief and because it is a piece (or is like pieces) that are frequently encountered in undergraduate theory classes. No single composition could illustrate all of the points or suggestions made in this book,[9] but even the application of a few analytical techniques can demonstrate how abstract ideas are made specific by connection to real music. One short composition can provide a starting point for discussion of a remarkably wide variety of issues.

The following analysis is presented in the form of questions with analysis of both the questions themselves and the music. Reinforcement of some points is provided by written commentary and symbols on the score (see below).

1. Most of the chords in this composition are coloristic (i.e., used non-functionally for their sound value) rather than serving some key-defining role. Within the first eight measures locate (by m. and beat) and discuss any three chords that operate in this way. Give a conventional quality description or

Prelude 4 in E minor

roman-numeral analysis, if possible, and explain how these labels *in*adequately describe how the chord really works (because of voice leading, context, lack of resolution, etc.).

Purpose of question: to distinguish between functional chords and those that are the byproduct of purely linear chromaticism; to distinguish vertical from horizontal influences and events. Notice that the slippage of the left-hand part occurs by half-step, one voice at a time; some of the "chords" are, therefore, intentional blurs—the side-effects of momentary "mis-alignments." Notice also the firm tonal/harmonic grounding of mm. 1, 9, 10, 11, 12, and the purely forward-directed push of mm. 2–8 as the chromatic voice-leading takes over (the "suspended" tonality is represented by a wavy line on the score).

2. Why does the bass line begin on G?

Purpose of question: to suggest how inversions affect "weight" (lightening, in this case, the departure point). The beginning is also made very slightly ambiguous by the assignment of tonic to an inconspicuous inner voice (with 3rd and 5th—could it be G major?—in outer voices). The most interesting point is that by beginning the bass on G, the lower voice has more room or space (notice subtle interplay of pitch content and register) for maneuvering down to its dominant goal, and, thus, indirectly affects the length of section one and its leisurely unfolding.

A question concerning such an unremarkable item can demonstrate to students the careful attention—whether it's conscious or not is immaterial here—that composers often pay to the smallest details. [An identical beginning—with i⁶ chord, descending chromaticism, downward soprano, etc.—is found in the Mazurka 49 in F minor, Op. posth. 68, no. 4.]

3. Describe the basic (i.e., undecorated) motion of the soprano line *in scale degree numbers* during mm. 1–11.

Purpose of question: to underline the frequent importance of links between *non-adjacent* pitches (embedded melodic step-progressions) and the distinction between embellishing and structural pitches (5–4–#3–2).

4. What note is conspicuously missing in m. 12? Why?

Purpose of question: an obvious follow-up to question 3. Questions can often duplicate the train-of-thought of the music itself. Every scale degree of e minor (even both leading-tone and subtonic) is present in m. 12 except the one pitch most

96

demanded by the harmonic set-up of mm. 9–11 and the melodic set-up of mm. 1–11: the tonic itself.

5. In light of the two previous questions, how is the arrival of m. 21 *both* the achievement of a long-awaited goal and the derailment of that goal? How could this measure be recomposed to make it the ending of the piece? Formally, why would this location (m. 21) be unsatisfactory as the end?

Purpose of question: another follow-up, but this time urging awareness of more *long-range* connections between the ending of part one and the ending of the whole piece. Such connections (often with intervening interruptions) between different sections (as opposed to simpler local relationships) are of the greatest importance in analytical work—especially for establishing the notion of hierarchy. (Note also the "starting-over" nature of part two.)

The question also implies that melodic and harmonic arrival are not always in phase and that this can be a source of tension. Two points need stressing with deceptive cadences: (*a*) the element of surprise; and (*b*) the element of frustration—the avoided goal thereby becoming all the more alluring. The notion of *recomposition* is extremely valuable in analysis since it often clarifies composer's choices and the understanding of "what might have been"—in its shadowy existence, a frequently overlooked aspect of aesthetic experience. Finally, the temporal factor (of balance, proportion, and timing) extends the range of inquiry beyond the more narrow realm of pitch.

6. Describe as many similarities *and* differences as you can between the two halves of this piece (melody, harmony, pacing, bass lines, register, and dynamics).

Purpose of question: to suggest that the second half is a variation of the first. Comparison questions are among the best since they prod students to account for facts in a larger context rather than in seclusion. The long list of comments that are possible even for this short piece should include both pitch *and* non-pitch items.

7. Where is the climax of the piece? Give as many reasons as you can to support your answer.

Purpose of question: to collect evidence to sustain a viewpoint. This question might lead to a discussion of definitions and determinants of musical climax for various kinds of pieces. A good analysis should teach something about both the piece under investigation and about music in general. Again, non-pitch factors (dynamics, location, density, range, pattern-breaking, compression of slippage, and environment) are important.

8. Discuss and contrast *several* possible harmonic explanations of m. 17 and of m. 23.

Purpose of question: to consider multiple interpretations of situations and to argue for and against these possibilities. The misspelled and inverted Ge^6 chord of m. 23 is especially interesting.

9. Which basic elements are the most static? What *does* provide the principal interest, drive, and intensity?

Purpose of question: to explore interactions and dependencies among parameters, and cause-and-effect relationships (in this case musical motion being a result more of harmonic thrust than of rhythm or melodic movement).

We should remember that the eventual goal of classroom work for the student is to provide the experience and background—the student will have to provide his own creativity—for doing analysis without being given ready-made questions. To find the proper questions on our own we must first observe and listen carefully enough to know what is worth including or excluding from the final result. We are left with a paradox: to do analysis we must first do analysis—of a preliminary kind. Analysis, then, is not done all at once; it proceeds in levels and layers of sifting and continues on and on and on.

So that the discussion of this Chopin prelude can finally be concluded, let me close by suggesting a short list of additional facts or perceptions that could be the foundation for yet additional questions for this piece:

1. The opening soprano motive of B–C (mm. 1–3) is echoed in the bass at crucial junctures of each half (mm. 9–12 and 18–22).

2. Examples of delay and resistance (harmonic, melodic, and rhythmic) are in evidence throughout.

3. Soprano octave displacement and a rift in the step-wise bass both occur at m. 16 (with contrary motion).

4. The climax point occurs at a golden-section proportional division (62%) giving a kind of wedge shape to the whole.

5. The tenuous surface details (extreme chromaticism and decorative overlays) are counterbalanced by firmly grounded

support points (see roman numerals in score) and P-D-T cadential formulas. Miraculously, the piece seems to be both securely anchored in e minor and at the same time outside of any key at all.

6. The root-position tonic triad occurs only once—at the last measure. The whole piece, in a way, is a struggle to achieve that solitary instant of stability. Before that point the tonal centricity exists by insinuation rather than realization.

7. The one moment of silence (m. 23) is filled with anticipation, not emptiness.

8. A whole series of questions involving historical context and style traits could be constructed: e.g., comparisons with (*a*) other Chopin preludes (note the remarkable correspondance with the mazurka mentioned earlier); (*b*) other romantic works; (*c*) the Bach or Debussy preludes; etc.

9. Finally, a whole series of hearing spin-offs is possible: e.g., (*a*) singing reduced soprano and bass lines; (*b*) singing the three-voice chromatic chord progressions as an ensemble in simplified rhythm; (*c*) harmonic dictation of the cadential patterns.

This final connection between analysis and listening leads to our next topic—ear training.

FIVE

Ear Training

Ear training in this chapter is defined in the broad sense of aural skills. Some teachers use the term to refer only to dictation (as opposed to sightsinging). My use covers both of these traditional skills as well as a whole range of related activities. Dictation and sightsinging should be thought of as opposite sides of the same coin. They are simply different avenues to the single goal of developing internal musical perception—the ability to hear musical relationships accurately and with understanding.

The purpose of dictation, for example, is not to produce correct written transcriptions but to produce a certain kind of listener who can hear sound as meaningful patterns. The purpose of sightsinging is not to provide a sight-reading service for music-department choral groups or to develop articulate vocal response—although these may be worthwhile fringe benefits. The goal again is to produce a listener who can hear musical patterns. The final step of externalizing one's hearing through notation or sung performance is useful for checking accomplishment and providing feedback but is not an inherent part of the activity itself. The sound-into-notes and notes-into-sound transference has been aptly described by Benward as developing the "seeing" ear and "hearing" eye.[1] From the standpoint of this book it might even more aptly be described as developing the *understanding* ear and the hearing *mind*.

Many dictation and sightsinging texts and even ear-training research projects have focused on the drill-and-repetition aspects of learning to hear. The weakness of this approach centers on a failure to distinguish between sound events (requiring just ears) and musical events (requiring ears *and* minds).

A well-rounded ear-training program includes at least two discernable phases—one preliminary and the other more terminal—just as true analysis in written work is prepared by the antecedent stage of description. In the case of ear training, the preliminary phase does not necessarily have to be mastered before moving on to the next level. The two stages can, to a large extent, be overlapped and in certain situations learned simultaneously. The second stage, in fact, like analysis itself, also incorporates the first, but moves beyond fragments to real musical contexts.

This first stage of ear training is concerned with the accurate perception and labeling of individual events: the quality of an interval, inversion of a chord, etc. The other stage involves the comprehension of musical relationships and for teaching purposes implies—almost demands—a holistic approach. The crucial distinction, then, is between raw unprocessed perception and informed structural hearing. The distinction is between letting sound simply strike the ear drum and plugging that sound into conceptual frameworks.

It is easy for teaching materials, a single course, or an entire ear-training program to become mired in the purely perceptual level of hearing. Because of the human need for security, we are always attracted to teaching situations, in both ear training and analysis, that favor absolute right or wrong answers. Since identification, recognition drills, and short isolated examples most satisfyingly fulfill these needs, more interpretive hearing situations tend to be ignored. Accuracy (figured always in terms of a percentage of correct responses) becomes too easily the measure of success in the program. And since percentages are so tangible and for almost everybody can be raised, the goal of perfect scores becomes the tail that wags the dog.

Longer or more cumbersome musical examples sometimes are eliminated from ear-training programs since they don't fit the preselected category of "problem-with-neat-solution." Often the best ear-training questions—again like analysis—are those that allow many right answers because legitimate differences in hearing are possible. Some listening situations have no answers at all since their goal is to steer the listener's attention toward features, connections, etc. that might otherwise have passed unnoticed. These types of questions stress the mental and musical processes involved in arriving at permissible answers rather than the answers themselves. Instead of responding passively to small doses of external stimuli, analytical listening binds individual surface traits together through short-term and long-term memory, and aural imagery. Teaching ear training from this point of view requires some knowledge of how we make sense of music—why do some combinations of sounds form music and others do not? It requires knowledge, in other words, of analysis.

This knowledge is not just about how notes are put together on paper but about how the brain groups, simplifies, stores, retrieves, manipulates, and constructs sensory input. Ear-training programs ultimately show their worth in their ability to teach students how the listening process itself operates.

More important even than getting the right note or answer is learning how to hear a sound in its contextual relationship and knowing its meaning. Right answers can even be irrelevant or injurious if proper listening habits are slighted. I am not encouraging a diminished regard for accuracy, but I am suggesting that too much emphasis on numerical measurement of results can work at cross-purposes to the goals of how to listen.

"How does what we listen for affect what we will or can hear?" is the main question to be pursued in the ear-training class. Psychologists would call this listening attitude our "mental set" (a perceptual adjustment for a certain kind of activity). Rahn describes the job of music theory as creating and refining mental filters through which sounds pass to become organized as music, and defines this process with the delightful term "constructive brainwashing."[2]

All of this discussion should sound suspiciously close to the goals of written theory. Ear training and analysis are usually treated as two topics within music theory—witness the organization of this book. The only reason for doing this, however, is for communication. Issues can only be discussed one at a time, so they must be presented in some order. In reality, there is no such thing as two parts to the study of theory. Ear training turns out to be the same thing as mind training. Listening is analysis and analysis is listening. Music theory has only one goal—to understand what we hear. The emphasis will vary only slightly in each component of the curriculum—first leaning toward the understanding, then the hearing, but never straying far from either. If we can understand, maybe we can hear even more; if we can hear more, maybe we can understand better.

This endless cycle of thinking and listening has already been elaborated in chapter 1 but needs reiteration here because the reciprocal relationship is not always fully appreciated in the teaching of ear training. The value of listening in doing musical analysis is obvious and widely recognized—if not always followed in practice. But the value of analysis in musical listening is less often acknowledged and hardly addressed at all in published teaching materials and the professional literature.

No topic in this book is more important than the merging of mind training with ear training through analysis. Whether ear training should be set up in a separate class with its own grading procedures or combined with analysis is a curricular-design issue that does not concern us here (see chapter 2). What is important is to remind ourselves that the arrows in the thinking/listening diagram go in both directions. We do not learn how to hear just to make analysis easier. We also do analysis to make listening easier, and it is this second possibility that is so often overlooked in the ear-training class.

It is surprising that such golden opportunities are often missed since analysis is the natural leader of the ear. Almost all students are more advanced conceptually than perceptually—at least most can absorb new thoughts faster than new hearing. For example, the basic facts concerning dominant 7ths can be understood in one or two nights of study, but they can take weeks or months to be heard. Think about how much easier it is to cram for a written test than for an ear-training test.

The road to follow can be simply stated: do as much listening as possible when teaching analysis and do as much analysis as possible when teaching ear training. The proper effect is achieved when the two topics are turned inside out, with the distinctions blurred and melded together by a commonality of purpose into a single unified topic. It is all one thing: music theory. I am recommending, then, an approach to ear training that brings the full underpinnings of analytical modes of thought into play because such an approach is both pedagogically sound—making the job easier through reinforcement with conceptual supports—and because it is musically sound. Structural hearing that grows out of organizational principles and psychological processes of the mind and music is the only way that music or music study makes sense—the only way it can make sense. Structured thinking and perception is the only way the world can make sense. This point is made clear by Murphy with regard to musical experience:

> Listening, in all degrees of intensity, is a *mental activity* dependent only in a very general sense upon actual physical hearing. This is shown by the fact that animals "hear" as well as humans. In fact, it is known that certain animals hear much more acutely. But for animals musical sounds are totally without musical meanings. Only through mental activity do musical sounds become meaningful. The mind selects, organizes, and clarifies what no human ear receives. "Ear training" is mind and sense training. The ear catches aural sensations but the mind evaluates, discriminates, and identifies what was heard. *We hear with our ears, but we listen with our minds.* It is a combination of intuition and knowledge. It includes remembering what was heard in the past and anticipating that which is to follow, i.e., listening is memory plus anticipation plus critical discrimination. It is hearing the present in relation to the past and the future. *These considerations imply that listening can be improved and developed consciously.* Aside from comparatively rare physical or psychological defects, there is no such thing as "a bad ear for music"; there are only untrained minds.[3]

Recognition

While recognition of isolated events is subsidiary to listening to real music, it can develop certain useful skills such as discrimination, comparison, and concentration habits that are useful and important for any kind of hearing activity. Recognition is also valuable because it avoids the problem of dealing with notation and music reading, thereby breaking down the listening process into manageable parts. Recognition is defined, then, as the identification of sound fragments by symbol or label (P4, major triad, etc.) independently of written notation.

Intervals are the most commonly studied fragments that fall into this category. Many schools and ear-training manuals spend enormous amounts of time (weeks, months, and even semesters) and space (chapters and even volumes) on interval identification. The justification for such study is often that intervals are eminently testable. They present a well-defined and tangible collection of sounds for training; and answers are clearly always right or wrong. This convenience factor, then, provides a ready-made topic for drill.

In some cases, drill is undertaken as an end in itself; in other situations, attempts are made to relate the skill of interval identification to the performance and hearing of melodies, chords, progressions, etc. The degree to which isolated interval practice transfers meaningfully to larger musical environments (tonal and nontonal) is debatable.[4] This controversy can be summarized under the "atomistic-vs.-contextual" heading. Such a distinction between approaches relates to the earlier discussion concerning perceptual-vs.-structural modes of listening.

The danger of dwelling on intervals (or any fragments) for too long is that they steal valuable time from other listening experiences. Some programs wait before moving on for a perfection that may never arrive. The habits, approaches, attitudes, and goals of these other listening experiences are often different enough that total proficiency in interval hearing is not necessarily a prerequisite. This is quite unlike the essential mastery of fundamentals for written work. Moderation and balance for these beginning ear-training steps are therefore recommended. The following specific comments are offered for interval practice:

1. Upward melodic intervals should be introduced first. Downward melodic and harmonic types are considerably harder and involve different listening strategies.

2. Interval study should be grouped by families with like problems or properties, not presented in order from small to large, or randomly, as happens in many texts. For example, stable intervals (3rds, P5, 6ths, and P8) vs. unstable (2nds, 7ths, tritone, P4 usually) form two large families. Interval classes (related by inversion) present pairs that are frequently confused (P4 vs. P5; m3 vs. M6; m2 vs. M7; etc.). Other kinds of confusion result from quality differences (M3 vs. m3), from similarity of dissonance type (tritone vs. M7; each being one half-step from a stable reference—P5 and P8 respectively—implying an appoggiatura-like

resolution of *one* note), or from similarity of function (tritone vs. m7; each contained within the same V^7 chord and implying a *two*-note resolution to the same tonic reference).

3. Each student will usually suffer from certain idiosyncratic confusions or problems. Each individual, with his teacher's aid, must discover what these special difficulties are and devise individually tailored solutions. These solutions will often contain the seeds for insightful discussion into the mysteries of the structural listening processes spoken of earlier. These discussions can often be made part of the class.

4. The tritone, m7, and m6 are the three most difficult (melodic and harmonic) types and are often confused with one another. Reserve them for last and give them special care.

5. The overuse of familiar tunes as a crutch (e.g., "Twinkle, Twinkle . . ." for a P5) should be discouraged, although experimenting with various scale-degree combinations can easily demonstrate the multiple functional possibilities for any interval. Almost every one can be made to sound stable, tension-provoking, compressed, expanding, etc., by imagining differing aural surroundings or key contexts. This demonstrates the fallacy in assigning one particular effect or meaning for each interval, which specific melody references tend to foster.

6. A harmonic interval can be practiced two ways: (*a*) separating out the two pitches, thus translating it into a melodic type (singing back the lower or higher of the two pitches can help); or (*b*) hearing the sound as a composite. Both approaches have merit for different reasons and illustrate beautifully the notion that what is heard is controlled by how one listens as well as the objective sound source itself, just as figure and background can seem to reverse themselves visually in optical illusions.

7. Intervals should be practiced in numerous ways, not just to perk up classroom interest through variety, but to expand and enhance the listening experience itself. Vocal and instrumental timbres, as well as the piano, will reveal striking illusions of change in interval hearing because of the differing overtone patterns. Registers outside the singing range should be explored. The experience of transferring pitches back into the student's own range is excellent practice. Reduction of compound intervals into a smaller, singable pattern can be used for similar purposes.

8. As basic sounds become familiar, spin-off activities going beyond simple naming can be added. Some of these include filling in the gap between two pitches by singing the intervening scale steps that connect them, mentally inverting sounds, spelling what was heard in notation or letter names (given one of the notes), making "same-or-different" comparisons (same sound with different notes, register, types—melodic vs. harmonic—timbres, tempos, or lengths), making selections from notation or symbols, matching sounds in a multiple-choice format, error detection (identifying a wrong pitch in notation or performance), and aurally imagining implied resolutions (e.g., a tritone expanding or contracting or a minor 6th leaning into a P5 with either the upper or lower note moving).

Triad and other chord identifications are also frequently encountered at beginning levels. Some points to keep in mind:

1. The four basic qualities (M, m, d, A) can be practiced in simple three-note root-position form and grouped into mini-families like intervals. Major is so rarely missed that it hardly qualifies for inclusion except for the useful comparison it provides with both minor and augmented (one note different in each case). Diminished is usefully presented as a variant (in construction, but not effect) of minor or it can be grouped with augmented as examples of instability (both lacking the P5 of the major and minor types).

2. Diminished and augmented triads, while both unstable, have opposite resolution tendencies—diminished wanting to cave in on itself and augmented pushing outward (top note up or bottom note down). Hearing these unrealized, but latent, tendencies is the point of this type of drill. If there is a strong value in working with fragments, it is in cultivating the aural imagery required for picturing probable larger contexts. The type of hearing that focuses on single sounds as dull, inert entities is much less valuable than imagined hearing that compels understanding of relationships—a linking of what is heard to what is not heard but can be conceived. This is where the habit of merging mind and ears can begin.

3. Inversions of triads present a whole additional realm for practice. Any one of three pitches obviously can be placed in the bass (or soprano for even extra identification practice) and a variety of available spacings provides a multitude of practice possibilities. Arpeggiated singing from the bass up is often

coordinated with this type of hearing. Some teachers feel, however, that too much emphasis on this vertical approach encourages listening habits that work against the linear clues that are so important when chords appear in progressions.

Since in real music chords do not exist alone but as part of something else—they come from somewhere and go somewhere—it may be more important to hear, for example, that a particular bass note represents scale degree 2 (uniting 1 with 3) rather than hearing it as the fifth of the chord (as in a V_4^6 between I and I⁶). A chordal pitch always has two relationships: (a) with those notes above and below (root, 3rd, 5th, etc.); and (b) with those before and after (scale degree function as part of a melodic line). Too much early practice with up and down can discourage the forward-directed hearing required to make sense of an unfolding soprano and bass *line*. The connection of a pitch to its key is often more important than to its root.

4. Seventh chords (Mm, mm, MM, dm, dd) offer five basic types for distinguishing quality and provide excellent discrimination practice because of the subtle differences. The possibilities for comparison are extensive. Each chord is like another except for one pitch being a half-step different. Starting with the Mm (of V⁷ fame) as probably the most familiar sound, all kinds of manipulations are suggested: lower the 3rd, and a mm results; raise the 7th, and a MM results; raise the root, and a dd results; etc. A vast network of such interconnections can be taught.

5. Each type seems to embody a particular flavor. The Mm strongly suggests its own tonic resolution (with inner-ear imagination again). The mm is the mildest and most content to lie still (having functional neutrality—is it a i⁷, ii⁷, iii⁷, iv⁷, v⁷, or vi⁷?). The MM is the most striking with its prominent and grinding M7 and most unlike the others (it is missed the least often). The dm is the most difficult to learn (ii⁰⁷ or vii⁰⁷?) and therefore the most pivotal in perfecting the whole set. It is confused most often, on the one hand, with the mm (in its predominant role) and, on the other, with dd (in its dominant role); master it and the others seem to fall in place. The dd is the most tension-filled with two tritones and its multi-faceted resolution capabilities; it radiates energy. I describe it to my students as the "trouble" chord: it's always heard (in rumbling

tremelo fashion) in the piano accompaniments of silent movies whenever trouble strikes—the heroine is tied to the railroad tracks or the black-hatted villain comes to collect the overdue rent.

6. Detailed study of inversions (and various soprano factors) is better handled in the context of (at least) a resolution or, better yet, a phrase or simple piece. Endless isolated-chord practice ("what's in the soprano?" and "what's in the bass?") tips the balance too far toward the vertical. Better than asking students, for example, to note that the bass of a Mm is the 7th and the soprano the 3rd, is to play the resolution of a V^2 to I^6 and to hear the 4-to-3 bass-line movement and the 7–8 soprano line. Our teaching should be aimed as much as possible toward the sources of directed motion, not toward frozen instants of time.

Dissociating sounds of augmented-sixth chords, for example, from their environment makes little sense. Again, #4–5 (in scale degrees—really a secondary 7–8) against ♭6–5 (in the bass) is far more important than the fleeting existence of the augmented 6th itself, just as ♭2–7–1 (soprano) against 4–5–1 (bass) outweighs the momentary "major" triad sound of the Neapolitan situation. In context the so-called root (normally thought of as a stable note—especially for a major triad) of the N^6 is a very dissonant pitch and is suffused with an urgency that emanates from its half-step displacement of the "normal" tonic (5th of the iv).

7. All chordal ear training can be presented in the assortment of ways already suggested for intervals; variety of timbres, registers, spacings, doublings, combining hearing with spelling (letter names and notation) eventually, multiple-choice formats, error detection, comparisons, keyboard drill and reinforcement, etc.

Behind all good teaching in ear training—even with these musical splinters—lurks the assumption that sounds should always be presented and heard in relation to other sounds. Even a single lonely interval invites comparisons with others that are similar or different; more or less stable—or can be made to sound that way; smaller or larger; that imply a goal which can be imagined or toward which another imagined sound has moved.

Sounds that are more familiar can always be used as reference pegs from which to hang the less familiar sounds. As the repertoire of familiarity expands, the data bank of potential comparisons, allusions, and security blankets grows. From this standpoint, the further one progresses in ear training (as in written work) the easier it becomes. Eventually each event is heard to have some connection with every other; everything becomes a clue. However, clues and their countless connections can become so paralyzing that we hardly know how to find our way around in such an aural maze. If the understanding of music can be thought of as a mystery, then the teaching of ear/mind training finally becomes a search for those clues that most efficiently guide our hearing process.

Melodic Dictation

Success in melodic dictation does not depend on mastery of intervals or other fragments. Tonal dictation—and, surprisingly, even nontonal material to a large extent—can be hindered, in fact, by over-reliance on a note-to-note type of hearing because it detracts from larger-scale connections that are both more important musically than surface details and also more important pedagogically because they make the learning of hearing easier.

The goal in melodic hearing is to comprehend the local movement of pitches through a system of structural points of reference. For tonal melodies, such a system is provided by functional tonality; for other pitch languages, similar networks of props are possible. It is the working out of the solution—the analytical act itself—that makes melodic dictation valuable, not the notating of a score from sound.

Melodic dictation is the ideal place to begin the integration of analysis and hearing since knowing *how and what to listen for* so clearly accounts for positive results more than highly accurate but raw, undisciplined hearing ability. This is why students with the best natural ears often score highest on fragments but not necessarily on longer patterns such as melodies. The student who can use his mind to cue and channel the ear into the proper perceptual grooves has a tremendous advantage over one who simply coasts on an inborn hearing gift. One with both good ears and a good mind can really bloom.

The grouping, relating, and connecting of single events into patterns is even more important for success than diligent but unfocused practice. Drill and repetition by themselves are inadequate. Many students (and some teachers) approach ear training as if repeating an activity over and over enough times will produce results. Working through tape-recorded and computer-assisted melodic practice exercises offers superb opportunities at many schools for extensive training and saving of class time, but unless such practice is prepared, followed up, and reinforced continuously by solid classroom study of the reasons for errors and analysis of how to listen—the clue-searching approach—the bustling impression of accomplishment will be an illusion. Even the time-saving aspect of computers and tapes is not, strictly speaking, a strong argument in favor of their use, since the kind of practice done in the labs is quite different from the combination of *practice-plus-analysis* that is part of good classroom teaching. In no sense is modern technology a replacement for proper class work but is rather an adjunct to it.

Spending thirty minutes in highly directed classroom dictation work with a skillful teacher on just two or three melodies can be worth more than hours of undirected tape or computer lab work on dozens of pratice melodies, just as thirty minutes of concentrated effort on an instrument in the practice room reaps more benefits than hours of daydreamy finger-twiddling. Going through the motions without thinking is not enough; it can actually be harmful (for both ear training and regular practicing) because of bad habits creeping in.

Guided, inventive classroom teaching will always reveal, from each example, something about how melodies are formed or how listeners hear that will apply to the next melody—and the next—so that learning is gradual and cumulative. Students are rarely able to do this effectively on their own although the goal is to make them become independent enough to be able to provide, without the teacher, a self-critique of their own listening through melodic analysis. It is this process that is refined outside the classroom in the practice lab. Ironically, by the time their own listening habits and critical awareness are sophisicated enough to provide self-analysis, students no longer need the kind of purely repetitive exercises that often make up the content of out-of-class practice material. The catch-22 situation is that drill is useless without analysis, but if analysis is understood, the drill is no longer necessary. The most effective ear-training classes are those that teach students how to practice outside of class on their own.

To have completed *x* number of lessons in the ear-training manual is no sign of progress. Even high scores (as measured by a number of correct pitches and rhythms) is not automatically a sign of true accomplishment since learning how to hear is not a matter of right answers but of musical insights and habits properly prepared and acquired. The difference between just "getting the notes" and how they are played (or heard) is well stated by Farkas:

> Have you ever heard someone read a sentence in a language not completely familiar to him? There is a peculiar lack of inflection in the reading which reveals that, although the individual words are understood, the speaker does not quite understand the thought which the sentence is trying to convey. So it is with a musical phrase. The composer has a musical thought which he can only approximate with a string of individual notes. If the performer plays only these notes, no matter how correctly, without grasping in his own mind the musical idea which the composer had, the phrase is bound to sound as lusterless and unintelligible as a sentence read aloud by an uncomprehending reader.[5]

All music teachers want correctness, of course, but they should want something else too—the understanding of that invisible thread that joins events together. Some teachers would even be willing to settle for less correctness and more understanding. Music should not be performed or heard as if it were a foreign language. To develop "native speakers," the difference between *getting the notes* and *grasping their sense* must be understood by the teacher and then conveyed to the student. Hearing and comprehending are not the same. True hearing success is probably best observed in sensitivity of interpretation through some performance medium. To nurture and cultivate such expressive values is a goal toward which valid ear training can contribute but which finally overflows far outside the confines of music theory classes.

The weakness of most poor classroom teaching in dictation is that the melodies are simply performed one after another with mistakes corrected, but no discussion of why mistakes

were made, what should have been noted to make the dictation task easier, what was learned from the previous melody
that could have made this one easier, or what can be learned
from this melody that will make the next one easier. Without
analysis the whole class might just as well be placed on tapes
with answer sheets passed out and with a wound-up robot
giving directions and substituting for the teacher. This type of
class is nothing more than a supervised rehearsal.

The following list of specific suggestions is intended to illustrate how to turn the classroom environment from a hearing
drill into a true listening lesson:

1. Students will usually try to write too much down *during*
a first hearing. They should instead be urged to *listen* first,
noting such general features of the tune as mode; meter;
length; phrases; melodic cadences (terminal vs. progressive);
parallel or contrasting periods; repetitions; sequences; motives
(rhythmic or pitch); contour; disjunct vs. conjunct motion;
high points; low points; important pitches because of duration, frequency, metric stress, register, etc.; how the key is
established at the beginning; how the final note compares with
the first; outlining of patterns (triadic; scalar); decorative
pitches; etc. Attention should also be directed to memorizing
its sound. The mind can be thought of as a tiny tape recorder
that can be rewound to play back the tune endlessly. From the
student's point of view it's like getting unlimited free playings.

2. *After* the first hearing (maybe not until after a second
hearing) some sketching can begin. It is often helpful to sing
back the melody silently (or with the whole class aloud) immediately after that first hearing so as to imprint it more firmly
rather than rushing to write notes down. I would recommend
a very short pause between first and second hearings and much
longer subsequent pauses as notation begins.

3. Invariably students work from left to right trying to perfect all of measure one before moving to measure two. Usually
students will remember the beginning and ending fairly well
with the middle somewhat blurred. Working backwards from
the end (i.e., figuring out how the final cadence was approached) is often a good way to connect the beginning to the
end—hoping the two meet in the center like tunneling out a
mountain from opposite sides.

4. Students should write quickly (chicken-tracks style) and

with pencils, of course. Stemless pitches can be jotted down with rhythms added later. Some students like to indicate rhythms early (perhaps above the staff) and add pitch details later. Students are sometimes shy about putting specific notes down until they are absolutely certain of their correctness. If carried too far, such an attitude can result in staring at a blank paper the whole time. Even making estimates is better than doing nothing. These can eventually be refined and brought into agreement with the aural facts. Committing notes to paper starts the analytical juices flowing even if numerous adjustments are required later.

5. Much of the sketching that is done should be of the structural sort. All of the repeated notes, passing and neighboring tones, and other foreground frills do not have to be indicated at once. Sometimes the downbeat pitch of each measure can provide a starting point, or writing down just the tonic pitches or just tonic and dominant will form a simple scaffold from which the remaining notes can be constructed with ease. Adding the mediant can complete what some have called the basic tonality frame—the unfurled tonic triad stretched out over the course of a given tonal melody. This can delineate register usage in relation to the central tonic and provide a group of goals toward which every other note can be related: no pitch is more than a step away from some skeletal reference.

Sometimes a background step-progression or actual harmonic analysis of the outlined chords will give the necessary clues for filling in the remaining gaps. Implied polyphony (a separate upper and lower level of melodic activity) sometimes emerges from such analysis (i.e., from such directed hearing).

6. For tonal melodies, one of the biggest clues of all is a sense of scale-degree function. Development of a sensitive feel for the psychological location and the pulls and attractions of each pitch within the major/minor system is one of the goals of doing dictation in the first place. Each scale degree embodies a particular personality of both realized and dormant tensions and tendencies for motion or arrival. The distinctive flavor of a crucial pitch will often provide the answer in dictation even when many surrounding notes are missing. This approach is both more musical and useful than trying to compute intervallically from point to point.

The best method for practicing recognition of scale-degree function is a dictation-type drill that does not even involve notation. This is a musical-chairs activity that consists of playing melodies that do not necessarily start or (especially) stop on tonic. Frequently, the stopping point can be made abrupt or unexpected rather than at a natural pause. The student is then asked to identify the final pitch by scale-degree number, syllable, functional name, letter name (if key is given), etc. Such practice forces the student, first of all, to gather accumulating aural clues and derive a feel for the tonic center of the tune from the *internal evidence* rather than from a given note or chord as in more conventional dictation. Attention is directed away from details (students are relieved of responsibility for each individual note) and toward the listening process and large-scale groupings that activate centricity.

The mysterious process of how the mind and ear together can find tonic (even in cases where the tonic pitch itself is never sounded but only felt) is one of the marvels of music experience and should be fully explored occasionally during class time. To articulate verbally how the mind makes such decisions as assigning tonic function to one specific note out of a whole collection of possibilities is part of learning to hear.

After a sense of tonic has been achieved, the final step of relating the ending note to the whole network is fairly easy. Ending on "frustration" notes (e.g., leading tones or supertonic) is especially telling since their closeness to their implied goal tones will almost make a class burst out in knowing smiles. Each of the other scale degrees has its own special aftereffect as well.

7. Multiple-choice material also involves recognition but not creation of written notation. In this case four slightly different versions of a melody are provided (choice A, B, C, or D) with students asked to match what they hear with the correct notation. This is really a type of error-detection exercise and relates well to the practical rehearsal situation of matching score with performance. A slightly more challenging variation can be created by including a choice E (none of the above).

Both this and the musical-chairs formats have the advantage of supporting the goals of traditional dictation without the messiness (from the student viewpoint) of writing down notes, or the messiness (from the teacher viewpoint) of grading dictation. Regular written dictation has numerous problems of evaluation: how are points distributed between rhythm and pitch; what happens if a student gets one interval or one beat off; should partial credit be given for any partially correct information; how can *partially correct* be defined? Grading with objective answers, though, eliminates these problems.

8. One of the most important principles in dictation is the concept of intelligent guessing. It is in this area that the use of both mind and ear become especially well coordinated. Where actual hearing fades out (from lack of attention, lack of perceptual acuity, failure of memory, or complexity of the music), the mind can often take over by making predictions. These predictions are always *educated* conjectures based on the likelihood of certain continuations and the perpetuation of evolving trends. Deviations, surprises, and obstructions must also be taken into account and frequently cause reassessment of expectations. Analysis and experience with dozens of similar patterns (this is where *thoughtful* drill and repetition can play a role in acquiring a storehouse of knowledge) will help to discover what must have happened in those blanks on paper and in the memory.

9. Melodic dictation can be broken down into two stages with the problems of each stage attacked separately. One problem involves the memory process of lodging the tune into the mind. Success at this first stage depends partly on what psychologists call the chunking process: the efficient grouping of large numbers of small events into a smaller number of large events so that fewer bits of information are needed. This is how we remember telephone numbers—not as ten separate units but as three or four chunks.

Selection of which groupings or which clues to use is also of crucial importance. Illogical or unmusical chunking might be worse than no chunking at all. Just as in speech (and telephone numbers), music is continuous and sounds run together, creating patterns and meanings that are not intended. With telephone numbers it doesn't matter what patterns are used so long as the purpose of memory aid is served; but with both music and speech it is critical for only the sensible groupings to be perceived. For example, it is just as necessary in music to distinguish between (or among) interval meanings as it is in language to distinguish between "I scream" and "ice cream."

To paraphrase what the psycholinguist Ronald Cole has said about speech: Grasping the intervallic structure of a tonal melody is only part of the knowledge we need to understand music. Even if we can identify all the intervals in a melody, additional knowledge is necessary if we are to recognize only the patterns the composer intends us to hear. Remember, a melody almost always contain patterns not intended. You might argue that only the intended patterns make sense. But that is just the point.[6]

To recognize the patterns we are meant to hear, we must make immediate sense of the sounds and hear only the intended combinations. To do that, we must use a knowledge of syntax and semantics—the same knowledge the composer used to create the sound combinations in the first place. In a sense, we recognize patterns by re-creating the composer's train of thought; the performer and the listener share in the process of giving meaning to the composer's sounds.

Verbal explanations of how this happens often seem clumsy and tedious since our understanding appears to occur by intuitive flash. At least some after-the-fact analysis of this process should be attempted, though, so that we can help to make it happen more often in the classroom. Much useful melodic-dictation practice can be restricted, then, to the tonal-memory level of just singing back what was played without bothering with the notation.

The second stage involves transferring the sounds themselves, once they are set in the brain, into written notation. This stage also involves analysis, as musical effects must be translated into actual pitches on the staff, and it can also be practiced separately. The best way to isolate this stage from the memory phase is to utilize familiar-tune dictation. This bypasses the memory problem altogether by asking the student to write down, in a given key, some well-known tune (dozens of folk tunes, nursery-rhyme tunes, patriotic songs, popular songs, and Christmas carols are available). This type of practice is especially good outside of the classroom (e.g., at the student's desk in the dorm) since it does not require any aurally sounding music. The playback exists entirely inside the mind's ear.

10. It is assumed throughout dictation work that practice material will be carefully chosen in a graduated sequence from

simple to complex, narrow range to wide, scale-wise to skipping, short to long, diatonic to chromatic, few harmonic implications to many, etc., so that learning and progress can be controlled and incremental. A careful balance should be sought between examples that are both reasonable and challenging.

11. The teacher should play a very active role during classroom practice and should not simply stand behind the piano plunking out the melodies. Hints should be provided on what to listen for; appropriate questions and suggestions should guide the listener to peculiar or prominent features of each example. Walking around the room, looking over shoulders, and examining answers as they evolve should help to subtly steer students back on track or offer encouragement. Solutions worked out at the blackboard can be used as models (good or bad) for the rest of the class of how to go about the hearing and notation tasks. Students can be asked to sing what they have written as well as what they have heard. They should be exposed to each other's mistakes. The stronger will sometimes be able to offer surprisingly perceptive suggestions for the weaker.

There is such a thing as too much talking (i.e., too much analysis) and not enough practicing during class. The relative weighting of the two can be varied periodically. In general, however, teachers will err on the side of slighting brain-training for fear of not getting far enough in the lesson book. Classroom effectiveness should be gauged not by how many melodies were covered but by how many listening ideas were covered. A healthy portion—although not all—of the melodies should be examined and discussed in considerable detail. Something of concrete practical value should be carried away from every listening example, not just the feeling that one more tune has been checked off in the book.

12. Conventional dictation can easily fall into a rut. Variety can be promoted by using voices or instruments other than the piano. Various kinds of information can be either given or withheld (e.g., the final note or notes in the middle can be provided rather than a starting or tonic pitch; structural hearing can be actively encouraged by providing a sketch of several important or critical pitches throughout; bar lines or meter can be given or not; etc.). For very difficult tunes, a partially completed version can be given. Constantly changing the format would be disruptive, but slight changes in the type of clues

provided (or the kinds of answers called for) over a period of time can both revitalize the student's attention and expose fresh approaches and goals for the listening process itself.

Straightforward error detection (in addition to the musical-chairs and multiple-choice types already mentioned) is a pragmatic alternative. This can be done easily by having students watch a specified melody in their sightsinging book, analysis anthology, or given score, while the teacher purposely slightly alters pitches or rhythms.

Hundreds of specific questions can be asked (especially) of familiar tunes; a performance need not even be provided. For example, what is the interval from lowest to highest pitches in *Silent Night?* The entire score can be visualized in the mind or the entire song can be silently sung. What functional degree of the scale does *Happy Birthday* begin on? What is its meter? In B♭ major, what is the letter name of the first altered pitch in *The Star-Spangled Banner?* What secondary dominant does it imply? An entire ear-training exam of this type could be administered without a single note being sounded aloud. The internalized aural imagination would receive, however, a concentrated and vigorous workout.

More creative approaches, yet, include listening to the difference between tonal and real answers using fugue subjects (this same-or-different format can apply to many other areas also), or distorting the rhythms or octave placements of certain pitches in familiar tunes. How drastic can the changes be before familiarity changes to unfamiliarity? Tunes used for recognition by title can be disguised in other ways too, such as texture changes, being reharmonized, or played simultaneously with other tunes in different keys.

For melodies too long or complex to be used as dictation examples, other more general, yet equally musical, questions can be constructed: identifying melodic cadences, number of phrases, overall form, location of climax points (perhaps on some kind of time line, listening chart, or graph), melodic curve, implied harmonic background, modulations, scale forms, etc. Dictation of a single line against a variety of textures is possible too. Two-part melodic dictation (soprano and bass only of chorales or other pieces) is especially effective since it teaches the ability to hear one line against another and provides, therefore, a useful transition to full-fledged harmonic dictation.

Harmonic Dictation

No job in ear training is more difficult than taking harmonic dictation. The following suggestions are an attempt to classify some specific approaches that many teachers have found helpful:

1. The difference between vertical and horizontal views of harmony is especially relevant here. Without repeating all that has been said earlier about this topic, the problem with regard to ear training involves how much relative importance to assign to the root. The vertical approach to hearing implies that since the root is the primary information given by roman numerals, a concentrated attempt to find this root will be the most meaningful way to reconstruct the roman numeral labels for a given progression. Such an approach involves a kind of arpeggiated hearing of individual chords by running the ears up and down the pattern of notes and intervals, quickly trying to locate the center of gravity or generative pitch for the entire vertical sound complex. Inversions, if applicable, are determined by comparison of root and bass.

The horizontal approach tends to stress the influence of the soprano and bass line as carriers of musical motion, de-emphasizing the limited (in this view) role that the root itself plays. While the outer voices are in the forefront of our perception, it is unclear how well most listeners can (or should) follow the internal root movements of a progression. Proponents of the linear approach believe that horizontal hearing reflects the way that listeners actually make sense of progressions.

Hearing outer voices as melodies makes obvious the importance of scale-degree functions (the relationship of pitches to the tonality) rather than the allegiance of a pitch to its chord (as root, 3rd, 5th, etc.). For example, it is more important, in the key of E^b, to hear D as the leading tone than as the 3rd of a dominant triad. Likewise, its voice-leading connection to the succeeding pitch should be perceived as movement to *tonic* rather than to a root. Of course in this case tonic and root (of the tonic triad) are the same pitch, but how it is conceived in the mind/ear is the whole point of the differing approaches.

In the linear view, soprano and bass pitches are always related to one reference: the tonic. In the chordal view, they are related to one of seven different references—or roots. Because of such constantly changing references and the required mixture of both arpeggiated and forward-directed hearing, some teachers feel that the vertical concept results in a disjointed and fidgety listening experience. Since the seven reference points (i.e., the roman numerals) have to be related eventually to a central tonic, why not just hear soprano and bass directly as belonging to a key rather than a chord?

Some might object that roman numerals cannot be figured without reference to root hearing. By thorough knowledge of the relationships between scale-degree meaning and chord symbols, however, and by knowledge of simple chord spelling (and even by common sense—a very useful tool in both theory learning and teaching), almost any progression can be heard in scale-degrees (of soprano and bass) and can be converted easily into roman numerals (including inversions) *through analysis,* but bypassing root-movement hearing entirely.

One additional advantage of linear hearing is that the activity of harmonic dictation is made to resemble melodic dictation as much as possible rather than appearing to be a totally different kind of thing. This alone has enormous psychological benefits, as one of the barriers to success in the harmonic realm is that students almost always think of it as something new and unconnected to all of their previous dictation work. Even the conventional names we apply to these enterprises (melodic vs. harmonic dictation) suggest they are not only different but even opposite. Any method, then, that presents harmonic dictation as a continuation and outgrowth of habits and routines already established in earlier single-line work, will provide a beneficial pedagogical edge. When such an approach is reinforced with musical advantages as well, teaching effectiveness is invariably enhanced.

2. The following plan offers one possible five-step method of converting such a linear hearing process into conventional labels:

 a. Write out the soprano line as one would for plain melodic dictation.

 b. Write out the bass line in the same way; note details of bass and soprano correlation.

 c. Identify chord quality—but not necessarily root—as required for distinguishing among implied choices (here

121

an element of the vertical is useful to sort out triads from seventh chords, basic intervallic tensions, etc.).

  d. The affective and psychological response of certain patterns will yield valuable clues (e.g., the surprise of deceptive moves; the gentle motion of plagal arrivals; the push of augmented-6th resolutions; etc.).

  e. For most progressions having some connection to real music (as opposed to the seemingly randomized exercises of many dictation texts), an element of built-in logic (learned first through analysis, part-writing, etc. and now through hearing) will offer the most valuable hints of all.

By combining clues from these five listening angles, students can construct a quite detailed account in roman numerals from a blending of both perceptual and conceptual knowledge. For example, by noting scale degree 2 in the soprano against 4 in the bass in a mm seventh-chord complex preparing a dominant, we have more than enough information to infer the existence of a ii$^6_5$. Of course, learning to hear a ii$^6_5$ (along with its normal environment) as a thing in itself is one goal also, but having the supporting and confirming facts at one's fingertips is part of what is meant when we talk about "understanding what is heard."

  3. The role of analysis is especially important in harmonic dictation. The concepts that are most useful include (*a*) the three basic functional families (it greatly simplifies the hearing task to realize that chords fall into particular slots in particular orders); and (*b*) variation—most progressions are transformations of a very few basic patterns using chord substitution, extension, condensation, interruption, prolongation, inversions, etc.

  4. The ideas of function and variation can be particularly well taught by presenting progressions through stereotyped cadence formulas. After early and simple comparisons (e.g., between I–V–I vs. I–IV–I; I–V–I vs. i–V–i; I–V–I vs. I–V^6–I; etc.) the I–IV–V–I pattern can be established as a foundation from which a whole series of harmonic-dictation lessons can emerge in gradually increasing complexity and length. An amazing number of elaborations on this one pattern alone are possible. In fact, almost all of tonal harmony can be taught

through this predominant-dominant-tonic model. Even long, involved phrases can either be boiled down to this cadential recipe or to a chain of such effects. Deviations and digressions from the norm, when they occur, can be understood and heard contextually rather than as arbitrary or purely capricious departures.

Hearing directed in this manner does not move from chord to chord but automatically, by habit, locks into larger groupings and the intelligent-guessing technique mentioned earlier. This is why the randomized patterns so favored in some published ear-training materials are so ineffective. They seek, evidently, to keep the student suspended in a continuous state of surprise by making one chord as likely as another in harmonic-progression exercises.

The result of such hearing experiences would seem to divorce the intellect from raw sense data, making the job of meaningful listening harder, not easier. Real music, or at least exercises based on the built-in logic of real music, will therefore have a better chance of providing relevant and productive practice material. Such material gives the student a fair chance of filling in scattered blanks by picking up the thread of reasoning that may temporarily have been lost aurally. The probability of some chords being more likely than others in particular locations or contexts can be used to advantage in filling vacancies or getting back on track. It's difficult to get back on track, though, when no track has been laid in the first place.

5. In no other area of dictation is it so important to start with simple examples and build slowly and progressively toward greater length and complication. Careful restrictions (of chord choice, inversions, type of question, etc.) must be imposed. Lesson by lesson, as new chords or variations are added, students must be kept fully aware of their expanding repertoire so the boundaries within which their hearing and choices (and intelligent guessing) take place are always clearly defined. By the time longer and expanded variations of short cadence formulas become suitable, transference to real music would be possible (Bach chorale phrases, or whole chorales, etc.). Modulation, of course, would be the next step to consider after relative mastery of diatonic and chromatic progressions.

6. One of the goals of harmonic dictation is to teach students to be able to make certain basic and, then later, finer

distinctions between or among similar but not identical details—a fine tuning of the ear. This can be done in longer contexts or zeroed in on through isolated practice. The following partial list suggests some of the comparisons that could be included in a beginning harmonic ear-training program:

    a. Major key vs. minor key
    b. Cadences: authentic vs. plagal vs. half vs. deceptive
    c. Presence or absence of tonic 6/4 chord
    d. Presence or absence of modal borrowing
    e. V vs. V^7
    f. V^7 vs. V^9 vs. V^{11} vs. V^{13}
    g. V^7 vs. V^6_5 vs. V^4_3 vs. V^2
    h. V^6 vs. V^6_5
    i. V^6_5 vs. vii^{o7} vs. $vii^{\varnothing7}$
    j. vi vs. IV^6 (or VI vs. iv^6)
    k. IV vs. ii^6 vs. ii^6_5 (or same chords in minor)
    l. ii^6_5 vs. $ii^{\varnothing6}_5$
    m. iv vs. N^6
    n. ii^6_5 vs. V^6_5/V
    o. N^6 vs. Aug^6
    p. vi (or VI) vs. Aug^6
    q. Aug^6 vs. V^6_5/V
    r. It^6 vs. Ge^6 vs. Fr^6

Many additional possibilities could be listed, such as various soprano and bass patterns or combinations, additional secondary dominants, various diatonic vs. chromatically altered scale degrees, chord qualities, inversions, and pivot-chord combinations for modulation.

7. One special problem for many students is hearing bass lines. Most student ears seem treble oriented—even sometimes for students who play bass-clef instruments. The reasons for this are probably superficial listening habits brought to college (assumptions about the melody "on top" are widespread) and the natural acoustical prominence of upper lines. This poses a great handicap since the bass includes so much valuable information. It provides not only a foundation note for each chord (root or otherwise) but, more importantly at the phrase level, acts as a rudder by piloting the ear toward goals—establishing, at times, momentary respites, delays, or alternate targets.

One approach for this problem is useful in various modified forms for a wide variety of other related hearing problems and entails starting with a task easy enough for instant success and boosting the challenge in stages. For example, to hear bass lines more clearly, start by playing progressions at the piano (simple four-part exercises, Bach chorales, etc.):

a. Play the bass by itself.
b. Sing *and* play the bass only.
c. Sing the bass alone.
d. Play all the lines; accentuate the bass; listen.
e. Play all the lines with bass at normal level.
f. Play again singing with the bass.
g. Play upper voices only while singing the bass.
h. Play upper voices only, hearing the bass (silently but very loudly) in the mind's ear.

This final phase takes immense concentration. The whole process should be repeated daily with new examples and continued over a period of weeks and months. Gradually the earlier steps can be dropped so that eventually bass lines can be heard immediately, clearly, and silently against other voices. Such an organized routine, if conscientiously applied over a period of time, could solve many bass-line (or inner-voice) hearing problems.

Bass lines, like any musical events, can be grouped into categories. The goal of most phrases is to arrive at the dominant, and most bass lines are launched from the tonic (sometimes with elaborate set-ups of the initial tonic departure first or embellishment of it before it continues its journey) and move toward scale degree 5 by either an ascent or descent. Certain roman-numeral patterns are associated with each type or their mixtures. Such knowledge in advance helps the mind to move along familiar channels rather than approaching each new progression as a special or infrequent case. Truly infrequent cases can often be assimilated into special categories of their own. At the least, having the stereotyped patterns clearly in mind invites ready comparisons and a method for measuring exceptional or unique instances. Unusual circumstances can only be recognized as being unusual if there is some available norm against which they can be compared.

8. Harmonic-dictation practice should include a great vari-

ety of response types and example types. Roman numerals can be derived from other clues, as I have suggested, or they can be written down directly without the supporting notation. Notation, for example of soprano and bass, can be written without the supporting analysis also. Four-part dictation (SATB) is a possibility although notation of inner voices becomes more a matter of common-sense voice leading than actual hearing (especially on the piano). Such an exercise does coincide, though, with my plea to extend analysis into perception. Partially completed progressions with subtle clues are especially effective for directing attention toward decisive junctures in the unfolding of a pattern.

Textures other than homo-rhythmic chorale types (e.g., two or three voice, imitative, Alberti bass, melody and chords, etc.) and sounds from chamber groups (woodwind, string, or brass quartets) provide welcome changes. Aural identification of non-harmonic tones can often be worked into exercises. Large-scale harmonic listening (cadences, changes of key, and pivots); identification of certain crucial harmonies (important because of their key-defining role, color, or surprise) rather than naming every single chord; or even sketching the overall tonal and formal plan for short pieces should all be part of a comprehensive course of study. Multiple-choice types (with either roman numerals or notation), error detection, and filling-in-the-blank types (providing a notated progression with missing notes—sometimes soprano, or bass, or an inner part) are all very effective since they practically impel students to apply conceptual knowledge to the listening situation. Some teachers and a few books are moving toward more use of real music—in many cases whole pieces and longer movements, not just snippets, as the basis for an entire program. Creative approaches can find ways to include all traditional activities, even recognition drills, in the context of music literature—in many cases using the same pieces that are also studied in separate analysis, history, or literature classes.

Sightsinging

The goals of sightsinging cannot be easily distinguished from those of dictation. For this reason, all of the foregoing material in this chapter has application for sightsinging. Within the sphere of sightsinging, however, two separate aspects, at least, can be singled out. The most obvious is the actual vocal performance itself which is used for testing. Beneath this external manifestation lies the more intangible, more important, and prior stage of aural imagery. Even this stage can be broken down further into two sub-stages: (*a*) the reading of notation (visual and mental grouping of symbols into patterns); and (*b*) the assignment of meaning in sound to these patterns. When diagnosing student difficulties, it is mandatory to analyze at which stage trouble occurs: (*a*) imagining the sound conjured up by the notation; or (*b*) reproducing that conception vocally as an audible sonic phenomenon. Making the breath and vocal cords match the sound inside one's head is quite a different problem from finding that sound in the first place in the silence of the mind's ear.

The goal of sightsinging, then, is not performance any more than the goal of learning to read is to recite aloud poetry or prose. According to Wedge, the goal, as in all ear training, is to *think sound*.

> To think sound means to hear it mentally, to listen to it with the inner ear. Most of us can think the tune America without actually singing it, just as we can think the words without actually saying them. To think sound demands concentration; and facility in it requires practice; but it may be acquired and it must be by the serious student. The beginner in ear training is always tempted to hum the sound he is trying to think. Singing has a vital part to play in training the ear, but only as a guide and not as a final necessity. Use it as a crutch which may be discarded as ability to think sound develops. In practising . . . it may at first be necessary to sing the exercises, but do not neglect constantly to make the effort to think sound.[7]

To be able to sing—to develop a well-supported, controlled voice that is reasonably attractive and accurate—is one of the most useful tools of practical musicianship. For any teacher or conductor it is almost indispensable for quick demonstrations of style and interpretation, or of pitch and rhythm. For just simple communication with another person it is often handy or even necessary to illustrate a point musically through vocal means. But for the theory class it remains secondary to internal hearing.

For testing—to make oral the aural—singing is the teacher's window into the mind and ear. If we had some way of crawling into a student's brain to observe, like a mouse in the corner, what mental processes were going on, then singing would not be necessary. In fact, other sound reproduction methods are available for variety, or for those with laryngitis or hopelessly uncontrollable voices. Whistling, rather than singing, is the first alternative that comes to mind. Humming into a kazoo (wax paper and comb) or a carnival toy is a sillier possibility, but the idea of making sightsinging an extension of the student's own performance medium is a serious and worthwhile suggestion, I think. The clearest application would be for brass players. To have them buzz pitch patterns, melodies, etc. on the mouthpiece alone duplicates exactly the hearing problems and solutions that are required in playing the instrument itself. The pitch must be heard first and matched to the proper lip setting before a correct answer can be performed.

For practicing, unlike testing, much of the student's work in sightsinging can be and should be done silently. Enough audible practice must be executed to achieve minimal vocal control but thinking sound or hearing silently should form a large part of a student's individual practice routine. Additional points, philosophy, and teaching suggestions concerning sightsinging are offered below:

1. Combining silent singing with regular singing can be an effective classroom technique. Phrases or measures of silent continuation in tempo can be alternated with audible performance. To enter "on pitch" or "in key" after silent interruptions of thinking sound is a satisfying experience and can reinforce the concept of inner hearing.

2. The use of tonality frames, structural reductions, or any simplification process is to be greatly encouraged. Nowhere are published textbook materials more deficient than in the area of structural sightsinging. Several good dictation texts are available that make use of such approaches, but most sightsinging books are simply collections of melodies organized by historical periods, or by interval, key, difficulty, etc. but with little inkling of a conceptual system or method of hearing around which to construct the student's practice. This leaves the instructor free to choose an approach, of course, but too often the teaching deteriorates to the kind of repetition and

supervised-rehearsal procedure that is so ineffective in dictation work also. Accomplishment cannot be measured by the number of pages covered in the book.

Structural reductions are now a well-established technique in most analysis work, many harmony texts, and increasingly so in dictation books, but the notion that reductions can be sung as well as drawn seems relatively unexplored. Just as seeing a simplified version aids in understanding a melody, performing it can aid in hearing. To sing the reduction side by side with the original breaks sightsinging down into at least two separate steps just as we have done already for many other topics. Theme-and-variation forms make excellent practice material for this reason as the elaborations grow from a tune in the same way that the foreground of a melody grows out of its skeletal background. The best place to practice melodic analysis, then, is not in analysis class but in sightsinging class. Or perhaps sightsinging should be practiced in analysis class. Better yet, do both.

Besides providing an easier point of entry by avoiding an immediate plunge into intricacy or chaos, reductions offer at least two additional advantages. Singing reductions can stress the long-range stepwise connections between notes that often are disguised by surface details. The most important connections are frequently not between adjacent notes at all. Interruptions, embellishments, and parenthetical insertions (often in contrasting registers) can conceal the true links between pitches. Most students—especially those reading by interval—perform a score with their noses too close to the notes, thereby losing sight of the forest for the trees. Reductions encourage perspective and develop an overview—the ability to stand back far enough to see the fusion of notes into units. Those embedded scales, as revealed by the reductions, provide a continuous series of checkpoints and guideposts for keeping on track. The common advice to look over a melody before singing—the preparatory step of scanning—is itself a kind of reductive technique.

The other advantage of reductions concerns the attitude that students bring to their sightsinging. The word *sight* (or "sight-reading") is unfortunate. It implies that each new melody is something new. This is true—but only at the surface level. Sight-reading (or singing) does not exist in the literal sense;

pattern perception would be more accurate. Every time a "new" melody is approached, a performer brings with him the accumulated experience of a lifetime of melodies and simply recognizes, in the newer surroundings, what he has already examined and heard in hundreds or thousands of more-or-less similar and previously experienced tunes. A storehouse of memories about their appearance, sound, and musical effect is brought into play. Reductions are helpful for their summarizing capacity since they can verify the underlying likenesses and provide categories for organizing types and subtypes. Psychologically, this approach thus removes somewhat the fear-of-the-unknown syndrome by making "sight" singing seem a little simpler. Reductions accomplish this by underscoring the larger system (modality, functional tonality, extended tonality, even atonality at times) of which individual cases are just a part.

To de-emphasize the "sight" aspects of singing, a considerable amount of prepared material can be included on examinations. This approach especially encourages practicing for the test as exams done totally at sight often leave students feeling that they are at the mercy of fate and that preparation is of little value. Some reading at sight can test the transfer of basic-pattern knowledge from familiar to unfamiliar material. A combination approach is possible too by rewriting prepared melodies, for example, by changing key, mode, clef, tempo, meter, rhythms, etc. or by literally combining the beginning of one tune with the middle of another, and the ending of a third.

3. Another underused teaching device is cassette tape recorders. For some unexplained reason (probably the inability to separate our ears from our mouth), students can identify mistakes in their classmates' performances more easily than in their own. Recording on tape a student's performance and then having him analyze it afterwards can help to make him more alert to his own flaws, intonation problems, rhythmic hesitations, etc. The recorder can be brought right into the classroom. Students are always genuinely astonished to discover how poor their sightsinging really is (not their vocal quality—usually a shock in itself—but the mistakes). They should be heartened, though, that their ears are good enough to detect these errors—some gross and some more subtle—as they are listening. The next step is to work for similar concen-

tration and discernment *while* they are singing so that e
can be consciously identified on the spot. The final step ↙
become so aware in listening that mistakes can be prevented.
Tape recorders are often used for dictation but their use in
sightsinging can be a real ear-opener.

One similar technique in the evaluation of sightsinging is to
test students in pairs. Each one, in turn, sings himself, is
graded by his partner, and then grades the other's performance. The teacher meanwhile grades both performances and
also grades their grading. While too complicated to use all the
time, occasional application will help to transfer the habits of
critical listening from external to internal hearing—from evaluation of peers to self-evaluation.

Such hearing projects also help to distinguish between two
kinds of problem students: (*a*) those who make mistakes and
know it—maybe not always with the ability to pinpoint where
or why, or the ability even to make corrections, but with a
feeling for "getting off;" and (*b*) those who make mistakes but
have no idea whether they were right or wrong. Such students
are the type who look up after the performance asking, with
their eyes, "Was it OK?" The first step is to promote them
from category *b* to *a*. With extremely weak students, their
tasks must be simplified enough for success. Often this means
going all the way back to matching pitches and then moving
forward again.

4. The functional method in singing tonal melodies offers a
corrective to over-reliance on intervals. Sensitivity to scale-
degree tendencies, internal tensions, and development of tonal
bearings provides a more musical sense of phrase and the long
line. One problem with the interval approach to hearing is that
it views sightsinging as a skill to be acquired (i.e., becoming
accurate at reproducing notated pitches and rhythms) rather
than as a means of gathering valuable information about how
music itself works. Sightsinging is not an aural xerographic
duplicating activity. Intervallic emphasis, when overdone, reduces the hearing process to a chain of localized hops from
point to point—all somehow equivalent, like undifferentiated
ticks on a clock.

The weak relationship between singing isolated intervals and
complete tonal melodies is trimly summarized by Lars Edlund:

A good knowledge of intervals implies quick recognition of any interval in the printed music and an ability to sing it at sight. This exercise is often applied only to isolated intervals. But it is by no means certain that skill in singing isolated intervals guarantees good sight reading of complete melodies. There are several reasons for this:

1. A melody is much more than a mechanical succession of larger and smaller intervals. When we read a literary text, we grasp syllables and whole words at a single glance, we see them as units, shapes. The same technique should be applied to reading music. Here the shapes are made up of melodic motives and phrases. But vital to the reading of major/minor melodies is the ability to see and feel the tonal quality of such shapes and to spot those notes which are "magnetic," thereby giving the other notes direction and function.

2. In major/minor tonality each interval always has some kind of tonal quality. The same interval can have several different tonal meanings, the response evoked being entirely different in different contexts.

3. In isolated intervallic exercises we ignore rhythm, which plays a great but subtle part in a melody. Rhythm also strongly influences our response to an interval. One reason for this is that rhythm often is related closely to the harmonic development of a melody.

4. A good command of isolated intervals (the ability to "hear" them mentally and to sing them from the printed page) is therefore only one requirement for good sight reading. This command is important, but is not enough in itself. *In actual practice there is constant interplay between this knowledge and a perception of the tonal and rhythmic shapes and sequences.*[8]

Even if intervallic awareness were the easiest and fastest method of learning to sightsing—a debatable premise—the goal remains to accomplish something more than getting the right note. Just getting that right note is such a major accomplishment for some students that when it happens, they tend to relax and expect no more. We, as teachers, hope ultimately that students learn not just about accuracy of performance or notation but also about shared and distinctive features of musical literature—not just about notes and spans but about listening habits that match in cogency the constructive and aesthetic principles of powerful language systems.

5. The use of syllables in sightsinging is one of the most

controversial issues facing teachers. Almost everyone has strong feelings on this subject. In general, three different systems can be distinguished:

a. The stationary "do" system assigns the same syllable always to the same note (do = C, for example) regardless of key. This method has been successful in certain European circles especially when studied intensively from an early age. Studies are not conclusive, but some feel that such a total-immersion approach can inculcate a sense of absolute pitch. The more concrete advantage is a visual one. Since the same syllable is always associated with the same line or space (within a given clef), music reading skills are promoted and reinforced.

b. The moveable "do" system assigns syllables by function. For example, do is always tonic, sol is always dominant regardless of key *or mode* (me, le, and te for scale degrees 3, 6, and 7 in minor as needed). This method stresses the development of hearing skills rather than music reading since the same musical and functional effects are always represented by the same symbols. Through association with the syllables, over a period of time, students gradually become tuned in to the nuances, directional tendencies, and structural relationships of tonality independently of particular keys or notational configurations. All keys, then, are treated, through transposition, as one, and the learning of the system becomes the goal rather than reading notes.

Functional syllables are also useful as analytical tools (like roman numerals) for making comparisons between melodies and for discussing and reinforcing stereotyped patterning. Their dangers include overuse as a crutch (causing difficulty, for example, in transferring to a nontonal context), and being sometimes too specific in meaning for modulating, highly chromatic, and especially ambiguous passages where perhaps two or more differing connotations are simultaneously intended for a single pitch. Using syllables forces one to choose only one of those possibilities.

c. A third system using semi-moveable do is a hybrid. In this case, the minor borrows syllables from the relative major, beginning with la-ti-do, etc. rather than do-re-me, etc. This system tends to use syllables as measuring sticks—the intervallic approach—rather than as symbols encoding latent or realized functional significance. In fact two sets of terms are required for every single functional event (e.g., the identical resolution of leading tone to tonic is ti-do in major but si-la in minor).

The minor-la system, as it is sometimes called, is handy for those bi-modal melodies (usually middle-baroque period) that switch quickly back and forth between major and relative minor without establishing convincingly either key. Of course, the do-re-me system is just as adept at moving from major to minor within parallel keys (e.g., the modal borrowing of much nineteenth-century music).

The weakness of minor-la is that parallel scales have both crucial structural (i.e., key-defining) pitches *and* function in common, while relative scales have only pitch similarity. While the pitch collections are almost identical with relative scales, the matrix of attractions and network of allegiances is re-aligned all over again by the domination and sway of the different tonic orientation of the relative key, just as a single twist of a kaleidoscope scrambles and regroups the same set of stones into a whole new pattern of relationships. Parallel scales represent a single tonality; relative scales represent two.

And Murphy comments on the difficulties resulting from assigning two different syllables to one functional meaning:

> The use of the moveable *do* in the minor mode is trouble-some. One of the most flagrant examples of the misuse of syl-lables is the practice of basing syllables on the relative rather than on the parallel relationship of the two modes. This results in calling tonic of a minor scale *la* instead of *do*. The aural and psychological fallacies are obvious: *la* has presumably been es-tablished as an active tone, when suddenly, for no conceivable reason except similarity of signature, *not of sound,* the student is asked to hear *la* as an inactive tone—and still worse, as the key center! Such a procedure is contrary to aural perception, psychology, and common sense. The tonic of a minor scale should be called *do,* as in major, and the other syllables altered accordingly. The only possible justification is for the use of melodies in the Aeolian mode, which apparently use the major and minor modes interchangeably.[9]

Many scalar and sequential patterns can be used with syl-lables to acquire fluency so they fly off the tongue lightly and automatically rather than operate as stumbling blocks. Simple chanting of exercises or melodies out of rhythm and without pitch is a good way to concentrate on syllables alone as a separate activity. Some teachers prefer to restrict singing in the early stages to just a few keys (e.g., C, G, F) to simplify reading problems and to set the feel and flavor of each syllable firmly in the ear with a minimum of notational distractions. Similar restrictions of using simple rhythms only and perhaps avoiding minor keys for a while make good sense also.

Singing familiar tunes with syllables is another good way of learning to associate location in a key with symbol. Pivot-pitch drills are also valuable for learning function and serve to prepare for work with modulation. In this case a designated note can be defined, heard, and sung first as do, then re, then mi/me, etc. with the appropriate supporting context. Flexibility of hearing and the ability to adjust to a new tonal center quickly are the goals. Any given note implies either actual or potential movement or rest depending on the environment. Flexibility of thinking is also crucial as the mental picture we form of a note while reading is what helps to recall the desired aural and functional effect.

Many teachers prefer to avoid syllables altogether because the investment in time (usually considerable) does not always seem to pay dividends. Some teachers and many students feel that syllables are more trouble than they're worth by clogging the sightsinging process with one extra layer of problems. Solfege takes time to develop and only those who are earnestly committed philosophically and willing to give the system a chance to crystalize should pursue such an approach.

A halfhearted effort with syllables (or anything else) is a waste of time. Teaching theory is more than teaching content. It involves the power of belief and the ability to sway students toward accepting that belief system—and its implied set of strengths and values. I have seen immensely sucessful sightsinging programs both with and without syllables, but the common feature is always the force of personality that convinces students that results will be forthcoming if they follow the prescribed routines. Some might call it the medicine-man or placebo effect, but it can work in theory teaching as effectively as in health.

6. For programs that choose not to use syllables, a very large number of other vocalization methods are available. The

easiest is singing with la. Full attention can be paid to listening feedback without the problem of hearing the note but forgetting its syllable. While the short-term advantage may be obvious, the long-term goal of instilling tonal function may be stunted.

A compromise solution is to sing with scale-degree numbers since these are more familiar and simpler to remember than syllables, yet represent essentially the same idea. Although simpler, numbers do not permit display of chromatic inflections and therefore are not able to reinforce or draw attention to alterations or modal borrowings with the same precision as syllables. Singing with letter names has some value from a music-reading standpoint (especially in the C clefs) but does not promote the development of hearing in the same way. The problem of whether to verbally acknowledge accidentals along with the letter names makes for a solution that is either simplistic (if not deceitful) on the one hand, or overly clumsy to perform on the other.

7. Teachers are frequently sharply divided on the relative merits of real music vs. exercises. One of the advantages of real music is the exposure to standard vocal and instrumental literature and the acquaintance with historical style periods. In addition, real music affords greater possibilities for expressing musicality; interpretation counts for more. Contrived material, however, lends itself to more teaching control and finer gradations of complexity. Literally any effect can be written into or out of a particular exercise. Pacing can suffer when using real music since examples cannot always be found at just exactly the appropriate level of difficulty or with just the right combination of complications or features. Real pieces almost always include some little pitfall that might better be left until later. Most teachers (and many books) construct a course of study by blending many kinds of examples—some specially written for warm-up, drill, or isolating trouble spots, and some from the literature for exposure to both technical *and* musical problems. Creative teachers are always on the lookout for opportunities to extract a practice pattern directly from musical examples.

8. Part-singing and creative performance are often undervalued in the sightsinging class. Duets, canons, and rounds are especially attractive ways to excite the interest of a class and provide experience in hearing one line against another. Playing

the piano while singing and improvisation activities are also both fun and worthwhile.

9. It is such an exhausting job to teach sightsinging that teachers often collapse after the accuracy level has been reached. Musical interpretation is an additional topic, though, that some will want to work on. A detailed study of how interpretive decisions (subtleties of phrasing, articulation, rubato, dynamics, etc.) are connected to analytical insights, although worthy of a whole course of its own, is probably beyond the scope of most undergraduate programs, but observing dynamics, style, tempo, and other expression marks that are already indicated in a score should be possible even at a beginner's level. It is simply a matter of doing it—of establishing a habit of performing music and not just notes. This is why some ear-training teachers prefer the more active mode of sightsinging performance rather than the passive listener's role in dictation or other hearing ventures. The difference is between making music and responding to it.

10. Practicing sightsinging in class should be combined with all the other ear-training drills already mentioned so that it's not put off into its own corner. Dictation material, for example, can practically be made interchangeable (although perhaps shortened) with sightsinging melodies. Every opportunity should be exploited for singing in analysis, harmony, and counterpoint classes also. Singing arpeggiated progressions is one obvious way to connect harmony to hearing. Singing intervals is still one of the best ways to learn recognition of them.

Practicing sightsinging—or any ear-training skill—out of class is best done in short doses repeated often. The repetition factor for basic skills (intervals, chords, simple melodic archetypes, etc.) plays an important role in implanting patterns in the mind. For example, it is far better to practice only ten minutes *every* day than two hours once a week. The more practice the better, of course, but regular continuing daily practice is what counts.

The temptation toward over-dependency on the piano or other sound source should be avoided. Simply copying aurally what has just been played only deludes the student that real hearing has taken place. Playing on the piano after performance as a check for accuracy is permissible. But when mistakes are made it is best (in tonal pieces) to try to sing or

137

remember tonic and use that knowledge for re-orientation rather than rushing too quickly to play the troublesome or missed note on the piano. The problem of hesitancy or constant stopping and starting should be avoided as well. Looking ahead (while reading) can help in moving ahead (while performing) and will facilitate pattern reading rather than note reading. Since we are all human, even more important than perfection as a reading goal, is learning how to recover from our mistakes, and that can be accomplished only by moving, not stopping.

Progress in ear training is often difficult to gauge since as improvement is made, the material becomes more advanced and so it often seems to the student that he is standing still—a steady stream of Cs in the grade book is a common sight. Progress is also frustrated by the plateau effect: long steady levels of accomplishment followed by sudden apparent jumps in hearing ability. Sometimes the most intensive practice is needed during the lulls where nothing observable seems to be happening, but all kinds of internal changes and readjustments are bubbling around beneath the surface of the mind. Keeping up student motivation during these long dry spells is a challenge. The progress of some students is like watching flowers grow—little change from day to day or even week to week but noticeable improvement over the longer run. The effects of practicing ear training are rarely immediately apparent as might be true for purely intellectual learning of factual material. The resulting discouragement that many students experience in ear training should be carefully explained and their efforts carefully nurtured so that workouts do not simply fizzle out through complete misunderstanding of how hearing skills are accumulated.

Twentieth-Century Ear Training

The problems of hearing nontonal music are special enough to deserve additional comment although many of the suggestions and ideas already mentioned will apply to much of twentieth-century material. It is commonly assumed that when functional relationships and familiar tonal landmarks are missing, note-to-note and interval-by-interval reading (and performing and hearing) are the only available methodological options. William Thomson vigorously challenges this position by arguing that an interval has no meaning or even life of its own by itself:

> One widely maintained (yet surprisingly underdeveloped) position maintains that only a reliance on the discrete pitch interval can yield a reading technique that is useful for complex music [highly chromatic or atonal]. The validity of this argument dissolves as soon as its ramifications are made clear. Its most significant implication is that intervals can be apprehended and conceived as *absolutes*, exclusive of any background context—that a perfect fifth, for example, can be conceptualized as a *thing in itself*, without reference to any broader pitch background. But attempting to imagine the two pitches of an interval exclusive of any context beyond themselves is like trying to imagine two points in vision without a spatial reference. Rigorous attempts at either seem equally fruitless; both must occupy positions in some form of auditory or visual background of space-time.
>
> [Thomson continues by discussing the need for referring pitches to some contextual frame] . . . either a frame that is made explicit by the patterns of the melody itself or . . . a frame that is imposed by the reader when the melody does not clearly project its own. The method is reliable and helpful even for those few who are blessed (or plagued?) by possessing absolute pitch recall (sometimes erroneously called "perfect pitch"), because this method stresses musical patterns greater than individual pitches, thereby forcing attention toward broad structure rather than details. Following its simple procedures, one can develop an aural imagery as efficacious for Boulez as for Bach, as logical for Monteverdi as for Menotti.[10]

Seen in this light of using structural frames as reference points, the problem of singing nontonal material is not necessarily different from that of the tonal literature, although the difficulty of true mastery is not usually comparable because of our culturally conditioned tonal ears. It is interesting to note the various combinations of approaches that different teachers choose to favor for melodic hearing. Some prefer a high degree of intervallic awareness for all music: "I have focused on the one musical element common to all styles and creative periods, namely the interval. I contend that if you sing by intervals at all times, you will be able to read music that is tonal, modal, pantonal, nontonal, or a combination of all of these means of organization and polarization."[11] Some, such as Thomson, prefer a structural model for all types. And some would advocate function for tonality and intervals for atonality.

The framework approach (a set of recurring reference points) for twentieth-century examples works especially well for the music of Debussy, Bartok, Hindemith, Copland, or Ives, where some type of extended tonality (i.e., pitch centricity) is present. For more instrumental idioms (large skips, jagged contours, and wide range) such as in some Stravinsky and much of Shostakovich, or for either serial or non-serial atonality (Schoenberg, Berg, or Webern), a combination of frames (often imagined) and intervals is possible.

Other methods besides two-note intervals and structural reductions can be used for teaching nontonal melodic hearing. The use of trichords involves a partitioning or extension of intervals into three-note (mostly) non-triadic patterns. These can be catalogued into twelve main types and identified by set-type numbers (e.g., 0–1–6). Through inversion, transposition, and combination, virtually every atonal situation can be covered. The trichords can be memorized and used as building blocks in the same way that scales, triads, and common functional groupings are used for tonal music. Although intervals are used in this approach, they are grouped into units larger than just two pitches.

Other systems use a set of similar (but not necessarily trichordal) recurrent nontonal patterns. These can also be memorized, transformed, varied, inverted, displaced by an octave, elided, and combined in limitless ways to cover most atonal possibilities. A small sample of some simple nontonal security blankets (some are outgrowths of tonal patterns) include:

1. Six basic four-note scalar tetrachords (major, minor, Phrygian, Lydian, harmonic, and Hungarian)
2. Eleven scales (major, three minors, four basic modes, plus Locrian, whole-tone, and Hungarian)
3. Twenty-five synthetic scales (from combinations of the six tetrachords, but not having names).
4. "Sandwich" patterns (whole-step followed by chromatic half-step filler: for example, G–A–G# or F–E♭–E)

5. Consecutive P4s and P5s; or M3s and m3s
6. "Envelope" patterns (P4 "tucked inside" a P5: C–G– F#–C# or A–D–E♭–A♭)

These can be practiced in many of the traditional ways:

1. Sing as written
2. Sing out of rhythm.
3. Transpose to other pitch levels (from memory and with notation).
4. Extract an "exercise" through simplifying a particular problem, then add back (step by step) the troublesome elements.
5. Make analytical structural reductions ("quasi" tonality frames).
6. Look and listen for long-range connections (step-wise or otherwise)—not just adjacent notes or intervals.
7. Read patterns rather than by interval.
8. Sing back from memory without using notation.
9. Use melodies for error detection and multiple choice.
10. Use for dictation.
11. Use for identification exercises:

   a. Name intervals.
   b. Give letter names (given starting note).
   c. Compare last note with first.
   d. Identify highest and lowest pitches.

13. Students critique each other.
14. Students critique their own performance.
15. Competition formats:

   a. Spelling bees (singing).
   b. Boys vs. girls.

Another method uses imaginary diatonic reference pitches as an aid to hearing chromatic "distortions." These distortions are conceptualized (and heard) as purposeful "wrong" notes a half step away from the plainer and more normal unaltered (and imagined) possibility. Successively more complex and numerous distortions of tonal examples can be constructed to eventually kick out all tonal props, resulting in completely atonal melodies.

Such a method suggests two contrasting approaches to teaching nontonal material. One follows the chronological evolution of the last phases of functional tonality through stages of increasing chromaticism with resulting gradual changes in the emerging twentieth-century languages. The other approach is based on the pedagogical concept of restriction—i.e., beginning with carefully limited exercises involving few problems or interval classes but making a clean break from tonality by starting immediately with simple atonal material rather than slowly easing into it through chromaticism.

This distinction might apply to hearing pre-tonal material as well. One approach might teach modal hearing as a language of its own, perhaps by using a more functionally neutral or objective solfege system such as fixed "do." Another method—using moveable "do," for example—teaches the church modes as "distortions" of the major/minor system (e.g., Dorian and Phrygian are forms of natural minor with raised scale degree 6 and lowered 2 respectively; Lydian and Mixolydian are forms of major with raised 4 and lowered 7 respectively). Modality is heard, then, as a somewhat milder form of functional tonality.

Such a view, historically speaking, is backwards; if anything, major and minor scales are "distortions" (or conjoinings) of modal scales. However, because of the strong tonal filters that students bring to college, this approach, pedagogically speaking, does have some teaching merit. It is probably not possible for us to hear medieval and Renaissance music with pure modal ears simply because, through centuries of collective exposure, we have been "tainted" by tonality.

Twentieth-century harmony can be studied using many of the above ear-training methods in vertical contexts. For example, the twelve trichord sounds, as simultaneities, can be learned just as triads and seventh chords are for tonal music. Multiple-choice and error-detection formats are especially helpful in avoiding the notational hassles of representing the closely packed intervals of more complicated chordal structures. Mutation exercises (starting with a basic sound—for example, superimposed P5s—and first changing one of the three notes, then another, then another, by perhaps whole-step or half-step voice leading) make very good dictation practice by combining harmonic and melodic hearing as one sound complex gradually evolves into another (not so different from Chopin) through small individual linear changes.

All of these methods are merely samples of things that can be done in teaching post-tonal (or pre-tonal) listening. Gradually, more twentieth-century ear-training materials are being published that support and extend these and other approaches. A hit-or-miss approach or avoidance altogether of nontonal hearing experiences is no longer an option that serious teachers will want to consider. Twentieth-century ear training can be as systematic, organized, and conceptually grounded as any other part of the curriculum.

Rhythm

Rhythm study is a topic that should certainly be mastered intellectually. Understanding the mathematical foundation of rhythm and meter (time values; meter signatures; subdivision; grouping and adding of beats within a measure; proper beamings and notations; simple vs. compound; duple vs. triple; etc.) is essential for any musician. For almost no other topic, however, is it so important to translate conceptual knowledge into sound and musical effect. To make sense, rhythm must finally be felt as a physical activity and not just understood as a formation of symbols.

Written exercises requiring students to fit long strings of given durations into prescribed meters (using ties as necessary, etc.) and other related notational exercises are all good methods of learning the mathematical properties of metric organization, but almost everything there is to know about rhythmic notation can be taught easily and naturally along with dictation and sightsinging—and with more impact than in a purely analytical environment. Some specifics:

1. Concepts of beat, pulse, strong vs. weak stress, schemes of accent patterns, basic duration, and tempo are among the most important topics for rhythmic ear training. All of these need to be organized and coordinated by some physical action in listening and performance. Many teachers prefer to use basic conducting patterns to reinforce metric organization. Others rely on simple foot tapping, pencil tapping, or even body movement. Regardless of the particular method employed, the point is the same: rhythm must be felt and experienced directly.

143

2. A course of rhythm study can be regularized, like melody and harmony, as a series of graduated steps from simple to complex. Beginning with easy meters ($\frac{2}{4}$, $\frac{3}{4}$, etc.) and quarter and half notes, exercises simple enough for almost anyone will allow a high success rate in singing and dictation. Such a program would continue by moving gradually through a greater variety of meters, pulse units, longer patterns, and eventually to deeper levels of subdivision, rests, dotted rhythms, ties, syncopation, hemiola, and finally covering the intricacies of twentieth-century notation (irregular and changing meters, polymeter, metric modulation, and proportional groupings).

3. In melodic work, rhythm can often be extracted and practiced separately, just like syllables or pitch, so that one problem at a time is spotlighted. In performance, rhythms are best sung (ta-ta-ta provides a crisp articulate syllable) rather than clapped so that both attack *and* duration can be properly represented. Singing rather than clapping relates more naturally to pitch singing too. Rhythmic-dictation melodies should use pitch content also for ease of memory.

4. One of the best devices for teaching rhythmic ear training is subdivision. Thinking in subdivisions involves nothing more than simple counting and keeping track of one's place within the measure or beat. The basic mathematical background (knowledge of time values, fractions, meter, etc.), of course, is assumed here so that reading problems do not create handicaps. Beating in time or even identifying upbeats and downbeats with pencil marks in the score (numbers or little upward and downward arrows) can help students identify precisely at which point a particular note begins or ends—was it just before a beat, just after, exactly in the middle? This is particularly crucial when ties, syncopations, dotted rhythms, or lots of rests are used, or when the surface notational values are drastically longer or shorter than the perceived pulse (lots of 16th notes, for example, in a slow $\frac{4}{4}$).

Simplification methods (similar to reduction technique in pitch analysis) for rhythm are very effective. For example, complex patterns can be made easier by performing very slowly (e.g., using eighths rather than quarters for the pulse), by eliminating ties (in tricky syncopations), counting beat numbers aloud during a long series of rests, singing only notes that occur on beats, etc. The imagination is the only limit in devising ways to triumph over snags. Subdivision benefits are most fully realized in rhythmic syllables (e.g., one-ee-and-a, two-ee-and-a, etc.). Such systems superimpose a steady stream of mini-beats—a meter within a meter—onto the actual durations themselves producing a detailed time grid of reference points. The beat and its internal divisions serve as an orientation for rhythm just as tonic does for tonality. The discipline of working with a metronome in this regard is beneficial for many but a distraction for others.

5. Perhaps the single most useful idea for singing and hearing rhythms is recognition of stock recurring patterns. A relatively small number of basic rhythmic kernels exist out of which grow innumerable longer and more involved designs (as in harmonic progressions). Such purely durational motives can be a few notes or even several measures in length. They always involve a small and distinctive grouping of time values that makes sense by itself. These can be contained neatly within a beat or measure or can cross bar lines or beats by using pick-ups. Samples include the first measure of *Silent Night* or the final section of *William Tell* Overture (the "Lone Ranger" theme).

Several dozen such germinal ideas could probably be identified, labeled (if desired), and listed; they must all be instantly recognized (visually and aurally) and memorized. Almost all rhythms that are encountered will be variations, extensions, combinations, or relatives of the shorter, more basic building blocks. Once these patterns are recognized as being familar friends, reading and hearing tasks are remarkably eased. The eye, ear, and brain find it much simpler to group rhythms together than to jump from individual note to note. Good sight readers are always looking far ahead of where they are actually performing at that second so as to prepare mentally for upcoming patterns. It is one of the miracles of perceptual processing that the mind can be setting up the groupings so far in advance of the actual vocalization while at the same time singing something different.

6. As with everything else, careful, organized, thoughtful, and purposeful practice is the best way to improve. Duets, trios, and canons are especially beneficial in rhythmic training. Performing one's own line against another tests tempo steadiness, the even flow of continuity, accuracy of conflicts, or exactness of alignment with another part.

Broader Ear-Training Approaches

Many overall ear-training programs lack variety, interest, and imagination because they are geared too closely with preparation for exams or because the concept of ear training is narrowly conceived. Some programs flounder because the amount of time spent in hearing is so meager or the emphasis so feeble that true ear training never gets off the ground. Thackray comments that in some circles "intellectual understanding, divorced from sound, has assumed such prominence that the actual hearing of music is often excluded. There are still teachers who teach "theory" lessons in which not a note is played; it is still possible to pass examinations in harmony without being able to hear what is written; the history of music is all too frequently studied largely from books; analysis is done by eye rather than by ear and even composition can be an intellectual exercise done in silence. These situations or practices are plainly difficult to justify."[12]

Some programs restrict all training to notation and music reading: traditional dictation and sightsinging. When notation is not used, activities are often of the conventional recognition type: verbal naming of intervals, scales, chords, meters, and cadences. There is, however, a much wider range of non-notational exercises and listening experiences that many schools and students have rarely probed or even glanced at. Specific suggestions (some by Thackray) for entering this relatively unexplored world follow:

1. Aural analysis of whole and real compositions or movements is the most obvious starting place. Recognition by ear of main sections and subdivisions, orchestration details, contrapuntal devices, rhythmic and melodic features, are good places to begin. Some additional areas of formal comparison include distinguishing between sonata-rondo and simple rondo or distinguishing between rounded binary and simple binary. Sonata-form pieces (e.g., first movements of Haydn symphonies) are especially rich in possibilities (was the exposition repeated?); describe the organization and origin of materials in the development; discuss differences (timbre, register, order, deletions, additions, extensions, etc.) between exposition and recapitulation; determine the form of the coda; etc.

Theme-and-variation types (e.g., the variation movement of

the Schubert *Trout* Quintet, or Ives' *America*) make excellent practice or exam material: specify the type of variation (figuration, ground bass, counter-melody, character, transformation, or free) and elements (meter, melody, tempo, harmony, rhythm, or mood) of retention and alteration for each variation; discuss the overall patterning of variations (order, climax, and relationships to each other). Comparisons between two pieces and multiple-choice questions about specific events can often be rewarding. Essay questions, or drawing charts, visualizations, time lines, or diagraming forms also are fruitful.

2. Types of texture provide a special area for much imaginative listening and response: single-line monophonic (Gregorianchant style); monophonic with implied polyphony (e.g., Bach cello suites); two, three, four or more voices in imitative vs. non-imitative polyphony; various degrees of independence among parts; numerous subcategories of homophony (melody and block chords; Alberti bass; melody, countermelody, and chords; and homorhythmic chorales); in-between categories (combinations or switchings of polyphony and homophony); heterophony; antiphony (spatial effects); planing (parallelism); Klangfarbenmelodie (pointillism); sound masses (density: thick/thin); dialogue texture (e.g., trio-sonata set-up: two equally important upper voices with register crossing and motivic interaction); ostinatos/pedals; aleatoric polyphony; hocket; layered effects; polytempo effects (e.g., Elliott Carter); and many more.

3. Listening situations involving composer and style identification overlap with traditional music-history listening. Test questions covering specific titles from an assigned listening list are usually less effective for establishing good listening habits than training in recognizing general traits or compositional procedures (who *might* have written this and why?). Recognizing style traits of unfamiliar works (based on prior listening experience) forces a student to notice a broad spectrum of clues (melodic content, harmonic vocabulary, orchestration, texture, meter/rhythm, stylistic fingerprints), while naming from memory a specific prepared piece by title and composer usually requires attention to a single obvious clue—almost always melodic. The difference is between learning how to listen (the more important goal for theory) and learning a required body of literature (often the goal in history).

4. The study of slight changes in tempo (by practicing accel-

erandos and ritardandos) and tempo steadiness are areas of rhythmic discrimination often overlooked.

5. Microtonal hearing is similarly undervalued in pitch. Ear-training programs are so wrapped up in getting the right note that almost no attention is ever given to problems of intonation, yet a more important aspect of performance can hardly be imagined.

6. Tuning drinking glasses in different scale systems or intervals by adding water provides practice in pitch discrimination.

Other ideas for ear training include the following briefly listed activities:

1. Identification of harmonics on a piano (hold one key down silently and strike various other pitches below)
2. Trying to hum and whistle the same pitch simultaneously
3. Recognition of the individual timbres that make up various composite instrumental sounds
4. Imitating in pitch and rhythm various environmental sounds (train whistles, auto horns, bird calls, tire squeals, etc.)
5. Trying to gauge a time interval (e.g., thirty seconds) by counting internally
6. Mentally hearing metronome clicks in groups of two, three, four, etc., changing the groupings internally at will; at slow tempos, groupings *within* (i.e., between) clicks are possible
7. Observation of vibrato styles, intonation problems, or mistakes in recordings
8. Comparison of varying recorded interpretations of the same piece by different performers or conductors; note details of rubato, dynamic shading, phrasing, balance, tempo, articulation, tone quality, expression, and style
9. Comparison of different languages or regional accents for pitch inflection, stress, timbre, and other nuances
10. Group improvisation activities involving changing pitches and rhythms according to pre-arranged plans

A much longer list could easily be made. In no area of theory teaching is imagination and creativity more valuable than in ear training. As Thackray summarizes, though, its goal remains something more than keeness of hearing:

It is possible, and not uncommon, for a person to develop a high degree of aural acuity and understanding, without sensitivity and aesthetic discrimination. Such a person might be highly skilled in sight singing and written dictation and be able to analyze by ear the harmony of a Brahms symphony, yet it does not follow that such abilities will ensure that his performance will be sensitive, that his taste will be discriminating or indeed that he will derive any pleasure or satisfaction from music. There is a real danger that "aural training", if it is narrow and unimaginative, may succeed in its immediate objective of "developing aural acuity", but fail to bring students any nearer to their higher goal, namely the joy and satisfaction to be gained from music.[13]

PART THREE

Achieving Teaching Success

SIX

Teaching Techniques

Strategies and Tactics

TEACHING TECHNIQUES have been discussed in many places scattered throughout this book. The following list will provide a brief summary of these and some additional practical ideas. Frequent reminders about the importance of such small details can help teachers to practice preventive medicine—that is, to anticipate and solve potential problems before they happen:

1. Perhaps the single most useful rule in presenting new material is to compare the strange with the familiar. The interrelationships among elements of music are so abundant that each new topic invariably can be connected in some way to many others already studied. The structure and content of music theory are beautifully arranged for this spiral-learning or disguised-repetition approach, yet many teachers and books continue to treat topics independently, reinforcing the widely held belief that theory is by its nature impenetrably complex. This myth has created, at the introductory/undergraduate level, waves of theory anxiety at many colleges akin to numbers anxiety in mathematics departments. Music theory, to be sure, is a broad, intellectually demanding domain with a genuine abundance of challenging ideas. Because of its conceptual richness and its inexhaustible levels of possible inquiry, though, music theory should guard all the more carefully against false or needless entanglements.

2. Distinctions between central, essential points and peri-

pheral supporting data must be made. Students have no way of sorting out the differences unless they are made explicit. The mass and maze of details—always the culprits of confusion—must be comprehended in relation to underlying principles. These principles, though, are themselves too often buried along with the details. When students are inundated by facts, the important and unimportant become indistinguishable.

3. Assume only the student's background in presenting new material; put yourself in the position of the beginner. It is very difficult, especially when teaching the same course many times, to imagine how a new topic impinges on the mind of someone hearing about it for the first time. The goal, once again, is to make music theory seem to the student simpler than it really is—that is, simpler than he thinks it is. This is not falsification, but represents, I think, one of the greatest creative spurs in theory teaching: to convince students that, properly understood, the important compositional systems are both versatile and lucid.

4. Present new topics in a way that sets the stage for the next, so that everything fits as part of a single continuum.

5. The principles of programmed instruction can be utilized in almost any kind of theory course: introduce information in small portions; identify the separate steps of each topic or task and master them in order. This is pertinent to both presentation of new material and to the important job of diagnosis when things go wrong. Much of a theory teacher's life is spent in tracing and retracing—forwards and backwards—the dozens of connections in a chain of reasoning or hearing in order to spot and repair that one weak link or, for more extreme cases, to reconstruct a whole new series of intertwined loops.

The self-pacing aspect of programmed learning can also be markedly beneficial for curriculums that can provide the flexibility of assignments, etc. to take advantage of the varying backgrounds and learning capabilities of each student. Many schools have classes that are too large or staffs too small to personalize the instructional program for individuals, so classes are often rather locked into an average kind of progress rate.

One goal in teaching should be to shift the responsibility of diagnosis from teacher to students. Students should be taught how to analyze their own mistakes. Categories of error types can be identified: (*a*) careless or silly mistakes; (*b*) spelling or thinking in a wrong clef; (*c*) working too fast; (*d*) working too slow so connections do not jell; (*e*) forgetting to consider alternatives; (*f*) lack of understanding of the current topic; (*g*) lack of previously assumed knowledge; etc.

6. The daily routine of running a class requires preparation and organization. Very few teachers have the background and panache to "wing it"—especially regularly. The specific topics of a class, examples, and illustrations must be prepared in advance. A precise mental list, or better yet, a written set of notes should outline the points to be covered on a given day. Planning more than can be accomplished is a good idea. Sometimes material is covered quickly and ten extra minutes to be packed with filler is embarrassing. The extra material can always be held over to help establish continuity with the next class. For most subjects, changing topics or approaches every ten or fifteen minutes will bring variety and freshened interest into the class. For example, spelling or recognizing intervals for an entire fifty-minute class would be deadly—unless practiced from more angles than most teachers would have in their repertoire. The opposite extreme of bombarding a class with dazzling and constantly changing activities would be equally preposterous. Balance is the guideline.

7. It is generally effective to verbally express high expectations. Research studies and practical experience bear out the "Pollyanna Hypothesis": students tend to live up to those standards and hopes that are assumed or instilled in the class room atmosphere.

8. The physical environment, although in many cases not open to change, will affect teaching quality. Any positive adjustments that can be made in temperature, air, light, windows, interferring sounds, neatness, placement of pianos, desks and chairs (e.g., sometimes circles—for discussion or seminar groups—will be more appropriate than rows), proximity of teacher to class, placement of stereo speakers, or general ambience should be taken advantage of.

9. Students should actively participate as much as possible during class time: assignments should be played and sung, discussed, revised, and improved; student compositions should be performed; and work at the blackboard (part-writing, dictation, etc.) should be encouraged. Discovery techniques—letting the students themselves actively create a definition, for

example—rather than always passively being handed information, should be mixed with lecture formats. Stimulation of curiosity will help to extend the teaching influence beyond the end of the course. To find out something alone is a joy in itself apart from the content of the idea. Responsive teachers cherish such moments of discovery when minds are set aflame. Each additional experience makes it more likely the student will crave a repeat of such learning sensations.

10. Analysis and listening should mutually reinforce one another regardless of the type or title of the class.

11. Multifaceted approaches are best for most teachers. Because of individual differences among learners, a variety of teaching methods will produce the greatest chance of success for each case. Most students will eventually, with gentle but steady instructional prodding and a certain amount of trial-and-error, discover what works for them. More rarely, teachers will organize their approach or style around a (sometimes narrow, but powerful) set of attitudes or a particular bias. This can be very effective also, especially when the teacher is one who has a forceful and persuasive personality and a strongly supported, well-prepared belief system.

12. One underdeveloped idea is to use students themselves as teachers. Frequently they will be able to elucidate a point with surprising clarity to a fellow classmate. In fact, one of the best ways to learn material is to explain it to someone else. Some schools even use undergraduate teaching assistants (sometimes giving academic credit—in pedagogy, for example—rather than remuneration for the work).

13. Distinctions between drilling and teaching should be made. Practicing a particular spelling, analytical, or hearing skill in class is different from explaining a process, diagnosing a problem (individual or group), comparing interpretations, or discussing issues. Classroom time will always require some combination of repetition and elucidation, but the tendency to gradually become more and more like an automaton should be resisted. Teachers should do what they do best (i.e., explaining) in class and leave routine practice for students to do outside of class or with machine assistance if available. Enough drilling should be demonstrated in class so that students know how to do it on their own elsewhere. Class time should not be

spent in simply practicing material, but in teaching students *how* to practice by themselves.

14. A brief review at the beginning of a new course or new year is usually desirable. This is especially true at the beginning of the sophomore year when students may have become rusty over the summer or where transfer students might bring a different background to the class.

15. Good teachers always seem interested in polishing their courses. Sometimes minor adjustments or changes in choice of pieces, textbooks, or pacing can help to keep the course fresh for the instructor. Sometimes revisions in assignments and exams are necessary simply to improve the course. Some teachers or whole faculties get carried away with constant experimentation or sudden shifts in orientation by trying out every teaching fad. If carried to extremes, this can be as disruptive to theory students over the course of an entire curriculum as changing applied teachers every semester would be for a performance major. The opposite type is the teacher who has taught for twenty years but has accumulated only one year of experience—repeated twenty times. Experience is only valuable if something is learned from it—knowledge that can result in tangible enhancement for learning. Self-evaluation, student evaluations, some trial-and-error, a little luck, and lots of practice and desire for improvement are necessary for "getting it right." Once that level of attainment is reached, a good teacher's notion of what "getting it right" means has usually advanced as well to act as a goad toward further betterment.

16. Tape recordings and computer-assisted instruction are very useful adjuncts to a theory program, but their limitations should be fully recognized as well. Tape labs (for recognition, dictation, etc.) are often not fully used by some students. The inconvenience of working the equipment, the poor quality of sound, the boring and (pedagogically) poor quality of many exercises all can contribute to a lack of enthusiasm. Many schools, on the other hand, do find tape labs—when well organized with very specific ear-training goals—to be helpful in saving class practice time. Saving class time is not always the issue, though, since good teaching rarely duplicates what goes on in the tape lab anyway.

Computer-assisted instruction, for fundamentals, analysis,

dictation, and even sightsinging, has recently made a great impact in numbers of both home-grown and commercially available instructional programs, types of computer systems and equipment (and supporting sound synthesizers, touch-sensitive screens, etc.), and in the numbers of schools that are making use of such advances in technology. Many students, in our game-playing age, are fervent supporters of such practice opportunities, can acclimate themselves to understanding directions and operations very quickly, and are genuinely inspired to study material in such a bewitching format.

There does not seem to be a danger, however, in the foreseeable future that CAI will supplant serious classroom teaching. One of the problems with computer instruction is that computers are very good at those things that are least important in music theory (labeling, description, facts, and answering questions) but are very weak at those things that are the most important *in teaching* (e.g., interpretive analysis, comparing arguments, choosing supporting evidence, making judgments; asking original questions, creating theories and hypotheses; learning from experience, tracing leads, diagnosing mistakes, and identifying problems). Many lessons that are used for labeling (scale and interval spelling, chord analysis, etc.) could just as easily, and much less expensively, be covered through the many fine programmed texts that are readily available. The texts have the added advantage of working directly in written notation for recording answers rather than punching keys at a terminal.

Computers can't really teach—they only test—because they have no imagination and until enormous gains are made in understanding how human beings accomplish such things as interpreting evidence, intuitively leaping into correct answers, and knowing precisely which special combination of perceptual clues to focus on (or ignore) and which conceptual follow-up patterns to retrieve from one's mental storage banks for maximum explanatory value, computers' help in teaching—as opposed to drilling—will be limited; these advances now seem, at the very earliest, decades off. Through advances—and setbacks—in artificial intelligence (applying the principles of human intelligence to machines), we are just now beginning to learn how truly difficult it is to replicate in computers the thought and hearing patterns that people use to process music (or language, or any complex system of relationships).

As recently as the late 1970s, it was believed that computer programs would soon be capable of beating the world champion in chess. Although small gains are gradually forthcoming, it is now apparent that such a possibility is many years away. Most powerful chess programs now use a brute-force method (literally examining every series of millions of possible moves each time), whereas grandmasters use a selective-search procedure (consideration of only sensible possibilities). It is not a problem of speed or memory storage that is holding back real progress, but a lack of thorough knowledge of how a grandmaster's mind works when selecting moves (the blend of accumulated experience; intuition; pattern perception; and the balancing of basic principles governing the choice of good moves vs. exceptional circumstances and special positions calling for changing temporarily the priorities of the normal principles).

Likewise, in programming ear-training lessons for computer practice, we simply do not understand enough about the psycho-acoustics of *music* listening (the physiology of hearing in general; why ear-training mistakes are made; what to do to correct them in differing musical situations; how to categorize these different situations; individual differences in hearing; and paradigm recognition and variation) to make the lessons very meaningful as musical experience or as real teaching aids. Just as in chess we do not fully understand the intuitive rules for choosing correct moves, in ear training we do not fully understand the intuitive rules for hearing correct notes rather than mistakes.

Many CAI ear-training lessons are of the isolated recognition type about which many teachers have reservations anyway. Because our knowledge of hearing and mental process is so limited, the branching techniques that classroom teachers use to *individualize* lessons (sending students through subroutines to review material or to receive extra practice on particular problem areas that may hinder further development) are extremely difficult to program into computer courseware.

It is frustrating and disappointing that so much time and money have been spent so far on developing such sophisticated technology for such trivial ends. It is almost as if the military had spent billions of dollars in research for the ultimate doomsday machine but instead reinvented the flyswatter. But such a preliminary stage of evolution is necessary before the future potential of CAI in music theory can be revealed. It now seems too early to tell whether CAI will be a fad of the 1970s and 1980s or will make, in the future, important contributions to teaching students *how* to listen and think in addition to its present more circumscribed and marginal role of providing supporting drill and repetition. An immense debt is owed to those pioneers who are exploring this area, and everyone who cares seriously about innovation and improvement in theory teaching, if not involved directly himself, is cheering from the sidelines to champion significant breakthroughs.

The necessary breakthroughs, though, are not so much in hardware (equipment), or in the programming languages themselves, but in the software (content of the lessons). The necessary breakthroughs do not concern advancements in programming techniques but in learning more about *what* to program. We need to clarify what the goals of ear training are and what kinds of listening experiences will achieve those goals. We need to learn more about the connections between ear training and mind training (use of solfege systems, structural reductions, reference guides, long-range liaisons, pattern grouping, and the similarities and differences among pitch language systems). We need to learn more about the connections between exercises, details, and whole, live compositions. We need to learn more from expert teachers about how they make decisions on what to say and when to say it. (How do instinct and intuition specifically guide the teaching process?) We need to learn more about how listeners learn to hear. (How do those pitch filtering systems—tonal and nontonal—really work?) We need to learn more about music and teaching, not more about computers. Computers are already more advanced (electronically speaking) than we know how to take pedagogical advantage of because of our comparatively rudimentary understanding of the listening process. When we can put the above knowledge into specific words, order the steps (i.e., formalize the problem), and delineate the thicket of sub-branches for all conceivable student mistakes (i.e., create software that can mimic the rich and rewarding learning environment of masterful human teachers), then we will be ready to begin making CAI a truly worthy component of a theory curriculum. But at the present, because of their right/wrong binary modes of "reasoning," computers are very strong on evaluation of student answers but very weak at real instruction. Perhaps "computer-assisted testing" would be a more accurate term.

Meanwhile, many other methods of out-of-class practice remain available for students: the "buddy" system (teaming up with a friend of similar ability to play dictation, correct one another, etc.); practicing ear training through keyboard or applied study on the major instrument; and working with a cassette recorder. The best method of perfecting aural skills is still probably through singing. No fancy equipment is needed: just a pair of ears, a brain (a voice is optional)—and motivation. And finally, nothing can substitute for the creative, flexible, and humanized teaching (in class or privately) of a real musician who can diagnose difficulties and prescribe remedies or antidotes and who, more importantly, can make the bond between pitch, timbre, volume, duration, and artistic expression—something that can never be quantified.

Teaching versus Learning

Classes (even large ones) are usually most effectively taught with some combination of lecture, discussion, and liberal doses of real music—both looking and listening. Students in very large lecture classes will not always have the opportunity for asking questions, but the instructor himself can still ask questions of the students. Such questions will help the students to engage more fully in the learning process, to actively participate in the classroom, and, therefore, to have more reason to pay attention.

A distinction should be made between teaching (i.e., transmitting information—for example, through a lecture) and learning (connecting the student's mind and needs in some way to what the instructor is talking about). Unless the information registers, is assimilated, applied, reinforced, and changes behavior, or affects intellectual growth, real learning is not taking place—even though teaching may be observed. "For most college teachers, lecturing is like throwing the shot: they spend all their time getting together a very heavy message and then they just fling it. Lecturing, in fact, is more like throwing a frisbee: the message has to be thrown in such a way that it can be caught and with some reasonable expectation that it can be returned."[1]

It almost, but not quite, goes without saying that lecturers should make reasonable attempts to package their material attractively or at least try to keep their students awake during presentations—or notice when they're not. The stereotyped professor who reads from written notes in a monotone, talks to the blackboard, or repeats "ah" eighty-seven times per class (students actually keep count of such things) is unfortunately still prevalent in many campus departments.

No one expects music theory to be presented with the intensity, dynamism, and charisma of an evangelist. But the normal communication courtesies of proper vocal delivery (volume, pacing, enunciation, etc.), eye contact, enthusiasm, sincerity, sense of humor, and appropriate gestures are much more important than most are willing to admit. Many teachers are defensive or embarrassed about such issues or believe that they apply only to other teachers. Many believe that even discussing them weights the balance between style and substance too far in the direction of empty theatrics or personality cults.

The fact remains, however, that skill in communication—in establishing and maintaining a warm rapport with individual students and whole classes—is as important as the goals and content of a course. Vacuous content presented with flair, while not seen quite so often, would be, of course, equally meaningless.

Most college teachers, or those studying to become teachers, would silently smile and nod in self-righteous approval at the following sentiment: "The profession of teaching is preeminently the art of developing [in students] the power of thinking, the habit of intelligent observation, the sense of discriminating taste, the capacities of appreciation, expression and effective communication."[2] Such a statement appeals to our loftiest view of ourselves and our mission as teachers.[3] We sometimes assume that accomplishing educational goals such as these is merely a function of knowledge in our own field. If we are competent, technically skilled, appropriately analytical, prepared for class, and involved in the subject ourselves, then students will be inspired automatically to learn the material we offer. Learning will be achieved miraculously: the fountain of knowledge and experience from which we have sipped will flow into eager mouths and minds, and the students, partaking, will grow into perceptive musicians and find the good life.

Alas, as Candide finally recognized, this is not the best of all possible worlds. What begins as a well-intentioned entry into a classroom can become a frustrating, draining, even puzzling experience. Students can become adversaries and over the years courses seem for some more and more like irritations to be endured while trying to carry out one's *real* work in research or performance. Repeated experiences of failure, student apathy, antagonism, and anti-intellectualism often produce a cynical attitude towards the practice and even the validity of one's profession. H. L. Mencken captures this mood when he states: "The truth is that the average school teacher . . . is and always must be essentially an ass, for how can one imagine an intelligent man engaging in so puerile an avocation."[4] Those who teach or express an interest in the quality of teaching are considered the juveniles in some music departments. The assumption—both tacit and false—in all of this is, of course, that anyone can teach if one knows the material. *What is consistently avoided is the recognition that teaching itself is a skill.*

Any of us who has walked into a classroom as a teacher has been immediately aware of the challenge of establishing some relationship with the assortment of individuals seated before us. Not only do the students bring a variety of backgrounds, interests, and skills to the class, they operate as a group in a manner that we may experience as irrational, or, at best, unpredictable. Walking out of that classroom, we may silently pat ourselves on the back or shake our heads in dismay because the class worked or didn't work. Sooner or later it dawns on those who consider such things that fine preparation in music theory is only part of the reason students learn from us; often it is only a very small part.

Consider the emphases possible in the sentence: I am teaching a class in music theory. In one statement, we are teaching a subject called theory. In the other, we are teaching a group of people a particular subject. Emphasizing the people as well as the subject helps us to understand why the learning environment is important. As the leader, we have a seemingly paradoxical task: to teach the overt material (the content of the course) and to attend to the group life of our class.

163

These problems have been enormously illuminated in recent years by research into group process. College theory teachers have been reluctant to make use of these studies (or are unaware of them) because music theory is so often taught in an atmosphere that stresses cognitive growth, intellectual development, and factual information rather than the changing of opinions and attitudes, the reworking of beliefs and habits, the judging of sides of an issue, and the development of a sense of values.

The dynamics of group process have been studied now for several decades and have their origin in psychotherapy group sessions although more recently have been applied also to many other types including classroom learning groups. The interaction between and among members of a class and between teacher and class are both subtle and complex. We sometimes even speak of the classroom chemistry. Awareness of such relationships and of various leadership roles that can be assumed (e.g., teacher as expert, as formal authority, as socializing agent, as facilitator, as ego ideal, and as person)[5] can go a long way toward establishing the goals of communication, rapport, and true learning.

For example, just one of dozens of group-process traits is the standard life-cycle that a normal class will pass through during the semester (or year). At least three psychological stages can be distinguished: (*a*) the dependency stage (first two or three weeks of a semester); (*b*) the affiliative stage (middle ten weeks); and (*c*) the closure stage (last two or three weeks). By understanding the differences among stages, a teacher can mold a class throughout the semester with a resulting and satisfying sense of movement and completion; constructing and directing a class in this sense is like constructing and composing a piece of music. A class operates, then, within a closed system with a clear beginning (setting attitudes and goals), middle (specific tasks towards fulfilling the goals), and end (achieving independence from the teacher).

Strong teachers will know how to steer classes through learning phases, how to create and maintain the positive empathy that is crucial to learning success, when to talk and when to listen, when to ask questions and when to ask *for* questions, when to adjust the teaching approach, and scores of other subtle details by being constantly in tune with feedback from the students. Strong teachers will also want to continually learn more and more about these mysteries of effective teaching by comparing notes with other teachers, through intensive self-evaluation, observation, study, experimentation, and rumination. These traits, more than anything else, define what strong teaching is.

The values of group process and their connections to learning have been well summarized by the psychologist and psychotherapist, Carl Rogers:

> When I have been able to transform a group—and here I mean all the members of a group, myself included—into a community of *learners,* then the excitement has been almost beyond belief. To free curiosity; to open everything to questioning and exploration; to recognize that everything is in process of change—here is an experience I can never forget. I cannot always achieve it in groups with which I am associated but when it is partially or largely achieved then it becomes a never-to-be-forgotten experience. Out of such a context arise true students, real learners, creative scientists and scholars and practitioners, the kind of individuals who can live in a delicate but ever-changing balance between what is known and the flowing, moving, altering, problems and facts of the future. . . . We know . . . that the initiation of such learning rests not upon the teaching skills of the leader, not upon his scholarly knowledge of the field, not upon his use of audio-visual aids, not upon the programmed learning he utilizes, not upon his lectures and presentations, not upon an abundance of books, though each of these might at one time or another be utilized as an important resource. No, the facilitation of significant learning rests upon certain attitudinal qualities which exist in the personal *relationship* between the facilitator and the learner.[6]

SEVEN

Evaluation and Curriculum Design

Testing and Grading

THE VERY BEST TEACHING and the best-designed courses can be undone through careless lack of attention to the subtleties of testing and grading. At least three different purposes can be stated for exams: measuring, learning, and motivating. Measurement of achievement is helpful both to the student (to find out what he has learned) and to the teacher (to spot gaps or weaknesses in the course). While the three central chapters of this book indicate the kinds of topics that should be included on both assignments and exams, the following list summarizes some suggestions for constructing a valuable test:

1. Try to make exams both fair and challenging. This is probably the most difficult aspect of construction.

2. Specifying the content, length, difficulty level, etc., of an exam in advance as much as possible will result in a greater likelihood of study and preparation. Practice exams, for no grade, are very helpful and especially appreciated by students for reducing anxiety. Not all regular exams even need to receive a grade.

3. Lots of shorter tests are best so that no single score is over-weighted. This is especially true of ear-training exams where the possibility of having an off day is more likely.

4. A variety of difficulty levels within each exam will help to spread the range of scores appropriately (too many scores at the top indicates an exam that was too easy, and clumps of

scores at the bottom, a test that was too hard). A good spread gives more opportunity for making distinctions among levels of accomplishment. It is wise (especially with dictation tests) to begin with a few simple items that nearly everyone can be successful with to build confidence and to help stabilize shaky nerves. It is helpful to include also at least a few very challenging items to extend the strongest students.

5. It is very good training to have students themselves construct exams as well as take them. Judging the difficulty level, appropriateness, and purpose of questions can help to clarify the point of a course.

6. Feedback (quick, if possible) and review of test questions and answers is important. Students should always learn something from a test through discussion afterward that can be applied to the next topic, test, or skill.

7. Creativity and imagination can be used in devising exam questions as much as in other areas of teaching. Especially tempting is the impulse in both teaching and testing to stress those topics or questions that are the easiest to grade—those that have clear-cut right or wrong answers or that mimic exactly the approach of preparation material. Look instead, where possible, for unusual questions involving startling comparisons, strange twists, humor, synthesis (combining separately studied topics in new conformations), or interpretations to help make exams more interesting, thought-provoking, and meaningful than a parroting of pre-digested facts. Students can actually be forced, on exams, to perform music theory (i.e., to create an original mental or aural conception of some piece, term, or situation).

8. One of the trickiest features of making up a test is to judge length. Since theory teachers, especially those teaching the same courses many times, often know the material so much more thoroughly and automatically than students, it is difficult to estimate the time needed for completion. Common sense, experience, and a sense of fair play are the best guidelines. In addition, distinctions between speed tests (for fluency and quickness) and power tests (for accuracy, knowledge, and thinking) are necessary.

9. Distinctions should also be made among domains of abilities to be tested and their various mixtures: (*a*) cognitive (mental, verbal, and non-verbal); (*b*) affective (awareness, aesthetic

response, values); and (c) psychomotor (perception, physical response, coordination). Testing must also match the appropriate level of learning: knowledge; comprehension; application; analysis; synthesis; evaluation. Use a variety of testing methods: both subjective and objective; some short answer, some essay; some verbal, some with symbols; some with skills, some with facts, some with opinions; etc.

10. Teachers should familiarize themselves with aspects of *reliability* (will repeated measures yield similar and consistent results?), and *validity* (does the test measure what it claims to measure?). The statistical procedure of *item analysis* is an especially useful tool in identifying very strong and very weak questions (i.e., good or poor discriminators of ability or understanding). Constant revision in exam construction is a must for serious theory teaching. Exams almost always can be made better each time around. Sometimes a completely new or different kind of test is called for; sometimes tiny adjustments or corrections are enough.

11. Pass/fail exams (usually with high cut-off points and covering very specified factual information—e.g., key signatures) can be distinguished from ranking types using letter grades.

12. Self-administered or self-paced testing can be very effective in programs that are flexible enough to allow for some variance in individual time tracks.

13. Distinctions between aptitude and achievement (a very complex issue) might be helpful in designing formats, and judging purposes of exams.

14. Grading schemes (i.e., translating results or raw scores into letter grades) is a whole topic in itself and is loaded with difficulty. A full range of options should be made available and not all work equally well for every subject or skill: (a) percentage methods (e.g., 90–100% = A; 80–90% = B; etc.)—considered too arbitrary by some; (b) curving (e.g., the five highest scores = A)—considered unfair and rigid by some; and (c) contract systems (a defined amount of work or level = A).

15. The most important part of grading, regardless of method, is to make clear the proficiency standards, the grading philosophy itself, and especially the weighting factors of each category in determining a final grade. This provides both in-

formation for the student and protection for the teacher in the event of a grade dispute or appeal.

16. Finally, teaching just for exams is a dangerous routine. Many of the most important goals of music theory cannot be tested at all, although perceptive teachers will nevertheless be aware of those subtler changes in habit, inquisitiveness, awareness, response, and maturity that signal growth in thinking and listening. A humanistic art such as music does not lend itself easily to quantification. And most teachers will want to include the intangibles of attitude, effort, long-range improvement (measured against oneself rather than others), and class participation in assigning grades. Testing and grading should be taken seriously in order to extract all of the value possible, but they should not be taken too seriously by teacher or student.

Organization of a Theory Program

It is both undesirable and impossible in a book such as this to try to set up an ideal undergraduate theory curriculum as a model of perfection toward which all music departments should strive. All theory teachers at one time in their fantasy lives have probably envisioned themselves as theory chairman at Utopia University with the opportunity to design from scratch a total theory program. The realities of college teaching, however, permit control, for most teachers, over only a small number of the issues that involve setting up a series of courses.

Many of the factors that affect curriculum design have already been discussed throughout the book—especially in part 1. I will attempt here a brief listing of some additional issues that are pertinent to an overall program:

1. There is no such thing as one correct theory program—or even a single faulty type. Some kinds of curriculums will be right for certain kinds of students, teachers, or schools while others would be totally wrong. The diversity of background and talent for both learners and faculty will be an important deciding factor. Most choices of content or organization will involve trade-offs. Simply being aware of what negative results might follow from given choices—along with the gains, of

course—can help to diminish their detrimental effects. The benefit/risk impact of all curricular selections and corresponding teaching approaches must be considered.

2. The three crucial factors for any program are order, pacing, and emphasis. Where to start and what to do next, how fast or slow to cover material, and which topics to omit (since there will never be enough time for everything that is important) are the questions that must be faced. Whether to cover a few topics thoroughly or many topics in abridgement is especially problematic.

Almost any kind of pacing will be too slow for about ten percent of the class and too fast for a different ten percent. The pacing, then, must be geared for the middle eighty percent. The issue of special classes for the very strong and/or very weak is raised occasionally at some schools. One problem here involves identifying strengths and weaknesses: are they in analysis, aural skills, or some combination? Another problem is that "strong or weak" is not necessarily a matter of previous background, inborn talent, or even test scores. Intangibles such as interest, attitude, maturity, conflicts in one's personal life, motivation, study habits, attendance, etc. also can affect success or potential placement in a particular section. Classroom performance often fluctuates widely (even wildly) for individuals during a semester's work. Placing students at an appropriate level is therefore a very ticklish matter.

The advantage of graded sections according to strength and weakness (assuming that proper definitions can be found) is that pacing can be more easily regulated according to needs. Quicker students can either be pushed ahead by covering current topics in greater depth and more detail—the enrichment option—or by moving to advanced topics sooner—the acceleration option. Likewise, the slower students can be allowed more breathing room and time to absorb material; this can backfire if at least moderate pressure to progress is not maintained. One advantage of mixed sections (random assignment) is that weaker students are sometimes more challenged in a setting with stronger peers. On the other hand, some are simply embarrassed and frustrated by constant failure in matching their classmates.

A related aspect of structuring courses is whether or not to include a one-semester pre-theory (i.e., rudiments) class in the curriculum. Once again, entrance exams—no matter how expertly constructed—can only estimate who might need such a course since background weaknesses are only part of the story in predicting future success in theory courses. Fundamentals are so essential (see chapter 3) that such knowledge cannot be presumed, yet when covered expeditiously, they need not take a whole semester to finish. Some beginning freshman courses solve the problem by including them at the beginning with a quick but thorough review.

3. Order and pacing are likely to be determined, at least partially, by choice of textbooks. Often the cart is put before the horse in choosing texts. A faculty will sometimes browse through current books, choose what strikes their fancy, use the text for a year or two, and discover defects. Another book will be chosen as a replacement to correct those deficiencies and, in turn, will disclose a different set of flaws. This cycle, then, is repeated endlessly with constant dissatisfaction.

The choice of textbook should be an outcome of the teaching philosophy of an individual or consensus of a group. Too often, though, the teaching style itself evolves from the book as an afterthought. Frequently, teaching philosophies or course goals are never defined clearly enough to be of any worth in evaluating books. The texts for a course, then, must reflect the objectives of the class—objectives that are determined *before* text selection takes place.

Many texts are not written to enlighten students coming to the subject for the first time but to impress theory teachers who might adopt them for class use. Even many of the very best texts—and some excellent examples are literally brimming with useful, original, and significant insights—often present so much material and some of it so soon that students are left drowning in a whirlpool of details. Some books are outstanding as reference works (for student *and* teacher) but unsatisfying to learn from. Because of too many ideas all competing for the student's attention, and sometimes because of poor organization, poor physical layout, or clogged writing style, basic distinctions between central key concepts and other supporting, but peripheral, issues are lost or never made.

Under these conditions teachers often spend their class time in translating the textbook into terms that a novice can understand. This can take two forms: (*a*) reading between the lines and elaborating on the main points of those texts that are cryptic and/or highly condensed—some just outlines; and (b) pruning those that are too wordy or loaded with needless jargon. Some schools solve the textbook problem by ambitiously, but rewardingly, creating their own materials in the form of continuous handouts—in effect writing their own text. Most good texts begin this way.

4. One aspect of emphasis involves the relative weighting and interrelationship of various perceptual and conceptual modes. Merrill Bradshaw has devised a chart to summarize the multiple combinations resulting from the interplay between words, notes, and sounds—the three most basic forms of stimulus and response in music theory teaching:

STIMULUS	RESPONSE	ACTIVITY
Words	Words	Talking about music
Words	Notes	Exercises; composing a song
Words	Sounds	Performance; improvisation
Notes	Words	Analysis
Notes	Notes	Exercises
Notes	Sounds	Sightsinging
Sounds	Words	Aural analysis
Sounds	Notes	Dictation; composition
Sounds	Sounds	Improvisation[1]

5. The number and type of courses and their relationships to one another are at the heart of an overall program. The plan of organization varies greatly from school to school. Whatever the plan, the courses themselves must relate to each other in some way that maintains or promotes coherence, just as individual topics within a course must relate; and at the highest level of the curricular hierarchy, the theory program as a whole must fit smoothly into the entire four-year undergraduate scheme of organization.

Almost all colleges require at least two years of theory. Many include requirements beyond this minimum—either specific courses or electives in the junior year. Some schools even extend the requirement to include the senior year. The underlying philosophy (see chapter 2) on a variety of issues will determine content and titles. Lack of a philosophy or conflicts among faculty members can just as potently also influence the program—often producing a strange or contradictory mixture of values.

The three Cs of curriculum design are correlation, coordination, and continuity. Correlation covers the alignment and overlap between music theory and other courses such as music literature, piano class, history, and conducting, or interconnections within the various aspects of theory itself, such as between harmony and counterpoint (either within a single class or between separate courses) or between analysis and sight-singing/dictation, etc. Close correlations are not necessarily better than distant ones, but the amount and nature of the correlations should be thought out and planned to avoid unnecessary duplications and, at the same time, encourage natural and logical associations. Some associations are logical and beneficial but not always immediately obvious. The problem of ingrown box-like compartments (see chapter 1) is of special concern here.

Correlated courses can be associated by various means. Topics can be related by covering similar material in different ways, by covering different material in similar ways, or by complementing one another through a dovetailing process—i.e., filling in one another's gaps in approach or subject matter.

Coordination refers to the connections—strong ones, ideally—between or among individual sections of the same course. When these sections are taught by different instructors or graduate assistants, it is especially important to share a set of common goals and skills for the students without stifling the creativity or distinctiveness of the teaching. If students are to be passed on to ensuing courses (perhaps with different teachers) and especially if they are to be re-mixed in later semesters (i.e., new sections formed from combinations of old ones), then at least roughly equivalent backgrounds seem necessary to avoid chaos.

Some schools assign a single teacher to lead one group of students through an entire curriculum. This has the double advantage and disadvantage of students' becoming thoroughly steeped in one particular approach or system (of analysis/hearing) but perhaps being oblivious to the variety of viewpoints that might come from exposure to several different instructors. A single teacher can stress more connections between earlier and later courses, whereas inheriting students from another teacher's class can limit those same tie-ins. Students can, however, become too attached to teachers and too dependent on or comfortable with a particular approach.

Transfer students often have a problem fitting into a program when switching from one school to another. Some programs vary so much that one curriculum can seem like a wholly different world; music theory almost appears, to the student, as an entirely different subject. Elaborate entrance exams for such students are not always the answer since alien terminology and analytical viewpoints will cloud the results and make evaluation both difficult and unfair. Brief interviews and a review of grades from previous courses can help to place students at the proper level.

No solution has yet been found for this advising problem. Surely the naive proposal to adopt some national standardization of theory curriculums would be undesirable even if it were not unworkable. (A single music department is lucky to get agreement among just three or four teachers on the same faculty.) Almost always students will end up being placed in courses that both reveal gaps in their previous knowledge while repeating material that they've already learned elsewhere. The best that can be done is to try to make the blanks and repetitions as small as possible since no course at one school will ever automatically be able to pick up where another course at a different school left off. Practical judgement and fairness are the best guides.

The third aspect of curriculum design, continuity, is concerned with the connections between one course and the next at the same school: are they all part of a single long course (only seemingly broken down into semesters or quarters because of the school-year calendar), do some stand alone as separate entities, or is some sub-grouping pattern in evidence? Again, there is no universally agreed-upon scheme, but most programs fit into one of the following categories:

a. For the purposes of illustration, a four-semester (two-year) program could be organized as a "1 + 3." This implies that the first semester would act as an introduction or overview of the whole program, perhaps by covering fundamentals, introducing terminology, and establishing parametric analytical categories. The final three semesters could then be conceived as a single unit starting with the second-semester freshman year as the beginning of a chronological historical sequence (only one of many possibilities). This course might cover medieval/Renaissance, with the sophomore year continuing, for example, in semester one with baroque/classical, and semester two with romantic/twentieth-century.

b. Another possibility (using a five-semester model for illustration) could be described as a "4 + 1," meaning that the final semester is thought of as a summary of all that has gone before. The first two years might blend harmony with counterpoint while a separate junior-level course in formal analysis pulls everything together at the end.

c. Yet another arrangement (using a six-semester model), might be organized as a "2 + 2 + 1 + 1." The first year (two semesters) might include, for example, a basic tonal harmony course. The second year might include a basic form-and-analysis course (all style periods) while the third year could contain two additional but independent classes such as counterpoint and orchestration.

d. A final example (back to four semesters) might simply be labeled as "4." No smaller groupings are apparent here as each semester grows out of the preceeding one, making a continuous stream. This represents the maximum in curricular continuity: four semesters blended into a single continuum. Each semester's work has no independent existence apart from the larger cohesive aggregate.

Dozens of variants and combinations of the above four basic types are possible. No one plan is superior or inferior to the others. A host of factors determines what is appropriate for a given department: definitions of theory and its goals, philosophical orientation, textbooks, type (conservatory, liberal arts, teachers college, etc.), size of school, number of faculty and extent of cooperation, availability of teaching assistants, faculty assignments (e.g., one faculty supervisor for each year vs. rotating teaching duties for all), amount of time in the curriculum, types of non-theory and non-music courses, overall degree requirements, examination techniques, teaching styles, relationships between mind and ear training, physical resources (rooms, stereos, labs, computers, etc.), and the needs and background of both students and teachers—in other words, everything in this book. No formula can be produced for choosing what will work, but I can recommend that the design *be chosen* with conscious awareness of the complete spectrum of alternatives. Knowledge of the full array of possibilities and their corresponding strengths and weaknesses will make it more likely that fitting solutions and blueprints will be found. It is in the spirit of providing such a background that this book has been written.

It should be emphasized one final time that there is room in music theory teaching for a wide variety of approaches. In evaluating the Julliard literature-and-materials program, Bergsma concludes that

> In music, where subjective reactions are the only valid ones, where final judgements cannot be proved objectively, the best guidance is a flexible one, given by "one skilled in the art."
>
> To defend a personal judgement nowadays is to be revolutionary and archaic at the same time. The world is full of experts on methodology, on "How To Do" something, step by prescribed step. Values are determined by the bell-shaped curve; fulfillment measured statistically. In music there is the idea of a "definitive" performance. No such thing exists. Music cannot be played, taught, or understood in only one manner. Its truths can be understood only in loving and willing participation in a work of art. Above the barest vocabulary of the art (and even there) no definition has absolute meaning. Behind every good musician there is a succession of his teachers, active interpreters whose musical activities took music off the page for him into the lovely world of sound. Each of us has that personal heritage.
>
> We therefore place reliance on the fruitful variety of the practice of good musicians. Diversity of procedure seems to us inevitable. It is neither forbidden nor encouraged. No instructor . . . need repeat his own teaching with any rigidity from year to year. Independence of thought and emphasis are admitted values in a high level of teaching. To discipline this diversity there is the *fact* of the literature, the repertory of perhaps five centuries of music. Freedom of approach cannot mean eccentricity. This repertory, commonly agreed to by performers and historians alike, is our touchstone of truth.[2]

The final goals, then, in teaching music theory are tolerance and flexibility. Besides acquiring knowledge of music theory itself, perhaps the most useful aid in preparing or improving one's teaching in theory—and one that recognizes the importance of the plural form of "approaches" in the title of this book—is to acquire knowledge of the trade-offs involved in choosing one approach over another. By forming and developing a set of consistent conceptual principles and a personalized belief system for teaching theory from an awareness of the similarities/differences and strengths/weaknesses of competing systems, we simultaneously solidify our own values and open our minds and ears to additional possibilities.

Notes
Suggested Reading
Index

Notes

1. The Purpose and Goals of Music Theory

1. Robert Bierstedt, ed., *The Making of Society,* rev. ed. (Random House, 1959), pp. xviii–xix.

2. Ibid., p. xix.

3. Leonard Meyer, *Explaining Music* (University of California Press, 1973), p. 25.

4. William Brandt et al., *Basic Principles of Music Theory* (Harper & Row, 1980), p. 3.

5. Meyer, p. 17.

6. Bruce Benward, *Music in Theory and Practice,* 2nd ed., 2 vols. (W. C. Brown, 1981), 1:ix.

7. William Thomson, *Music for Listeners* (Prentice-Hall, 1978), pp. xvi–xvii.

8. Frederic Homan, *Components of Music, Expanded, Part I* (Central Missouri State University, 1980), p. 1.

9. William Schuman, "On Teaching the Literature and Materials of Music," *Musical Quarterly* (April 1948):159.

10. Peter Westergaard, "What Theorists Do," *College Music Symposium* (Spring 1977):143–49.

2. Philosophical Orientations

1. See Quentin Norgren, "Traditional and Comprehensive Musicianship: A Survey," *American Music Teacher* (January 1980):34–36.

2. The notion that ideas can create even more ideas (in an almost biological sense) is explored in Douglas R. Hofstadter, "Virus-like

Sentences and Self-replicating Structures," *Scientific American* 248/1 (January 1983):14.

3. Ian Polster, "Theory Preparation for Future Teachers: Process vs. Information" (paper presented at Michigan Conference of Music Theory, Ann Arbor, October 1975), p. 8.

3. Mind Training

1. W. Francis McBeth, *Helpful New Ideas for the Understanding of 18th Century Harmony* (Southern Music, 1979), p. 45.

2. Leland Smith, *Handbook of Harmonic Analysis* (San Andreas Press, 1979), p. 8. See also pp. 40ff.

3. Charles Rosen, "An Exchange on the New Grove," *New York Review of Books* (13 August 1981):52.

4. Leo Kraft, *Gradus*, 2 vols. (Norton, 1976), 1:30.

5. Allen McHose, *Basic Principles of the Technique of Eighteenth- and Nineteenth-Century Composition* (Appleton-Century-Crofts, 1951); and *The Contrapuntal Harmonic Technique of the Eighteenth Century* (Appleton-Century-Crofts, 1947).

6. The closest in both title and intent is Peter Westergaard, *An Introduction to Tonal Theory* (Norton, 1975).

7. Terminology and interpretation are adapted from J. Fétis, *Traité complet de la Theorie et de la pratique de l'harmonie* (Paris and Brussells, 1844).

4. Musical Analysis

1. André Gide, *If It Die* [Si le grain ne meurt . . .], trans. Dorothy Bussy (Random House, 1957), pp. 6–7.

2. Meyer, *Explaining Music*, pp. 6–7.

3. John D. White, *The Analysis of Music* (Prentice-Hall, 1976), p. 1.

4. William Thomson, "Style Analysis: or the Perils of Pigeonholes," *Journal of Music Theory* (1970):191–208.

5. See Gary E. Wittlich, ed., *Aspects of Twentieth-Century Music* (Prentice-Hall, 1975), p. 48.

6. Wallace Berry, *Structural Functions in Music* (Prentice-Hall, 1976), p. 20. This brilliant book unfortunately is written entirely in overly technical jargon thereby obscuring considerably its many and profound insights.

7. G. M. Trevelyn, "Clio, A Muse," quoted in Richard D. Altick, *The Art of Literary Research*, rev. ed. (Norton, 1975), p. 200.

8. Claude Lévi-Strauss, *The Raw and the Cooked,* trans. John and Doreen Weightman (Harper & Row, 1969), p. 17.

9. The single best source of model analyses for classroom discussion, assignments, exams, etc. is Ralph Turek, *Analytical Anthology of Music* (Knopf, 1983) with accompaniment volume including answers for students and/or teachers. This collection of music *and* analysis includes all historical epochs (with summaries of traits for major periods and composers), a balanced treatment of all parameters and methodologies, both stylistic and structural approaches, and both simple and complex ideas.

The readings list for this chapter, of course, provides a detailed selection of additional analytical work illustrating the widest possible variety of analytical systems and philosophies.

5. Ear Training

1. Benward, *Music in Theory and Practice,* p. xi.

2. John Rahn, *Basic Atonal Theory* (Longman, 1980), p. 1.

3. Howard A. Murphy, *Teaching Musicianship* (Coleman-Ross, 1950), p. 61.

4. See Michael R. Rogers, "Beyond Intervals: The Teaching of Tonal Hearing," *Indiana Theory Review,* in press.

5. Philip Farkas, *The Art of French Horn Playing* (Summy-Birchard, 1956), p. 54.

6. Ronald A. Cole, "Navigating the Slippery Stream of Speech," *Psychology Today* (April 1979):77–87.

7. George A. Wedge, *Ear Training and Sight Singing* (Schirmer Books, 1921), p. 7.

8. Lars Edlund, *Modus Vetus: Sight Singing and Ear-Training in Major/Minor Tonality* (Broude, 1974), p. 31.

9. Murphy, p. 46.

10. William Thomson, *Advanced Music Reading* (Sonora Music, 1969), p. x.

11. Samuel Adler, *Sight Singing: Pitch, Interval, and Rhythm* (Norton, 1979), p. x.

12. Rupert Thackray, "Some Thoughts on Aural Training," *Australian Journal of Music Education* (October 1975):25.

13. Ibid., p. 30.

6. Teaching Techniques

1. James R. Davis, *Teaching Strategies for the College Classroom* (Westview Press, 1976), p. 57

2. Sidney Hook, "Teaching as a Profession," *Education & the Taming of Power* (Open Court Publishing Co., 1973), p. 267.

3. Adapted from Faith Gabelnick, "Creating an Active Learning Environment in the College Classroom," Northeast Modern Language Association Meeting, 1979.

4. H. L. Mencken, *Prejudices,* as cited in Hook, p. 263.

5. See Richard D. Mann et al., *College Classroom: Conflict, Change and Learning* (Wiley & Sons, 1970), pp. 1–19.

6. Carl Rogers, "The Interpersonal Relationship in the Facilitation of Learning" (lecture given at Harvard University, April 12, 1966).

7. *Evaluation and Curriculum Design*

1. Merrill Bradshaw, "Improvisation and Comprehensive Musicianship," *Music Educators Journal* (January 1980):113–15.

2. William Bergsma, "L & M Revisited," *Julliard Review* (Fall 1955):30–31.

Suggested Reading

1. The Purpose and Goals of Music Theory

Barford, Philip. "Preface to the Study of Music Theory." *Music Review* 31/1 (1972):22–33. Good ideas on defining music theory.

Benjamin, William. "Report on the National Theory Meeting, Boston, 1976." *Perspectives of New Music* (Fall/Winter 1975):218–21. Discussion about forming the Society for Music Theory.

Clifton, Thomas. "Training in Music Theory: Process and Product." *Journal of Music Theory* 13/1 (1969):38–65.

Cone, Edward T. "Music Theory as a Humanistic Discipline." *The Julliard Review* 5/1 (Winter 1957/58):3–12.

Kirchner, Leon. "The Lag of Theory Behind Practice." *College Music Symposium* (Fall 1961):23–48. Four articles and a panel discussion.

Kraehenbuhl, David. "On the Nature and Value of Theoretical Training: A Forum." *Journal of Music Theory* (April 1959):31–69. Four articles; see especially the discussion by Stanley Fletcher on the relationship of music theory to performance.

McGee, William J. "Music Theory—Or Music Practice?" *Music Educators Journal* (October 1970):52–55.

"Music Theory: The Art, the Profession and the Future." *College Music Symposium* 17/1 (Spring 1977):135–62. A group of articles defining the discipline; see especially the Peter Westergaard article, "What Theorists Do."

"Pedagogy in Perspective: Music Theory in Higher Education." *Journal of Music Theory* (Spring 1974):44–122. A comprehensive forum discussion about differing theory goals in a wide variety of educational settings.

"The Professional Music Theorist—His Habits and Training: A Forum." *Journal of Music Theory* (April 1960):62–84. A paper by David Kraehenbuehl with four responses; see especially the comments by Robert Melcher on the training of theory teachers.

Rosen, Charles. "The Proper Study of Music." *Perspectives of New Music* (Fall 1962):80–88.

"The Teaching of Music Theory in the University." *College Music Symposium* (Fall 1964):103–12. A panel discussion with much disagreement.

Thompson, Randall. *College Music.* Macmillan, 1935. See chap. 3 on music theory for an older viewpoint.

"Undergraduate Preparation for Graduate Study in Music." *College Music Symposium* 11/2 (Fall 1971):23–46.

"Undergraduate Training in Music Theory." *College Music Symposium* (Fall 1965):21–60. Four articles defining the purposes of music theory.

2. Philosophical Orientations

Bergsma, William. "L & M Revisited." *Julliard Review* (Fall 1955):29–36.

Bland, Leland. "The College Music Theory Curriculum: The Synthesis of Traditional and Comprehensive Musicianship Approaches." *College Music Symposium* (Fall 1977):167–74.

"Contemporary Music Project." *Music Educators Journal* (March 1968):41–72; and (May 1973):33–48. A good summary of the evolution of the comprehensive musicianship movement.

Duyk, Joan M. "Historical-Analytical Versus Common Practice Period Approach in Junior College Music Theory." Ph.D. dissertation, University of North Carolina at Chapel Hill, 1977.

Jackson, Roland. "A Single or Multiple View." *College Music Symposium* (Fall 1973):65–69. A stylistic vs. historical tonality.

Kraft, Leo. "In Search of a New Pedagogy." *College Music Symposium* (Fall 1968):109–16.

———. "Reflections on CMP[6]." *College Music Symposium* (Fall 1972):84–93.

Mark, Michael L. *Contemporary Music Education.* Schirmer, 1978. A summary of recent innovations and trends in philosophies.

Mitchell, William. "CMP Workshop at Eastman (June 1969)." *College Music Symposium* (Fall 1969):65–81.

Norgren, Quentin. "Traditional and Comprehensive Musicianship: A Survey." *American Music Teacher* (January 1980):34–36.

Polster, Ian. "Theory Preparation for Future Teachers: Process vs. Information." Paper presented at Michigan Conference on Music

Theory, Ann Arbor, October 1975. A stimulating discussion of composition approaches in freshman theory.

Rowell, Louis. "Comparative Theory: A Systematic Approach to the Study of World Music." *College Music Symposium* (Fall 1972):66–83.

Schuman, William. "On Teaching the Literature and Materials of Music." *Musical Quarterly* (April 1948):155–68. The guiding philosophy behind L & M.

———. *The Julliard Report.* Norton, 1953. Gives detailed outlines and assignments from the famous Literature and Materials curriculum.

Silliman, A. Cutler. "Comprehensive Musicianship: Some Cautionary Words." *College Music Symposium* (Fall 1980):125–29.

Thomson, William. "New Math, New Science, New Music." *Music Educators Journal* (March 1967):30.

———. "The Core Committment in Theory and Literature for Tomorrow's Musician." *College Music Symposium* (Fall 1970):35–45.

Walton, Charles. "Three Trends in the Teaching of Theory." *Music Educators Journal* (November/December 1961):73–76.

———. "A Visit to a Theory Class." *Music Educators Journal* (April/May 1965):70–74.

Watson, Walter, "New Approach to Teaching Theory." *Music Journal* (March 1966):98.

Werner, W. K. "Music Theory: Pedagogical Philosophies at the Munich Hochschule für Musik." *American Music Teacher* (April/May 1972):36–37.

Willoughby, David. *Comprehensive Musicianship and the Undergraduate Music Curricula.* MENC, 1971.

———. "Comprehensive Musicianship: Some Encouraging Words." *College Music Symposium* (Spring 1982):55–64.

3. Mind Training

FUNDAMENTALS TEXTBOOKS

Benward, Bruce, and Jackson, Barbara Garvey. *Practical Beginning Theory.* 5th ed. W. C. Brown, 1983.

Clough, John. *Scales, Intervals, Keys, and Triads.* 2nd ed. Norton, 1983. Programmed format; excellent ordering and pacing; includes rhythm and part-writing.

Duncan, James, and Ochse, Orpha. *Fundamentals of Music Theory.* Holt, Rinehart and Winston, 1983.

Hanson, John. *Music Fundamentals Workbook.* Longman, 1979.

Harder, Paul O. *Basic Materials in Music Theory.* 5th ed. Allyn and Bacon, 1982. Includes rhythm and pitch; very thorough; does intervals before scales.

Howard, Bertrand. *Fundamentals of Music Theory.* Harcourt, Brace & World, 1966. Very good; programmed.

Irwin, Phyllis. *Music Fundamentals: A Performance Approach.* Holt, Rinehart and Winston, 1982. Includes singing and keyboard exercises.

Kiely, Dennis K. *Essentials of Music for New Musicians.* Prentice-Hall, 1975.

Lefkoff, Gerald. *Reading and Writing Intervals: A Self-Instruction Book.* Glyphic Press, 1980.

Mankin, Linda, et al. *Prelude to Musicianship: Fundamental Concepts and Skills.* Holt, Rinehart and Winston, 1979. Includes a book of worksheets.

Manoff, Tom. *The Music Kit.* Norton, 1976. A very creative group of materials including workbook, rhythm reader, scorebook (a brief anthology), and four small records.

Montgomery, Michael F. *Music: A Step-by-Step Guide to the Foundations of Musicianship.* Prentice-Hall, 1981. One of the best nonprogrammed texts; very clearly and engagingly written.

Ottman, Robert, and Mainous, Frank D. *Programmed Rudiments of Music.* Prentice-Hall, 1979.

Reed, H. Owen, and Sidnell, Robert G. *The Materials of Music Composition.* Book 1: *Fundamentals;* book 2: *Exploring the Parameters.* Addison-Wesley, 1978, 1980.

Steele, Janet, and McDowell, Bonney. *Elementary Musicianship.* Knopf, 1981. Includes ear-training material.

Winold, Allen, and Rehm, John. *Introduction to Music Theory.* 2nd ed. Prentice-Hall, 1979. Semi-programmed; includes music literature and ear training.

NOTATION AND CALLIGRAPHY

Cundick, Robert, and Dayley, Newell. *Music Manuscript.* Sonos Music Resources, 1974.

Donato, Anthony. *Preparing Music Manuscript.* Prentice-Hall, 1963.

Read, Gardner. *Music Notation.* Crescendo, 1969.

———. *Modern Rhythmic Notation.* Indiana University Press, 1978.

Roemer, Clinton. *The Art of Music Copying.* Roerick Music, 1973. Very detailed and authoritative; a standard text.

Stone, Kurt. *Music Notation in the Twentieth Century: A Practical Guidebook.* Norton, 1981. The definitive book on contemporary practice.

Warfield, Gerald. *How to Write Music Manuscript (in Pencil)*. McKay, 1977. Very practical.

HARMONY TEACHING

Appledorn, Mary Jeanne. "In Quest of the Roman Numeral." *College Music Symposium* (Fall 1970):47–51. A defense of roman numerals.

Austin, John C. "A Survey of the Influence of Heinrich Schenker on American Music Theory and its Pedagogy Since 1940." M.M. thesis, North Texas State University, 1974.

Beach, David. "Schenker's Theories: A Pedagogic View." In *Aspects of Schenkerian Theory*. Yale University Press, 1982.

Block, Adrienne Fried. "And Now We Begin—A Survey of Recent Theory Texts." *College Music Symposium* (Fall 1973):97–105. A comparison of different types of texts.

DeLone, Richard P. "On the Question of Music Reading." *Musical Cue* (May 1967).

Fletcher, Stanley. "Music Reading Reconsidered as a Code-Learning Problem." *Journal of Music Theory* (March 1957):76–96.

Gould, Murry. "Schenker's Theory in the World of Teacher and Student." *College Music Symposium* (Spring 1975):133–49.

Harris, John M. "The Pedagogical Development of College Harmony Textbooks in the United States." D.M.A. dissertation, University of Texas at Austin, 1969.

Hurwitz, Robert. "A Critical Examination of Some Traditional Approaches to Music Theory." Paper presented at the Annual Meeting of the Society for Music Theory, Minneapolis, October 1978. Presents carefully worked out definitions of familiar terminology.

Jones, Robert P. "The Design and Application of a Model for the Assessment and Development of College Harmony Texts." Ed.D. dissertation, University of Virginia, 1977.

Joseph, Charles. "Classroom Use of Composer's Sketches." Paper presented at the Annual Meeting of the College Music Society, Cincinnati, October 1981.

Komar, Arthur. "Schenkerian Analysis and Classroom Harmony Pedagogy." Paper presented at the Annual Meeting of the College Music Society, Denver, November 1980.

Kraft, Leo. "A New Approach to Species Counterpoint." *College Music Symposium* (Spring 1981):60–66.

Kudlawiec, Dennis P. "The Application of Schenkerian Concepts of Musical Structure to the Analysis Segment of Basic Theory Courses at the College Level." Ed.D. dissertation, University of Illinois, 1970.

Lewin, David. "An Interesting Global Rule for Species Counterpoint." *In Theory Only* 6/8 (March 1983):19–44. Discussion of rules for writing musical as well as correct exercises.

Lieberman, Ira. "The Music Theory Teacher and the Elements of Music." *College Music Symposium* (Fall 1972):20–28.

Loach, Donald. "A Stylistic Approach to Species Counterpoint." *Journal of Music Theory* (November 1957):181–200.

Müller-Hartman, Robert. "On Teaching Harmony." *Music & Letters* (October 1947):364–68.

Novak, Saul. "Recent Approaches to the Study of Harmony." *Perspectives of New Music* (Spring/Summer 1964):150–58.

Rogers, Michael R. "A Critique of *Sonic Design*." Paper presented at the Central Midwest Theory Society, University of Iowa, April 1977.

Rothgeb, John. "Schenkerian Theory: Its Implication for the Undergraduate Curriculum" *Music Theory Spectrum* (1981):142–49.

Salop, Arnold. "J. S. Bach: The Chorale Harmonizations and the Principles of Harmony." In *Studies on the History of Musical Style*. Wayne State University Press, 1971.

Smith, F. J. "Traditional Harmony? A Radical Question." *Music Review* (1974):63–75.

"The Teaching of Traditional Harmony." *Australian Journal of Music Education* (October 1978):39–46.

Thompson, David. *A History of Harmonic Theory in the United States*. Kent State University Press, 1980. The evolution of harmony textbooks up to the 1960s.

HARMONY TEXTBOOKS

Aldwell, Edward, and Schachter, Carl. *Harmony and Voice Leading*. 2 vols. with workbooks. Harcourt Brace Jovanovich, 1978, 1979. Heavily influenced by Schenker.

Benjamin, Thomas, et al. *Techniques and Materials of Tonal Music: With an Introduction to Twentieth-Century Techniques*. 2nd ed. Houghton Mifflin, 1979. In outline format; a neutral theoretical bias; good summaries of topics in appendices.

Forte, Allen. *Tonal Harmony in Concept and Practice*. 3rd ed. Holt, Rinehart and Winston, 1979. Some Schenkerian orientation; exercises based on real music with stress on part-writing and voice leading.

Goldman, Richard Franko. *Harmony in Western Music*. Norton, 1965. A theoretical treatise and text; stresses root-movement principles and a history of chromaticism.

Green, Douglas. *Harmony through Counterpoint*. New Century, 1970.

Harder, Paul O. *Harmonic Materials in Tonal Music*. 4th ed. 2 vols.

Allyn and Bacon, 1980. Traditional vertical approach; programmed format; includes cassette tapes of many examples.

Lester, Joel. *Harmony in Tonal Music.* 2 vols. with workbooks. A combination of traditional and Schenkerian approaches.

McBeth, W. Francis. *Helpful New Ideas for the Understanding of Eighteenth Century Harmony.* Southern Music, 1979. A brief supplementary aid for students.

McHose, Allen. *The Contrapuntal Harmonic Technique of the Eighteenth Century.* Appleton-Century-Crofts, 1947.

———. *Basic Principles of the Technique of Eighteenth- and Nineteenth-Century Composition.* Appleton-Century-Crofts, 1951.

Ottman, Robert W. *Elementary Harmony; Advanced Harmony.* 3rd ed. Prentice-Hall, 1983. Traditional approach including related ear-training and keyboard drills.

Piston, Walter, *Harmony.* 4th ed., rev. and enl. by Mark DeVoto. Norton, 1978. A standard classic; traditional approach.

Ratner, Leonard G. *Harmony: Structure and Style.* McGraw-Hill, 1962. Based on functional families.

Sadai, Yizhak. *Harmony: In Its Systematic and Phenomenological Aspects.* Jerusalem: Yanetz Ltd., n.d.

Siegmeister, Elie. *Harmony and Melody.* 2 vols. with workbooks. Wadsworth, 1965, 1966. Alternates chapters between harmony and melody but without integration of the two.

Smith, Leland. *Handbook of Harmonic Analysis.* San Andreas Press, 1979. An excellent text for advanced harmony.

Spencer, Peter. *The Practice of Harmony.* Prentice-Hall, 1983. Condensed explanations with many workbook exercises.

Thostenson, Marvin S. *Fundamentals, Harmony, and Musicianship.* W. C. Brown, 1963. Includes a complete ear-training (with sight-singing) program.

COUNTERPOINT TEXTBOOKS

Benjamin, Thomas. *The Craft of Modal Counterpoint: A Practical Approach.* Schirmer Books, 1979. Sixteenth-century style (Palestrina); non-species approach.

Fux, J. J. *The Study of Counterpoint.* Translated and edited by Alfred Mann. Norton, 1943. From the classic treatise, *Gradus ad Parnassum* (1725); still amazingly useable and useful as a general counterpoint text; the original species approach.

Horsley, Imogene. *Fugue: History and Practice.* Free Press, 1966. Includes a useful workbook.

Kennan, Kent. *Counterpoint.* 2nd ed. With workbook. Prentice-Hall, 1972. The standard eighteenth-century style (Bach); strict species approach.

Marquis, Welton. *Twentieth-Century Music Idioms*. Greenwood Press, 1964. Both extended tonal and non-tonal styles represented.

Merriman, Margarita. *A New Look at Sixteenth-Century Counterpoint*. University Press of America, 1982.

Norden, Hugo. *Fundamental Counterpoint*. Crescendo, 1969. Species approach.

————. *Foundation Studies in Fugue*. Crescendo, 1977.

Oldroyd, George. *The Technique and Spirit of Fugue*. Oxford University Press, 1948.

Salzer, Felix, and Schachter, Carl. *Counterpoint in Composition: The Study of Voice Leading*. McGraw-Hill, 1969. The Schenkerian approach in counterpoint; tonal but completely astylistic.

Soderlund, Gustave. *Direct Approach to Counterpoint in Sixteenth-Century Style*. Appleton-Century-Crofts, 1947.

Westergaard, Peter. *An Introduction to Tonal Theory*. Norton, 1975. A blend of Fux and Schenker for beginning theory students; includes a theory of rhythm and perceptive chapter on musical performance.

COMPREHENSIVE MUSICIANSHIP TEXTBOOKS

Benward, Bruce. *Music in Theory and Practice*. 2nd ed. With workbooks. W. C. Brown, 1981. Includes historical style but not chronological ordering.

Brandt, William, et al. *The Comprehensive Study of Music*. Harper & Row, 1977–. Includes a core text, *Basic Principles of Music Theory;* 5 vols. of anthologies (all style periods); corresponding history/theory texts; and additional materials (not all available yet).

Carter, Earl, ed. *Workbook: Theory I. Workbook: Theory II.* Manhattan School of Music, 1982. Cover rudiments, melodic harmonization, counterpoint, form, etc.

Christ, William, et al. *Materials and Structure of Music*. 3rd ed. 2 vols. with workbooks. Prentice-Hall, 1981. Astylistic; excellent material on melodic analysis.

Cogan, Robert, and Escot, Pozzi. *Sonic Design: The Nature of Sound and Music*. Prentice-Hall, 1976. Perhaps the most innovative book of recent years; uses analytical categories of space (register and melody); language (pitch); time (rhythm and proportion); and color (timbre and acoustics); range of ideas is very sophisticated.

Cooper, Paul. *Perspectives in Music Theory: An Historical-Analytical Approach*. 2nd ed. With workbooks. Harper & Row, 1981. Follows a chronological order through all style periods; anthology within the text.

Duckworth, William, and Brown, Edward. *Theoretical Foundations of Music.* Wadsworth, 1978. Follows historical sequence; parametric analysis approach.

Kraft, Leo. *Gradus.* 2 vols. With anthologies. Norton, 1976. Combines harmony, counterpoint, music literature, and analysis; all periods but not strictly chronological; very insightful and well-written commentary; excellent sightsinging material in vol. 1.

COMPOSITION (ARTICLES AND TEXTBOOKS)

Benjamin, Thomas. "On Teaching Composition." Paper presented at the Annual Meeting of the College Music Society, Denver, November 1980.

Bennett, Stan. "The Process of Musical Creator: Interviews with 8 Composers." *Journal of Research in Music Education* (Spring 1976):3–13.

Brindle, Reginald Smith. *Serial Composition.* Oxford University Press, 1966.

Cope, David. *New Music Composition.* Schirmer Books, 1977. Extremely wide range of styles and projects.

Etler, Alvin. *Making Music: An Introduction to Theory.* Harcourt Brace Jovanovich, 1974. Teaching beginning theory students through a composition approach based on the consonance/dissonance system of Hindemith.

Jones, George Thaddeus. *Music Composition: A Manual for Training the Young Composer.* Summy-Birchard, 1963.

Kohs, Ellis B. *Musical Composition: Projects in Ways and Means.* Scarecrow Press, 1980.

Kramer, Jonathan D. "Teaching Music to the Amateur Through Composition." *Proceedings of the American Society of University Composers* (1976/77):60–65.

Law, Daniel. "Teaching Contemporary Composition Theory: The Use of Simulation Games in the College Level Music Theory Course." Ph.D. dissertation, Northwestern University, 1979.

"Learning to Compose." *Composer* (Winter 1980/81):1–20. Five articles from various countries.

Mandelbaum, Joel. "Should Composition Be Taught in Universities, and if so, How?" *Proceedings of the American Society of University Composers* (1969):57–87.

Schoenberg, Arnold. *Models for Beginners in Composition: Syllabus, Music Examples and Glossary.* Rev. ed. Belmont, 1972.

Seltzer, George. *Music Making.* McFarland, 1983. Composition activities for non-music majors.

Strange, Allen. *Electronic Music: Systems, Techniques, and Controls.* 2nd ed. W. C. Brown, 1982. Textbook for using an electronic studio.

Westergaard, Peter. "What do you, as a Composer Try to get the Student to hear in a Piece of Music?" *Proceedings of the American Society of University Composers* (1966):59–81.

Wuorinen, Charles. *Simple Composition.* Longman, 1979. The twelve-tone and time-point systems.

Yannatos, James. *Exploration in Musical Materials: A Working Approach to Making Music.* Prentice-Hall, 1978. An astylistic orientation for learning theory through composition; assumes no background.

KEYBOARD

Berkowitz, Sol. *Improvisation through Keyboard Harmony.* Prentice-Hall, 1975.

Brings, Allen, et al. *A New Approach to Keyboard Harmony.* Norton, 1979. An excellent and versatile course of study.

Cho, Gene J. *Melody Harmonization at the Keyboard.* Kendall/Hunt, 1983.

Duckworth, Guy. *Keyboard Musicianship.* Free Press, 1970.

Lloyd, Ruth, and Lloyd, Norman. *Creative Keyboard Musicianship.* Dodd, Mead, 1975.

Lowder, Jerry E. "How Comprehensive Musicianship Is Promoted in Group Piano Instruction." *Music Educators Journal* (November 1973):56–58.

Shumway, Stanley. *Harmony and Ear Training at the Keyboard.* 2nd ed. W. C. Brown, 1976.

Trantham, William E. "A Music Theory Approach to Beginning Piano Instruction for the College Music Major." *Journal of Research in Music Education* (Spring 1970):49–56.

Wittlich, Gary E., and DeLone, Richard P. *Harmonic Patterns and Elaboration: for Keyboard, Other Instrumentalists, and Voice.* Knopf, forthcoming.

TWENTIETH-CENTURY MUSIC

Brindle, Reginald Smith. *The New Music: Avant Garde Since 1945.* Oxford University Press, 1975.

Cope, David H. *New Directions in Music.* 2nd ed. W. C. Brown, 1976. A survey of experimental and avant-garde music.

Dallin, Leon. *Techniques of Twentieth Century Composition.* 3rd ed. W. C. Brown, 1974.

"Differing Approaches to the Teaching of Contemporary Techniques." *College Music Symposium* (Fall 1965):111–18. Group discussion.

Faulk, Harry R. "A Curriculum Guide Designed to Teach a Basic

Knowledge of Electronic Music to Undergraduate Music Education Students." D.A. dissertation, Carnegie-Mellon University, 1978.

Griffiths, Paul. *A Concise History of Avant-Garde Music from Debussy to Boulez.* Oxford University Press, 1978. Good mixture of history and theory.

———. *A Guide to Electronic Music.* Thames and Hudson, 1979.

———. *Modern Music: The Avant Garde since 1945.* George Braziller, 1981. Especially good on the evolution of total serialism.

Harder, Paul O. *Bridge to Twentieth-Century Music.* Allyn and Bacon, 1973. A study of impressionism and its antecedents; programmed format.

Hyde, Martha MacLean. "Schoenberg's Sketches and the Teaching of Atonal Theory." *College Music Symposium* (Fall 1980):130–37. A persuasive plea for considering fully the differences between tonal and atonal music and analytical techniques in teaching approaches.

Kramer, Jonathan. "Can You Teach Anti-Academy Music in the Academy?" *Numus West* (1974):64–67. A very thought-provoking outline for presenting avant-garde music; gives specific pieces and specific teaching techniques.

Machlis, Joseph. *Introduction to Contemporary Music.* 2nd ed. Norton, 1979. A music literature/appreciation approach (biographical background, etc.).

Nyman, Michael. *Experimental Music: Cage and Beyond.* Studio Vista, 1974.

Persichetti, Vincent. *Twentieth-Century Harmony.* Norton, 1961. A compositional approach.

Peyser, Joan. *Twentieth-Century Music: The Sense Behind the Sound.* Schirmer Books, 1980. Concentrates on Stravinsky, Schoenberg, and Varese.

Rockwell, John. *All American Music: Composition in the Late Twentieth Century.* Knopf, 1983. Recent trends and influences crossing between genres.

Taylor, Clifford. "Contemporary Music." *College Music Symposium* (Fall 1972):34–40.

Ulehla, Ludmilla. *Contemporary Harmony: Romanticism through the Twelve-Tone Row.* Free Press, 1966.

Vander Ark, Sherman D. "Programmed Instruction in Twentieth Century Music: A Feasibility Study." Ph.D. dissertation, Ohio State University, 1970.

Wittlich, Gary E., ed. *Aspects of Twentieth-Century Music.* Prentice-Hall, 1975. A very comprehensive parametric approach; no historical context; chapters on form, texture, and set theory are particularly strong; stress on concepts and analytical techniques.

Suggested Reading

MUSIC LITERATURE/APPRECIATION

DeLone, Richard P. *Music: Patterns and Style.* Addison-Wesley, 1970. Theory orientation.

Funes, Donald, and Munson, Kenneth. *Musical Involvement.* Harcourt Brace Jovanovich, 1975. Universals-of-music approach; no history or style.

Hopkins, Antony. *Understanding Music.* Dent, 1979. Miscellaneous topics for the non-specialist.

Komar, Arthur. *Music and Human Experience.* Schirmer Books, 1980.

Levy, Kenneth. *Music: A Listener's Introduction.* Harper & Row, 1983. Chronological.

Manoff, Tom. *Music: A Living Language.* Norton, 1982. Excellent comparisons and connections drawn between style traits and periods; excellent teacher's manual.

Neumeyer, David, and Wennerstrom, Mary. *An Introduction to the Literature and Structure of Music.* Waveland Press, 1980. Uses listener's score diagrams.

O'Brien, James. *Non-Western Music for the Western Listener.* Kendall/Hunt, 1977.

Ratner, Leonard G. *Music: The Listener's Art.* 3rd ed. McGraw-Hill, 1977. A central set of concepts is applied to all style periods.

Thomson, William. *Music for Listeners.* Prentice-Hall, 1978. Organized chronologically within each genre.

ANTHOLOGIES OF MUSIC

Arlin, Mary I., et al. *Music Sources.* Prentice-Hall, 1979. Excerpts and complete movements.

Benjamin, Thomas, et al. *Music for Analysis.* Houghton Mifflin, 1978. Excerpts and short whole pieces.

Berry, Wallace, and Chudacoff, Edward. *Eighteenth-Century Imitative Counterpoint.* Appleton-Century-Crofts, 1969.

Brandt, William, et al. *The Comprehensive Study of Music.* Harper's College Press, 1977–80. Five volumes covering all style periods and piano reductions.

Burkhart, Charles. *Anthology for Musical Analysis.* 3rd ed. Holt, Rinehart and Winston, 1978. Chronological span with brief historical background and analytical questions.

Davison, Archibald, and Apel, Willi. *Historical Anthology of Music.* 2 vols. Harvard University Press, 1949. Through pre-classical; emphasis on early music.

Devine, George F., and Starr, William J. *Music Scores Omnibus.* 2 vols. Prentice-Hall, 1964. Excellent for style identification practice.

Godwin, Jocelyn. *Schirmer Scores.* Schirmer Books, 1975. Organized by genre.

Hardy, Gordon, and Fish, Arnold. *Music Literature.* 2 vols. (homophony; polyphony). Dodd, Mead, 1966. Common-practice period.

Johnson, Roger, ed. *Scores: An Anthology of New Music.* Schirmer Books, 1981. Recent experimental pieces with performance instructions.

Kamien, Roger. *The Norton Scores.* 3rd ed., enl. 2 vols. Norton, 1977. All style periods; uses highlighted shading.

Kirby, F. E. *Music in the Classic Period: An Anthology with Commentary.* Schirmer Books, 1979.

Lang, Paul Henry. *The Symphony: 1800–1900.* Norton, 1969.

Palisca, Claude, ed. *Norton Anthology of Western Music.* 2 vols. Norton, 1980. Keyed to Grout's *History of Western Music.*

Parrish, Carl, and Ohl, John F. *Masterpieces of Music Before 1750.* Norton, 1951.

Turek, Ralph. *Analytical Anthology of Music.* Knopf, 1983. A complete analysis textbook with anthology; includes detailed analysis questions, historical background, and composer style traits; optional student answer book; unusually creative.

Ward-Steinman, David, and Ward-Steinman, Susan L. *Comparative Anthology of Musical Forms.* 2 vols. Wadsworth, 1976. Arranged by genre; analogies made with other arts; strong CM philosophy.

Wennerstrom, Mary H. *Anthology of Twentieth-Century Music.* Prentice-Hall, 1969. Includes study questions.

———. *Anthology of Music Structure & Style.* Prentice-Hall, 1983. All periods and types; includes a brief but useful study guide.

MISCELLANEOUS

Adler, Samuel. *The Study of Orchestration.* Norton, 1982. Includes workbook and tape of examples.

Amadie, Jimmy. *Harmonic Foundation for Jazz and Popular Music.* Thornton Publications, 1982. Chord voicings, melody harmonization, etc.

Arnold, F. T. *The Art of Accompaniment from a Thorough-Bass as Practiced in the Seventeenth and Eighteenth Centuries.* 2 vols. Dover, 1965. Historical treatise on figured-bass realization.

Backus, John. *The Acoustical Foundations of Music.* Norton, 1969.

Blake, Ran. "Teaching Third Stream." *Music Educators Journal* (December 1976):30–33. Teaching jazz theory at the New England Conservatory.

Blatter, Alfred. *Instrumentation/Orchestration.* Longman, 1980.

Block, Adrienne Fried. "Teaching Music History: An Interview with

William Kimmel." *College Music Symposium* (Spring 1980):105–19. Ideas applicable to music theory also.

Bradshaw, Merrill. "Improvisation and Comprehensive Musicianship." *Music Educators Journal* (January 1980):113–15.

Burton, Steven Douglas. *Orchestration*. Prentice-Hall, 1982. Includes workbook and instructor's manual.

Crowder, Laurin P. "The Development of a Self-Tutoring Program in the Fundamentals of Orchestration." Ph.D. dissertation, Louisiana State University and Agricultural and Mechanical College, 1971.

Davies, John. *The Psychology of Music*. Hutchinson, 1978. An interesting, helpful, and very readable introduction.

Hall, Donald E. *Musical Acoustics: An Introduction*. Wadsworth, 1980. Emphasizes many music-theory related issues.

Kennan, Kent. *The Technique of Orchestration*. 2nd ed. Prentice-Hall, 1970. With workbooks.

Lindley, Mark. "Preface to a Graduate Course in the History of Music Theory." *College Music Symposium* (Fall 1982):83–102. Good bibliography.

Martin, F. David, and Jacobus, Lee A. *The Humanities Through the Arts*. 2nd ed. McGraw-Hill, 1978. Interdisciplinary approach; with study guide.

Poultney, David. *Studying Music History: Learning, Reasoning and Writing about Music History and Literature*. Prentice-Hall, 1983. A student supplement for history textbooks.

Riley, James R. *Graduate Music Theory Review*. Southern Music, 1980. In brief outline form.

Salzman, Eric, and Sahl, Michael. *Making Changes: A Practical Guide to Vernacular Harmony*. Schirmer Books, 1982. Harmonic language and style in jazz, folk, country, blues, rag, rock, and pop.

Stanton, Kenneth. *Jazz Theory: A Creative Approach*. Taplinger, 1982.

Ultan, Lloyd. *Music Theory: Problems and Practices in the Middle Ages and Renaissance*. University of Minnesota Press, 1977. A beginning theory text; with workbook/anthology.

Wold, Milo, and Cykler, Edmund. *An Introduction to Music and Art in the Western World*. 7th ed. W. C. Brown, 1983.

4. Musical Analysis

Aldrich, Putnam. "An Approach to the Analysis of Renaissance Music." *Music Review* (1969):1–21.

Ballentine, Christopher. "Towards an Aesthetic of Experimental Music." *Musical Quarterly* (April 1977):224–46.

Barra, Donald. *The Dynamic Performance: Guide to Musical Expression and Interpretation*. Prentice-Hall, 1982. Relationships between analysis and performance.

Bashour, Frederick J. "Towards a More Rigorous Methodology For the Analysis of the Pre-Tonal Repertory." *College Music Symposium* (Fall 1979):140–53.

Batstone, Philip. "Musical Analysis as Phenomenology." *Perspectives of New Music* (1969):94–110.

Battock, Gregory. *Breaking the Sound Barrier*. E. P. Dutton, 1981. An anthology of essays about recent music.

Beach, David. "A Schenker Bibliography." *Journal of Music Theory* (1969):2–37. "A Schenker Bibliography: 1969–1979." *JMT* (Fall 1979):275–86.

———. "Pitch Structure and the Analytic Process in Atonal Music: An Interpretation of the Theory of Sets." *Music Theory Spectrum* (1979):7–22.

Beeson, Roger. "Background and Model: A Concept in Musical Analysis." *Music Review* (1971):349–59.

Bent, Ian D. "Current Methods in Stylistic Analysis, Summary of Remarks." *Report of the Eleventh Congress, 1972*. International Musicological Society, vol. 1. Copenhagen: Wilhelm Hansen, 1974.

———. "Analysis." *The New Grove Dictionary of Music and Musicians*. Edited by Stanley Sadie. Macmillan and Co., 1980. The single best summary of the history and methods of analysis; includes a detailed bibliography.

Berger, Karol. "Tonality and Atonality in the Prologue to Orlando di Lasso's Prophetiae Sibyllarum: Some Methodological Problems in Analysis of Sixteenth-Century Music." *Musical Quarterly* (October 1980):484–504.

Bernstein, Leonard. *The Unanswered Question: Six Talks at Harvard*. Harvard University Press, 1976. Music and language comparisons and evolution of nineteenth- and twentieth-century music. These lectures in their recorded form are frequently beneficial for classroom demonstrations.

Berry, Wallace. *Form in Music*. Prentice-Hall, 1966.

———. *Structural Functions in Music*. Prentice-Hall, 1976. An advanced text in tonality, texture, and rhythm.

Carpenter, Patricia. "The Musical Object." *Current Musicology* (1967):56–87. A stimulating philosophical discussion.

Clifton, Thomas. *Music As Heard: A Study in Applied Phenomenology*. Yale University Press, 1983. Penetrating analysis of musical time, space, and related issues.

———. "The Poetics of Musical Silence." *Musical Quarterly* (April 1976):163–81.

Cogan, Robert. "Reconceiving Theory: The Analysis of Tone Color." *College Music Symposium* (1975):52–69.

Cone, Edward T. "Analysis Today." *Musical Quarterly* (April 1960):172–88. Discusses distinctions between description, analysis, and prescription in twentieth-century music.

———. "Music: A View from Delft." *Musical Quarterly* (October 1961):439–53.

———. "Beyond Analysis." *Perspectives of New Music* (Fall/Winter 1967):33–51. Discusses problems of twelve-tone analysis. See the follow-up article by David Lewin, "Behind the Beyond," *PNM* (Spring/Summer 1969):59–72.

———. *Musical Form and Musical Performance.* Norton, 1968.

———. "Three Ways of Reading a Detective Story—or a Brahms Intermezzo." *Georgia Review* (Fall 1977):544–77. A comparison of analytical approaches.

———. "One Hundred Metronomes." *Journal of Aesthetic Education* (January 1979):53–68. An excellent and amusing discussion of the values of experimental music (and art).

Cooper, Grosvenor, and Meyer Leonard B. *The Rhythmic Structure of Music.* University of Chicago Press, 1960. Uses patterns of prosody and hierarchic levels.

Dahlhaus, Carl. "Some Models of Unity in Musical Form." *Journal of Music Theory* (1975):2–31.

———. *Analysis and Value Judgement.* Translated by Sigmund Levarie. Pendragon Press, 1983.

DeStwolinski, Gail. *Form and Content in Instrumental Music.* W. C. Brown, 1977.

Epstein, David. *Beyond Orpheus: Studies in Musical Structure.* MIT Press, 1979. Based on Schoenberg's concept of Grundgestalt (basic shape).

Erickson, Robert. *Sound Structure in Music.* University of California Press, 1975. A study of timbre.

Ernst, Roy E., and Green, Douglass M. *Structure and Performance.* Ergo Publications, 1978.

Flynn, George W. "Listening to Berio's Music." *Musical Quarterly* (July 1975):388–421.

Forte, Allen. "Schenker's Conception of Musical Structure." *Journal of Music Theory* (1959):1–30. The best brief summary of Schenker's ideas.

———. *The Structure of Atonal Music.* Yale University Press, 1973. A major work on set theory.

————. "Schoenberg's Creative Evolution: The Path to Atonality." *Musical Quarterly* (April 1978):133–76.

Forte, Allen, and Gilbert, Steven E. *Introduction to Schenkerian Analysis*. Norton, 1982. Very detailed and thorough textbook; includes an extensive teacher's manual.

George, Graham. *Tonality and Musical Structure*. London, 1970.

Green, Douglass M. *Form in Tonal Music: An Introduction to Analysis*. Holt, Rinehart and Winston, 1979.

Howell, Almonte. "An Essay in Structural Analysis." *Musical Quarterly* (January 1964):18–30.

Hutcheson, Jere T. *Musical Form and Analysis*. 2 vols. Allyn and Bacon, 1972, 1977. Programmed format.

Johnson, Douglass. "Beethoven Scholars and Beethoven's Sketches." *Nineteenth-Century Music* (July 1978):3–17.

Johnson, Theodore O. *An Analytical Survey of the Fifteen Two-Part Inventions by J. S. Bach*. University Press of America, 1982.

Jonas, Oswald. *Introduction to the Theory of Heinrich Schenker*. Translated by John Rothgeb. Longman, 1982. A summary written by a Schenker student and scholar in 1934.

Katz, Adele. "Heinrich Schenker's Method of Analysis." *Musical Quarterly* (July 1935):311–29.

Keller, Hans. "Strict Serial Technique in Classical Music." *Tempo* (Autumn 1955):12–24.

————. "Functional Analysis: Its Pure Application." *Music Review* (1957):202–6. A non-verbal system using recorded musical examples.

————. "Knowing Things Backwards." *Tempo* (Winter 1958):14–20.

Kerman, Joseph. "How We Got Into Analysis and How to Get Out." *Critical Inquiry* (1980):311–31.

Kidd, James. "Wit and Humor in Tonal Syntax." *Current Musicology* (1976):70–82.

Kohs, Ellis B. *Musical Form: Studies in Analysis and Synthesis*. Houghton Mifflin, 1976.

Kraehenbuhl, David. "Information as a Measure of the Experience of Music." *Journal of Aesthetics and Art Criticism* (June 1959):510–22.

Kramer, Jonathan. "Multiple and Non-Linear Time in Beethoven's Opus 135." *Perspectives of New Music* (1973):122–45.

————. "Moment Form in Twentieth Century Music." *Musical Quarterly* (April 1978):177–94.

Kresky, Jeffrey. *Tonal Music: Twelve Analytic Studies*. Indiana University Press, 1978. Corelli to Debussy.

Lang, Berel, ed. *The Concept of Style*. University of Pennsylvania

Press, 1979. A collection of essays on all the arts; see especially Leonard Meyer, "Toward a Theory of Style."

LaRue, Jan. "What Is Analysis." *Music Educators Journal* (October 1968):35–37.

———. *Guidelines for Style Analysis*. Norton, 1970. Parametric approach.

Lerdahl, Fred, and Jackendorf, Ray. *A Generative Theory of Tonal Music*. MIT Press, 1983. An analysis of musical structure based on Noam Chomsky's transformational grammar.

Levarie, Siegmund. *Musical Morphology: A Discourse and a Dictionary*. Kent State University Press, 1983. Brief essays on aspects of musical form.

Levy, Edward. "Analysis Applied to Performance." *College Music Symposium* (Spring 1979):128–38.

Madell, Geoffrey. "Thematic Unity and the Language of Music." *Music Review* (1962):30–33.

Mann, Michael. "Schenker's Contribution to Music Theory." *Music Review* 10 (February 1949):3–26.

Meyer, Leonard. *Emotion and Meaning in Music*. University of Chicago Press, 1956. A classic; based on a theory of musical expectation.

———. *Music: The Arts and Ideas*. University of Chicago Press, 1967.

———. *Explaining Music: Essays and Explorations*. University of California Press, 1973. Further development of the implication concept.

———. "Exploiting Limits: Creation, Archetypes, and Style Change." *Daedalus* (Spring 1980):177–205.

———. "Process and Morphology in the Music of Mozart." *Journal of Musicology* (January 1982):67–94.

———. *Style in Music: Theory, Analysis, and History*. Forthcoming.

Mitchell, William, and Salzer, Felix, eds. *The Music Forum*. 5 vols. Columbia University Press, 1967– . Essays in Schenkerian analysis.

Morgan, Robert. "On the Analysis of Recent Music." *Critical Inquiry* (1977):33–54. How analysis must be redefined to explain experimental music.

———. "Schenker and the Theoretical Tradition." *College Music Symposium* (Spring 1978):72–96.

———. "The Theory and Analysis of Tonal Rhythm." *Musical Quarterly* (October 1978):435–73.

Music Analysis. Basil Blackwell, 1982. A new journal from England.

Nordmark, Jan. "New Problems of Form and the Problem of Thematic Identities." *Journal of Music Theory* (1960):210–17.

Narmour, Eugene. *Beyond Schenkerism: The Need for Alternatives in Music Analysis.* University of Chicago Press, 1977. A study of the implication-realization model and deficiencies of Schenkerian analysis.

———. *The Melodic Structure of Tonal Music.* University of Chicago Press, forthcoming.

O'Grady, Terrence J. "Aesthetic Value in Indeterminate Music." *Musical Quarterly* (July 1981):366–81.

Perle, George. *Serial Composition and Atonality.* 4th ed. University of California Press, 1977. A standard reference.

Pike, Alfred. "Perception and Meaning in Serial Music." *Journal of Aesthetics and Art Criticism* (Fall 1963):55–61.

———. "The Theory of Unconscious Perception in Music: A Phenomenological Criticism." *Journal of Aesthetics and Art Criticism* (Summer 1967):395–400.

Pinkerton, Richard. "Information Theory and Melody." *Scientific American* 194/2 (February 1956):77–87.

Rahn, John. *Basic Atonal Theory.* Longman, 1980.

Ratner, Leonard. *Classic Music: Expression, Form, and Style.* Schirmer Books, 1980. Very comprehensive; includes views of theorists of the era.

Reti, Rudolph. *The Thematic Process in Music.* London, 1961.

Rogers, Michael R. "Chopin, Prelude in A Minor, Op. 28, No. 2." *Nineteenth-Century Music* (Spring 1981):244–50. Illustrates use of the golden section.

Rosen, Charles. *The Classical Style: Haydn, Mozart, Beethoven.* Norton, 1971. A masterpiece of analysis and energetic, elegant writing.

———. *Sonata Forms.* Norton, 1980.

Rowell, Lewis. *Thinking About Music.* University of Massachusetts Press, 1983.

Russell, Carlton. "The Analysis and Evaluation of Music: A Philosophical Inquiry." *Musical Quarterly* (April 1972):161–84.

Salzer, Felix. *Structural Hearing: Tonal Coherence in Music.* 2 vols. Dover, 1962. An interpretation of Schenkerian analysis.

Samson, Jim. *Music in Transition: A Study of Tonal Expansion and Atonality, 1900–1920.* Norton, 1977.

Schenker, Heinrich. *Der Freie Satz.* 2 vols. Translated by Ernst Oster. Longman, 1979.

Schueller, Herbert M. "The Aesthetic Implications of Avant-Garde Music." *Journal of Aesthetics and Art Criticism* (Summer 1977): 397–410.

Sessions, Roger. "Heinrich Schenker's Contribution." *Modern Music* 12/4 (May/June 1935):170–78.

Silbert, Doris. "Ambiguity in the String Quartets of Joseph Haydn." *Musical Quarterly* (October 1950):562–73.

Singer, Andre. "Kaleidoscope and Silly Putty." *Current Musicology* (1972):83–89.

Slatin, Sonia. "The Theories of Heinrich Schenker in Perspective." Ph.D. dissertation, Columbia University, 1967. An excellent study of the development of Schenker's ideas.

Temperley, Nicholas. "Testing the Significance of Thematic Relationships." *Music Review* (1961):177–80.

Thomson, William. "The Problem of Musical Analysis and Universals." *College Music Symposium* (1966):89–107.

———. "Style Analysis: or The Perils of Pigeonholes." *Journal of Music Theory* (1970):191–208.

Thurmond, James Morgan. *Note Grouping: A Method for Achieving Expression and Style in Musical Performance.* JMT Publications, 1982. Interrelationships of rhythm, phrasing, and interpretation.

Tovey, Donald. *Essays in Musical Analysis.* 6 vols. Oxford University Press, 1935–39.

Treitler, Leo. "Musical Analysis in an Historical Context." *College Music Symposium* (1966):75–88.

Walker, Alan. *A Study in Musical Analysis.* London, 1962. The thematic-unity school.

———. *An Anatomy of Musical Criticism.* London, 1966.

Wallace, Robert. "The Murders in the Rue Morgue and Sonata-Allegro Form." *Journal of Aesthetics and Art Criticism* (Summer 1977):457–63.

Walton, Charles. "Analyzing Analysis." *Music Educators Journal* (February 1969):57.

Warfield, Gerald. *Layer Analysis.* McKay, 1976. An introduction to a simplified version of Schenkerian analysis for undergraduates.

Wenk, Arthur. *Analyses of Twentieth-Century Music, 1940–1970.* MLA, 1975.

———. *Analyses of Nineteenth-Century Music, 1940–1975.* MLA, 1976.

———. *Analyses of Twentieth-Century Music, 1970–1975.* MLA, 1976.

Westergaard, Peter. "Some Problems in Rhythmic Theory and Analysis." *Perspectives of New Music* (Fall 1962):180–91.

White, John D. *The Analysis of Music.* Prentice-Hall, 1976. Parametric approach.

Wienpahl, Robert W. "Modality, Monality, and Tonality in the Sixteenth and Seventeenth Centuries." *Music & Letters* (October 1971):407–17; and (January 1972):59–73.

Wilkinson, Christopher. "Teaching Musical Analysis by Guided Design." Paper presented at the Mid-Atlantic Chapter Meeting of the College Music Society, University of North Carolina at Greensboro, March 1981.

Williams, B. M. "Time and the Structure of Stravinsky's Symphony in C." *Musical Quarterly* (July 1973):355–69.

Winold, Allen. "Competence and Performance in Language and Music." *Indiana Theory Review* (Spring 1979):13–29. Applications of linguistics to analysis.

Wright, Rayburn. *Inside the Score.* Kendor, 1982. Analyses of jazz charts.

Yanal, Robert J. "What is Set-Theoretical Musical Analysis?" *Journal of Aesthetics and Art Criticism* (Summer 1977):471–73.

Yeston, Maury. *The Stratification of Musical Rhythm.* Yale University Press, 1976.

———. *Readings in Schenker Analysis and other Approaches.* Yale University Press, 1977.

5. Ear Training

TEACHING EAR TRAINING

Abramson, Robert M. "A Demonstration of the 'Solfege rhythmique' of Jaques-Dalcroze." Paper presented at the Northeast Chapter Meeting of the College Music Society, State University of New York at Buffalo, March 1980.

Alvarez, Manuel. "A Comparison of Scalar and Root Harmonic Aural Perception Techniques." *Journal of Research in Music Education* (Winter 1980):229–35.

Autry, Mollie R. "A Study of the Effect of Hand Signs in the Development of Sight Singing Skills." D.M.A. dissertation, University of Texas at Austin, 1975.

Barnes, James W. "An Experimental Study of Interval Drill as it Affects Sight-Singing Skill." Ph.D. dissertation, Indiana University, 1960.

Benham, John L. "Rhythm Pedagogy by Syllabic Imitation Through Conceptualization of Regular and Irregular Metric and Beat Subdivisions." Ed.D. dissertation, University of Northern Colorado, 1971.

Blum, Beula B. "Solmization in Nineteenth-Century American Sight-Singing Instruction." Ed.D. dissertation, University of Michigan, 1968.

Boberg, Robert M. "Ear-Opening Experiences with Rhythm and Pitch." *Music Educators Journal* (December 1975):32–39.

Bolden, Joyce. "The Influence of Selected Factors in Growth in Sight Singing and Rhythmic Reading." Ph.D. dissertation, Michigan State University, 1967.

Bradley, Ian. "Effect of Student Musical Preference of a Listening Program in Contemporary Art Music." *Journal of Research in Music Education* (Fall 1972):344–53.

Bridges, Nicholas. "The Development of Aural Perception of Selected Percepts of Musical Form Utilizing Programmed Instruction." Ed.D. dissertation, Boston University, 1982.

Brink, Emily R. "A Cognitive Approach to the Teaching of Aural Skills Viewed as Applied Music Theory." Ph.D. dissertation, Northwestern University, 1980. Perceptual vs. structural approaches to ear training; one of the best pedagogy dissertations.

Buchanan, Walter. "Comparison of Fixed and Movable Solfege in Teaching Sight Singing from Staff." Ph.D. dissertation, University of Michigan, 1946.

Carlsen, James C. "Programmed Learning in Melodic Dictation." *Journal of Research in Music Education* (Summer 1964):139–48.

Chittum, Donald. "Diagnosis and Therapy in Interval Dictation." *Music Educators Journal* (September 1967):71–73.

Clarke, Henry Leland. "Home Syllables for Singing and Wordtones for Composition." Paper presented at the Northeast Chapter Meeting of the College Music Society, State University of New York at Buffalo, March 1980.

Collins, Irma. "Current Attitudes and Trends in the Teaching of Sight Singing in Higher Education." D.M.A. dissertation, Temple University, 1979.

Connor, Aikin O. "The Perception of Musical Intervals: The Theory of Property Arrays." Ed.D. dissertation, University of the Pacific, 1967.

Cope, David. "The Mechanics of Listening to Electronic Music." *Music Educators Journal* (October 1977):47–51. Practical classroom activities with specific compositions discussed.

Cowell, Richard. *The Theory of Expectation Applied to Musical Listening*. Cooperative Research Project No. H106 (Office of HEW), University of Illinois, 1966. Leonard Meyer's ideas extended to a classroom setting.

Danfelt, Lewis. "An Experimental Study of Sight Singing of Selected Groups of College Music Students." Ed.D. dissertation, Florida State University, 1970.

Daniels, Melvin L., Jr. "An Investigation of the Effectiveness of Programmed Learning in the Teaching of Harmonic Dictation in a Beginning College Music Theory Course." Ed.D. dissertation, North Texas State University, 1964.

Davidhazy, Andrew. "Hopsichords in the Theory Class." *Music Educators Journal* (September 1971):44–47.

Davidson, Jerry Frank. "An Investigation into the Systematic Application of Performance Objectives to Ear Training." Ph.D. dissertation, Northwestern University, 1982.

Dean, J. "A History of Solmization and a Comparative Study of American Pitch Verbalization Methods." M.M. thesis, University of Texas, 1965.

Domek, Richard C. "Teaching Aural Skills to High School Students." *Music Educators Journal* (January 1979):54–57.

Foltz, Roger E. "Sight Singing: Some New Ideas on an Old Institution." *College Music Symposium* (Fall 1976):95–100. A twentieth-century intervallic approach.

———. "Sight Singing in Relation to the Total Theory Program." *Indiana Theory Review* (Winter 1981):3–10.

Fowler, William L. "How to Augment Your Aural Assets." *Downbeat* (November 3, 1977):38–39.

Franklin, Elda. "Monotonism." *Music Educators Journal* (March 1981):56–58.

Funk, Curtis H. "An Investigation with Pedagogical Implications into the Aural Perception of Root in Trichords." D.Mus.Ed. dissertation, Indiana University, 1976.

Jeffries, Thomas B. "The Effects of Order of Presentation and Knowledge of the Results on the Aural Recognition of Melodic Intervals." *Journal of Research in Music Education* (Fall 1967): 179–90.

Johnson, Marjorie S. "A Comparison of Tonic Orientation Versus Isolated Interval Approach to Teaching Pitch Relations." Ph.D. dissertation, Catholic University of America, 1977.

Justus, Lane Dale. "Evaluation of an Innovative Instructional Design for Sight Singing." Ed.D. dissertation, University of Arizona, 1970.

Karl, Harold T. "The Effects of Melodic Dictation and Sight Singing on Music Reading Achievement." Ph.D. dissertation, Michigan State University, 1971.

Killam, Rosemary, and Lorton, Schubert. "Interval Recognition: Identification of Harmonic and Melodic Intervals." *Journal of Music Theory* (Fall 1975):212–34.

Kuhn, Wolfgard. "CAI in Music Drill and Practice in Dictation." *College Music Symposium* (Fall 1974):89–101.

Lora, Doris. "Musical Pattern Perception." *College Music Symposium* (Spring 1979):166–82. Extensive references and bibliography.

Malm, William. "Teaching Rhythmic Concepts in Ethnic Music." *Music Educators Journal* (October 1972):95–99.

Marquis, James H. "A Study of Interval Problems in Sight-Singers'

Performance with Consideration of the Effects of Context." Ph.D. dissertation, University of Iowa, 1963.

Martin, Louis. "Solmization: Getting the Facts Straight." *Theory and Practice* (September 1978):21–25. An argument against the use of solfege.

Massinggale, George W. "A Study to Determine the Effect of a Program of Rhythmic Training on the Ability to Perform Music at Sight." Ph.D. dissertation, North Texas State University, 1979.

Multer, Walt. "Solmization and Musical Perception." *Theory and Practice* (February 1978):29–51. The definitive discussion of the pros and cons of moveable vs. fixed "do."

Music Perception. University of California Press, 1983. A new interdisciplinary journal covering theory, psychology, linguistics, neurology, artificial intelligence, physiology, ethology, etc.

Neidlinger, Robert J. "Bring Learning Theory to the Listening Lesson." *Music Educators Journal* (March 1972):52.

Nelson, John C. "A Comparison of Two Methods of Measuring Achievement in Sight Singing." Ph.D. dissertation, University of Iowa, 1970.

Ortmann, Otto. *Problems in the Elements of Ear Dictation.* Baltimore: Peabody Conservatory Publication, 1934.

Placek, Robert W. "Design and Trial of a Computer-Assisted Lesson in Rhythm." *Journal of Research in Music Education* (Spring 1974):13–23.

Rogers, Michael R. "Integration of Analytical and Aural Skills: Structural Analysis and Sight Singing." Paper presented at the National Conference on the Teaching of Music Theory, North Texas State University, July 1981.

————. "Beyond Intervals: The Teaching of Tonal Hearing." *Indiana Theory Review,* in press.

Rosner, Burton S., and Meyer, Leonard B. "Melodic Process and the Perception of Music." In *The Psychology of Music.* Edited by Diana Deutsch. Academic Press, 1982. Includes many other relevant articles (e.g., absolute pitch, information processing, performance, singing, listening, etc.).

Schafer, R. Murray. *Creative Music Education.* Schirmer, 1976. See especially the ear-cleaning exercises.

Scofield, William R. "The Construction and Validation of a Method for the Measurement of the Sight Singing Abilities of High School and College Students." Ph.D. dissertation, Michigan State University, 1980.

Sears, Margaret F. "Musical Listening Skills, Musical Insight and Visual-Auditory Perception: A Statistical Investigation of their Relationships." Ph.D. dissertation, Southern Illinois University, 1976.

Shannon, Don Wayne. "Aural-Visual Interval Recognition in Music Instruction: A Comparison of a Computer-Assisted Approach and a Traditional In-Class Approach." D.M.A. dissertation, University of Southern California, 1982.

Shatzkin, Merton. "A Review of Marjorie Scott Johnson: A Comparison of Tonic Orientation Versus Isolated Interval Approach to Teaching Pitch Relations." *Council for Research in Music Education* (Winter 1980):43–49.

Sherman, Robert, and Hill, Robert. "Aural and Visual Perception of Melody in Tonal and Atonal Environments." *Council for Research in Music Education* (Fall 1968):1–10.

Smith, Charles. "Duplets, Triplets, Quadruplets." *Instrumentalist* (April 1981):11–13. Practical advice for teaching rhythm.

Smith, James C. "A Performance Test of Kanable's 'A Program for Self-Instruction in Sight Singing.'." Ph.D. dissertation, Florida State University, 1968.

Spohn, Charles. "Programming the Basic Materials for Self-Instructional Development of Aural Skills." *Journal of Research in Music Education* (Fall 1963):91–98.

Starr, Lawrence. "Educating the Ear: Strategies for Teaching 20th Century Music Analysis." *Music Educators Journal* (November 1977):52–56.

Steckman, Harry. "The Development and Trial of a College Course in Music Literacy Based Upon the Kodaly Method." Ed.D. dissertation, University of Illinois, 1979.

Stockton, James Larry. "An Experimental Study of Two Approaches to the Development of Aural Meter Discrimination Among Students in a College Introductory Music Class." D.M.A. dissertation, Temple University, 1982.

Sudano, Gary R. "Perceptual Problems in Teaching Form and Analysis." *Music Educators Journal* (February 1979):48–51.

Szende, O. *Intervallic Hearing: Its Nature and Pedagogy.* Budapest: Akademiai Kiado, n.d.

Taylor, Jack A. "The Perception of Melodic Intervals within Melodic Context." Ph.D. dissertation, University of Washington, 1971.

Thackray, Rupert. "Some Thoughts on Aural Training." *Australian Journal of Music Education* (October 1975):25–30. An excellent summary of unusual and highly imaginative ear-training classroom activities.

Tucker, Gerald L. "The Influence of Isolated Rhythmic Drill on Growth in Sight Singing." D.Mus.Ed. dissertation, University of Oklahoma, 1969.

West, George. "An Experimental Study of Proficiency in Sight Sing-

ing a Series of Atonal Intervals with Accompanying Sonorities."
Ph.D. dissertation, Michigan State University, 1971.

Will, R. T. "The History and Development of Musical Dictation."
M.M. thesis, Eastman School of Music, 1939.

Winking, John T. "The Application of Monroe Beardsley's Theory of
Aesthetics to the Structuring of Music Listening Experiences."
Ed.D. dissertation, University of Illinois, 1977.

Wunsch, Ilse Gerda. "Brainwriting in the Theory Class: The Importance of Perception in Taking Dictation." *Music Educators Journal*
(September 1973):55–59.

DICTATION TEXTBOOKS

Benward, Bruce. *Ear Training: A Technique for Listening.* 2nd. ed.
W. C. Brown, 1983. Includes sections on melody, harmony, and
rhythm; with tapes.

Bockmon, Guy, and Starr, William J. *Perceiving Music: Problems in
Sight and Sound.* Harcourt, Brace & World, 1962. With records.

Brooks, Richard, and Warfield, Gerald. *Layer Dictation: A New
Approach to the Bach Chorales.* Longman, 1978. Begins with one-
voice, then two-voice melodic dictation, finally building to harmonic progressions; uses structural reductions and programmed
format with fold-up answers in the book.

Carlson, James C. *Melodic Perception: A Program for Self-Instruction.* McGraw-Hill, 1965. With tapes.

Hansen, Ted. *Twentieth-Century Harmonic and Aural Perception.*
University Press of America, 1982. For dictation and sightsinging.

Horacek, Leo, and Lefkoff, Gerald. *Programed Ear Training.* 4 vols.
Harcourt Brace Jovanovich, 1970. Intervals, chords, melody, and
rhythm; with tapes.

Kliewer, Vernon. *Aural Training: A Comprehensive Approach.* Prentice-Hall, 1974.

Kraft, Leo. *A New Approach to Ear Training: A Programmed
Course in Melodic Dictation.* Norton, 1967. Structural hearing;
answers in book; with tapes.

Kreter, Leo. *Sight and Sound: A Manual of Aural Musicianship.* 2
vols. Prentice-Hall, 1976.

Lefkoff, Gerald. *Audio Companion for Analyzed Examples of Four-
Part Harmony.* Glyphic Press, 1980. Recorded harmonic progressions for dictation practice.

McGaughey, Janet McLoud. *Practical Ear Training.* Allyn and Bacon, 1961.

Sherman, Robert W., and Knight, Morris H. *Aural Comprehension in Music.* 2 vols. McGraw-Hill, 1972. With records.

Thomson, William, and DeLone, Richard P. *Introduction to Ear Training.* Wadsworth, 1967. One of the few texts to use analytical supports.

Trubitt, Allen R., and Hines, Robert S. *Ear Training and Sight Singing: An Integrated Approach.* 2 vols. Schirmer Books, 1979, 1980. One of the few texts to combine dictation and sightsinging; with tapes.

Wittlich, Gary, and Humphries, Lee. *Ear Training: An Approach through Music Literature.* Harcourt Brace Jovanovich, 1974. One of the few texts to derive dictation material from *whole* and real pieces.

SIGHTSINGING TEXTBOOKS

Adler, Samuel. *Sight Singing: Pitch, Interval, Rhythm.* Norton, 1979. Intervallic approach for all styles; excellent course of study for rhythm.

Benward, Bruce. *Sightsinging Complete.* W. C. Brown, 1965. Contrived melodies.

Berkowitz, Sol, et al. *A New Approach to Sight Singing.* Rev. ed. Norton, 1976. Contrived examples with excellent pedagogical ordering; includes duets, improvisation studies, etc.

Cho, Gene J. *Melodic, Dyadic, and Harmonic Singing: Graded Exercises.* Kendall/Hunt, 1981. Good practice material; minor-la syllable system.

Cole, Samuel W., and Lewis, Leo R. *Melodia: A Course in Sight-Singing Solfeggio.* 4 books. Oliver Ditson, 1909. Very extensive set of contrived exercises.

Cooper, Paul. *Dimensions of Sight Singing: An Anthology.* Longman, 1981. Music literature in chronological order; includes a section of folk songs.

DeLone, Richard P. *Literature and Materials for Sightsinging.* Holt, Rinehart and Winston, 1981. Music literature in historical order; contains an excellent set of supplementary practice exercises and drills.

de Zeeuw, Anne Marie, and Foltz, Roger E. *Sight Singing and Related Skills.* Sterling Swift, 1975. Includes all style periods, intervals, rhythms.

———. *Sight Singing: Melodic Structures in Functional Tonality.* Sterling Swift, 1978.

Edlund, Lars. *Modus Novus: Studies in Reading Atonal Melodies.* Broude, 1963. Adds new interval patterns each chapter; some exercises and some literature.

———. *Modus Vetus: Sight Singing and Ear-Training in Major/Mi-*

nor Tonality. Broude, 1974. Composed exercises in carefully graduated order; includes rhythm, harmony, keyboard, etc.

Fish, Arnold, and Lloyd, Norman. *Fundamentals of Sight Singing and Ear Training*. Dodd, Mead & Co., 1964. Lots of simple-level material.

Ghezzo, Marta Arkossy. *Solfege, Ear Training, Rhythm, Dictation, and Music Theory: A Comprehensive Course*. University of Alabama Press, 1980. Individually packaged lessons; contrived melodies.

Gould, Murray J. *Paths to Musical Thought: An Approach to Ear Training through Sight Singing*. Holt, Rinehart and Winston, 1979. Contrived melodies; harmonic arpeggiations; trichords.

Hegyi, Erzsebet. *Solfege According to the Kodaly Concept*. 2 vols. Budapest: Editio Musica, 1975, 1979. A wealth of practice material in ear training, sightsinging, and musical memory based on the pentatonic scale and traditional tonal literature.

Herder, Ronald. *Tonal/Atonal: Progressive Ear Training, Singing, and Dictation Studies in Diatonic, Chromatic and Atonal Music*. Rev. ed. Continuo Music Press, 1977. Makes use of imaginary diatonic reference notes.

Hickman, David. *Music Speed Reading for Melodic Instruments*. Wimbledon Music, 1979. A method for training the eye to read notation in groups.

Hindemith, Paul. *Elementary Training for Musicians*. 2nd rev. ed. Associated Music Publishers, 1949.

Kliewer, Vernon. *Music Reading: A Comprehensive Approach*. 2 vols. Prentice-Hall, 1973. Includes some very advanced sight-reading material.

Lloyd, Norman; Lloyd, Ruth; and DeGaetani, Jan. *The Complete Sightsinger: A Stylistic and Historical Approach*. Harper & Row, 1980. An anthology of compositions for sightsinging.

McHose, Allen, and Tibbs, Ruth. *Sight-Singing Manual*. Appleton-Century-Crofts, 1957. Snippets of real pieces.

Ottman, Robert W. *Music for Sight Singing*. Prentice-Hall, 1967.

———. *More Music for Sight Singing*. Prentice-Hall, 1981. Real musical examples.

Préval, Martin. *Exercette*. Quebec: Les éditions Ad lib. inc., 1982. An ear-training computer with a touch-sensitive matrix.

Shrader, David L., and Scott, Carol R. *TAP Master*. Temporal Acuity Products. Not a text but a set of recorded rhythms against which a performance can be measured.

Starer, Robert. *Rhythmic Training*. MCA, 1969.

Thomson, William. *Advanced Music Reading*. Sonora Music, 1969. Real or imagined tonality frames used with highly chromatic and twentieth-century music literature.

————. *Introduction to Music Reading: Concepts and Applications.* 2nd ed. Wadsworth, 1981. The original tonality-frame approach.

Wedge, George. *Ear Training and Sight Singing.* Schirmer Books, 1921. Very exercisy but well organized in a programmed manner; uses tendency-tone concept.

Wehner, Walter L. *Rhythmic Sightsinging.* University Press of America, 1979.

6. Teaching Techniques

Arenson, Michael A. "A Model for the First Steps in the Development of Computer-Assisted Instruction Materials in Music Theory." Ph.D. dissertation, Ohio State University, 1976.

Arnold, Charles. "Use of Mood Effects in the Teaching of Music Theory." Ph.D. dissertation, Columbia University, 1952.

Benjamin, Thomas. "The Learning Process and Teaching." *College Music Symposium* (Fall 1982):120–32.

Boatwright, Howard. "Paul Hindemith as a Teacher." *Musical Quarterly* (July 1964):279–89.

Boehle, William. "Unlocking the Undergraduate Music Student." *Music Educators Journal* (February 1972):48–50.

Bower, Gordon H., and Hilgard, Ernest R. *Theories of Learning.* 5th ed. Prentice-Hall, 1981. The definitive summary of behavioral vs. cognitive theories.

Brand, Manny. "Toward Greater Teaching Effectiveness." *College Music Symposium* (Fall 1980):138–41.

"Computer-Assisted Instruction." *College Music Symposium* (Fall 1981):7–53. A collection of six articles on the history and recent developments in CAI.

Davis, James R. *Teaching Strategies for the College Classroom.* Westview Press, 1976. Discusses the four strategies of instructional systems, lectures, inquiry, and group process.

Davis, Samuel E. "Predicting Probable Failure in College-Level Music Theory Courses." Ed.D. dissertation, University of Montana, 1968.

Devine, Thomas G. *Teaching Study Skills: A Guide for Teachers.* Allyn and Bacon, 1981. Discusses thinking, academic ability, and intelligence as they affect academic success.

de Zeeuw, Anne. "Teaching College Music Theory Classes that Include Blind Students." *College Music Symposium* (Fall 1977):89–101.

Documentary Report of the Ann Arbor Symposium: National Symposium on the Applications of Psychology to the Teaching and

Learning of Music. MENC, 1981. Complete text of papers and responses by both psychologists and musicians.

Dressel, Paul L., and Marcus, Dora. *On Teaching and Learning in College.* Jossey-Bass, 1982.

Eble, Kenneth. *The Craft of Teaching: A Guide to Mastering the Professor's Art.* Jossey-Bass, 1976. Excellent advice on giving lectures, conducting discussions, etc.

Elrod, Wilburn T. "The Effects of Programmed Instruction on Achievement and Attitude of College Freshman Music Theory Students." Ed.D. dissertation, University of Illinois. 1971.

Emig, Sandra J. "The Relationships of Selected Musical, Academic, and Personal Factors to Performance in the Freshman and Sophomore Music Theory and Ear Training Sequences at the Ohio State University." Ph.D. dissertation, Ohio State University, 1978.

Eschman, Karl. *Teaching Music Theory.* Schirmer, 1965. Stresses fundamentals and harmony more than teaching ideas.

Fowler, Charles B. "Discovery: One of the Best Ways to Teach a Musical Concept." *Music Educators Journal* (October 1970):25–30.

Goldiamond, I., and Pliskoff, S. "Music Education and the Rationale Underlying Programmed Instruction." *Music Educators Journal* (February/March 1965):43.

Gordon, Edwin. *The Psychology of Music Teaching.* Prentice-Hall, 1971.

———. *Learning Sequence and Patterns in Music.* G.I.A. Publications, 1976.

Greer, R. Douglas. *Design for Music Learning.* Teachers College Press, 1980.

Griffel, L. Michael. "Teaching Music." In *Scholars Who Teach,* edited by Steven M. Cahn, pp. 193–216. Nelson-Hall, 1978. College-level teaching.

Gullette, Margaret Morganroth, ed. *The Art and Craft of Teaching.* Harvard-Danforth Center for Teaching and Learning, 1982. The best collection of practical advice that I have seen for college teachers; covers the first day in class, lecturing, questioning, grading, the rhythms of the semester, etc. Should be required reading for all theory teachers, especially beginners.

Hall, John F. *An Invitation to Learning and Memory.* Allyn and Bacon, 1982.

Hofstetter, Fred T. "Microelectronics and Music Education." *Music Educators Journal* (April 1979):34–45. A good introduction to current trends in CAI.

———. "Computer-Based Aural Training: The Guido System." *Journal of Computer-Based Instruction* (February 1981):84–92. See also the annual yearbook of CAI music articles.

Hogg, Merle. "Teaching Comprehensive Musicianship Using the Personalized System of Instruction." Paper presented at the Annual Meeting of the Society for Music Theory, Minneapolis, October 1978. Based on the positive reinforcement principles of psychologist Fred Keller and the behavior modification principles of B. F. Skinner.

Hoover, Suzanne R. "Nadia Boulanger." In *Masters: Portraits of Great Teachers,* edited by Joseph Epstein, pp. 88–102. Basic Books, 1981. Fascinating account of the personality and teaching techniques of the famous composition and musicianship mentor by a former student; see also the other equally fascinating accounts of famous university teachers.

Killam, Rosemary. "Papers About the NTSU CAI System." North Texas State University, 1981. A bibliography with reprints of all articles available from the author.

Killam, Rosemary; Baczewski, Philip; Bales, W. Kenton; and Bertsche, Steven. *CAI Workshop Guidebook.* North Texas State University, 1981. Twenty-five outlined units of instruction in do-it-yourself CAI authoring.

Knapper, Christopher. *Evaluating Instructional Technology.* John Wiley & Sons, 1980. Discussion of many types of teaching and learning systems, not just computer-based technology.

Kuhn, Wolfgard, and Lorton, Paul. "Computer Assisted Instruction in Music: Ten Years of Evolution." Paper presented at the Third World Conference on Computers in Education, Lausanne, Switzerland, July, 1981.

Linton, Stanley. "Newer Systems of Individualized Learning." *College Music Symposium* (Fall 1978):136–47.

McKeachie, Wilbert. *Teaching Tips: A Guide Book for the Beginning College Teacher.* 7th ed. Heath & Co., 1978. A standard reference filled with practical advice.

Mann, Richard, ed. *The College Classroom: Conflict, Change and Learning.* Wiley & Sons, 1970. Valuable essays on structuring a positive learning environment, group process, and group dynamics; detailed analysis of actual classroom situations.

Milton, Ohmer, and associates. *On College Teaching.* Jossey-Bass, 1978.

Murphy, Howard A. *Teaching Musicianship.* Coleman-Ross, 1950. Perhaps the first thorough theory pedagogy book; many issues are still timely; includes an excellent bibliography of pre-1950 articles and books on teaching theory.

Murphy, Judith. "National Symposium on the Applications of Psychology to the Teaching and Learning of Music." *Music Educators Journal* (March 1980):47–78. A summary of the important Ann Arbor meetings.

Music Educators Journal (January 1983). A whole issue devoted to technology and computers in teaching music.

Music Theory Research Newsletter. Reports on current trends in CAI, published by North Texas State University School of Music.

Olsen, Richard N. "Howard A. Murphy, Theorist and Teacher: His Influence on the Teaching of Basic Music Theory in American Colleges and Universities from 1940–1973." Ed.D. dissertation, University of Illinois, 1973.

O'Neil, Harold F., ed. *Computer-Based Instruction: A State-of-the-Art Assessment.* Academic Press, 1981.

Peters, G. David, and Eddins, John. *A Planning Guide to Successful Computer Instruction.* Champaign: Electronic Courseware Systems, 1981. Selection and evaluation of hardware and software.

Rogers, Michael R. "On the Teaching of Theory Teaching: A Selected Bibliography of Music Theory Pedagogy." *Indiana Theory Review* (Fall 1981):61–82.

———. "Preventive Medicine in Theory Teaching." *American Music Teacher* (April/May 1983):12–16.

Rosenstiel, Leonie. *Nadia Boulanger: A Life in Music.* Norton, 1982. The pre-eminent theory teacher of the twentieth century.

Shepherd, Arthur. " 'Papa' Goetschius in Retrospect." *Musical Quarterly* (July 1944):307–18.

Skilling, Hugh H. *Do You Teach? Views on College Teaching.* Holt, Rinehart and Winston, 1969. Good examples for conducting classroom discussions.

Sledge, Larry J. "The Application of Selected Writings by Gagné, Bruner, and Ausebel to Music Theory Pedagogy." Ph.D. dissertation, Florida State University, 1971.

Timpson, William M., and Tobin, David N. *Teaching As Performing: A Guide for Energizing Your Public Presentation.* Prentice-Hall, 1982. Comparisons between acting and teaching; contains much practical advice.

White, John D. *Guidelines for College Teaching of Music Theory.* Scarecrow Press, 1981. A brief introductory treatment based on the author's experience and the ideas of Piaget; no bibliography; a brief list of textbooks.

7. Evaluation and Curriculum Design

Applebaum, Edward. "A Practice of Narrowing Options: How the Theory-Based Curriculum Destroys Creativity." *Music Educators Journal* (March 1972):43–45.

Blachly, Alexander, and Rahn, D. Jay. "A Survey of Recent Comprehensive Examinations Administered by Departments of Music in Nineteen North American Graduate Schools." *Current Musicology* (1971):7–54. Excellent examples of advanced music theory exam questions.

Cahn, Steven M. "The Uses and Abuses of Grades and Examinations." In *Scholars Who Teach,* edited by Steven M. Cahn, pp. 217–41. Nelson-Hall, 1978.

Coleman, Randolph. "New Music in the Undergraduate Music Program: The Composer-Theorist View." *Proceedings of the American Society of University Composers* (1970):95–108.

Coulter, Ronald S., Jr. "A Compositional Approach to Music Theory." Ph.D. dissertation, Claremont Graduate School, 1975.

Fitch, John R. "An Instructional Design using Selected Contemporary Compositional Practices as the Basis for a Beginning Theory Course." A.Mus.D. dissertation, University of Arizona, 1970. A freshman textbook.

———. "Twentieth-Century Students Should Start with Twentieth-Century Techniques." *Music Educators Journal* (April 1973):46–47.

Fleisher, Robert. "Non-Western Music in the Theory Curriculum." Paper presented at the Annual Meeting of the College Music Society, Denver, November, 1980.

Frye, Ellen. "First Year Theory for the Guitar and Bongo Set." *Music Educators Journal* (December 1971):38–42.

Kohs, Ellis B. "Teaching Music Theory: Current Needs and Problems in the Teaching of Undergraduate Music Theory." *Music Theory Spectrum* (1980):135–42.

Paul, Philip M. "The Development and Validation of Two Music Theory Achievement Tests." Ed.D. dissertation, University of Georgia, 1973.

Peters, G. David, and Miller, Robert F. *Music Teaching and Learning*. Longman, 1982. Includes valuable information on curriculum design.

Popham, W. James. *Modern Educational Measurement*. Prentice-Hall, 1981. A comprehensive study on constructing and grading tests.

Sherman, Robert W. "As Taught, Music Theory is an Anachronism." *Music Educators Journal* (October 1969):39–41.

Taylor, Jack, and Urquhart, Dan. "FSU: An Experimental Approach to Comprehensive Musicianship for Freshman Music Majors." *College Music Symposium* (Fall 1974):76–88.

"The Theory Curriculum: Styles and Ideas." *College Music Symposium* (Spring 1977):174–78. Summary of a panel discussion.

"Theory with a Thrust." 4 parts. *Music Educators Journal* (September 1968):56–59; (October 1968):49–51; (December 1968):57–61; (January 1969):55–57. A discussion of the design and philosophy of the theory/history program at American University.

Trani, Lynda A. "Comparison and Evaluation of Four Collegiate Curricula Which Integrate or Coordinate Music History and Theory." M.A. thesis, California State University at Long Beach, 1978.

Youngblood, Joseph. "Improving Teaching and Testing Through Item Analysis." *College Music Symposium* (Spring 1981):67–75.

Index

Index

Harmony: augmented-6th chords, 57–58, 109; Bach chorales, 53, 55; chord functions, 45–48; chromaticism, 54–55, 64; harmonizing a melody, 61–62; linear approaches, 51–52; modulation, 57; Neapolitan-6th chord (N⁶), 57, 109; non-harmonic tones (NHTs), 58–59, 59–60; prolongation, 48, 49–50; roman numerals, 44–45; secondary dominants, 57, 60–61. *See also* Tonality

Hearing eye, 100

Hearing vs. listening, 10

Hierarchy, 68, 75–76; foreground, background, and middleground, 50. *See also* Schenker

Homan, Frederick, 10

Integration: of ear training and analysis, 16–19

Intelligent guessing. *See* Ear training; Harmonic dictation; Melodic dictation

Interpolation, 83

Interpretation, 24, 77, 79, 84–85, 137, 148

Interval singing, 131–32, 139–40

Intuition, 9–10

Isolated courses, 23–24

Jazz, 20

Julliard. *See* Literature and materials

Juxtaposition, 83

Kaleidoscope, 75, 134

Keyboard: place in curriculum, 69; reinforcement of conceptual skills, 70; relationship with ear training, 70–71

Kraft, Leo, 51

Learning: class life-cycle, 164; definition, 161; group process, 163–64, 165; leadership roles, 164; lecturing, 161–62. *See also* Teaching

Lévi-Strauss, Claude, 93

Linguistics, 10, 17, 27, 35, 38, 53, 90; music vs. language understanding, 112, 116–17

Literature (music), 20–21

Literature (non-music): comparisons with music, 3, 75

Literature and materials (L & M), 20, 176

Loose ends, 6, 40, 63

McBeth, W. Francis, 36

McHose, Allen, 53

Macrorhythm, 55

Magnetic notes, 132

"Man-climbs-the-mountain" view, 13

Map-like vs. time-like: in analysis, 78

Maslow, Andrew, 28

Mastery, 34–36

Melodic analysis: harmonization of a melody, 61–62; of phrases, 67–68; of tonality, 67

Melodic dictation: chunking, 116–17; error detection, 119; familiar tunes, 117, 119; integration of analysis and hearing, 110–12; intelligent guessing, 116; multiple-choice, 115; musical chairs, 115; programmed learning, 118; scale-degree function, 114; structural sketching, 114. *See also* Ear training; Sightsinging

Memory, 83

Mencken, H. L., 163

Meyer, Leonard, 6–7, 9, 49, 76

Mictrotonal hearing, 148

Mind training: definition, 33: as ear training, 18; intuition, 9–10; thinking, 4, 10, 27. *See also* Ear training

Minor-la system (syllables), 133–34

Minor scale: as a variant of major, 37, 134

Modality, 55

Modulation, 54, 57

Moveable "do," 133, 142

Murphy, Howard, 104, 134

Musical emotions, 93–94

Musicianship, 12–13; as skills, 28. *See also* Comprehensive musicianship

Nature vs. nurture, 52

Neapolitan-6th chord, 57, 109

Non-harmonic tones (NHTs). *See* Harmony

Non-pitch factors, 86

Non-Western music, 20

Notation, 44

Omnitonic, 56

Palestrina, 55

Paper-and-pencil musicians, 16

Parametric analysis, 21

Parkinson's Law, 34

Patterns, 75

Perfect pitch, 139

MICHAEL R. ROGERS is Associate Professor of Music Theory at the University of Oklahoma and has graduate degrees from the University of Illinois and University of Iowa. He has published articles on both musical analysis and music theory ped agogy in professional journals. He is also an active performer (euphonium and trombone) and is currently doing research on relationships between musical analysis and performance and on temporal proportion in tonal music.